MONEY-
SAVING
T I P S
FOR GOOD TIMES
AND BAD

CONSUMER REPORTS

MONEY-SAVING TIPS

FOR GOOD TIMES AND BAD

Walter B. Leonard

AND THE EDITORS OF CONSUMER REPORTS BOOKS

CONSUMER REPORTS BOOKS
A Division of Consumers Union
Yonkers, New York

LIBRARY OF CONGRESS CATALOGING-IN-PUBLICATION DATA

Leonard, Walter B.
   Consumer Reports money-saving tips for good times and bad /
Walter B. Leonard and the editors of Consumer Reports Books.
      p.   cm.
   Includes index.
   ISBN 0-89043-459-X
   1. Finance, Personal.   2. Savings and thrift.   I. Consumer
Reports.   II. Title.   III. Title: Money-saving tips for good times
and bad.
HG179.L443 1992   91-46354
332.024′ 01—dc20   CIP

First printing, April 1992

Manufactured in the United States of America

Consumer Reports Money-Saving Tips for Good Times and Bad is a Consumer Reports Book published by Consumers Union, the nonprofit organization that publishes *Consumer Reports*, the monthly magazine of test reports, product Ratings, and buying guidance. Established in 1936, Consumers Union is chartered under the Not-for-Profit Corporation Law of the State of New York.

The purposes of Consumers Union, as stated in its charter, are to provide consumers with information and counsel on consumer goods and services, to give information on all matters relating to the expenditure of the family income, and to initiate and to cooperate with individual and group efforts seeking to create and maintain decent living standards.

CONTENTS

MONEY- SAVING T I P S

FOR GOOD TIMES AND BAD

INTRODUCTION

Thrift is the watchword for the nineties. The blow-it-all, got-to-have-it-now eighties have been shown the door by a leaner, meaner decade. Current statistics show consumer debt and personal bankruptcies at all-time highs. Recent years have fixed consumers' attention on pocketbook issues; everyone wants to save in ways large and small.

This book is intended to help both the newly budget-conscious and the habitually frugal get more out of their dollars. *Consumer Reports Money-Saving Tips* tells you the cheapest meal to eat out, suggests ways to save on painting costs, and offers tips on cooling your house with a fan rather than air-conditioning. It shows how raising the collision deductible of your car insurance can save you money. It gives you a hand in sorting the necessities from the frills in baby products, health needs, and travel purchases. It presents money-saving strategies for buying, running, and repairing your car. And it points you toward wise buys in a variety of products ranging from electronics and cameras to mascara and panty hose.

All the tips in this book are presented briefly, to help you get to information and strategies quickly. The material, all published in recent years in *Consumer Reports, Consumer Reports Travel Letter,* or *Consumer Reports on Health,* has been selected to give you information you'll find useful in saving money.

To assure the accuracy and currency of the information, specialists from Consumers Union's technical departments have reviewed and updated the product-testing, product-using, and product-buying sections. Similarly, CU's medical, travel, and financial consultants have reviewed and revised the information within their areas of expertise.

Every item in this book reflects our best advice to consumers. We hope that you find our dollar-stretching tips valuable.

ONE

Eating Well, Eating for Less

A considerable part of every household's budget goes toward putting food on the table. But this cost is often higher than need be—careless buying without comparing prices or automatically reaching for packaged, highly processed foods in the supermarket can result in higher expenses at the checkout counter. Here's a dollar-wise guide to saving without stinting when you shop for food.

Eating Out

Eating Out Needn't Break Your Budget

Roadside restaurants such as Denny's, Ponderosa, Friendly, Red Lobster, and Shoney's offer less speed but more variety and ambience than the fast feeders and pizza chains. Not only are they competing with one another but they are also engaged in a tug-of-war with such chains as McDonald's and Pizza Hut for your dining-out dollar.

Fast-Food Breakfasts

A solitary inventor, working the grill at the McDonald's he owned in Santa Barbara, California, cooked up the world's first **Egg McMuffin** 20

3

years ago. He fashioned a unique tool—a cluster of nonstick rings—to fry a batch of eggs that would each have a poached look and the right shape for an English muffin. Then he added melted cheese to lend the recipe an eggs Benedict consistency, crowned his handiwork with Canadian bacon, and thus created the quintessential fast-food breakfast: portable bacon and eggs that even drivers in traffic could handle.

As the backbone of a new breakfast menu, the **Egg McMuffin** let McDonald's owners open their doors not just for lunch but for the profitable morning crowd. As of this writing, breakfast brings in about 20 cents of every dollar the McDonald's cash registers ring up. Not to be outdone, the number two and three fast-food chains have also served up breakfast fare, although they do it *their* way: Burger King makes breakfast sandwiches on croissants and bagels, while Hardee's is partial to biscuits. (Wendy's has all but given up on the breakfast trade.)

From the beginning, the fast-food chains have given Americans breakfasts designed for convenience and taste appeal, and not for nutritional value. The first breakfast food introduced at Burger King was its **Croissan'wich,** an egg-and-cheese sandwich on a croissant, one of the fattiest kinds of bread around. Today the morning mainstays at the chains include hotcakes and sausage, scrambled-egg platters, and meat sandwiches with or without eggs—all dishes with serious nutritional drawbacks.

Most people certainly think of fast-food outlets as places to get a quick breakfast rather than a nourishing one. When we polled more than 750 of our readers in spring of 1991, we found that fully one-quarter of them had eaten breakfast at a major fast-food chain in the month before our survey. Readers often said they ate fast-food breakfasts when they were traveling or in a hurry. But two-thirds of all readers surveyed believe the meals aren't nutritious.

Recently, McDonald's has led the move toward lighter breakfast fare. In 1990, the chain switched from 2 percent to 1 percent lowfat milk and began serving prepackaged bowls of cereal. McDonald's now also offers fat-free apple-bran muffins side by side with Danish pastry.

But such innovations don't constitute an entire menu make-over. The question remains: Can a fast breakfast be both tasty and nutritious?

The right start? There's no single, clear definition of a healthful breakfast. When we spoke with nutritionists, we were surprised to hear how little consensus there is about the morning meal. The U.S. Department of Agriculture (USDA) doesn't even recommend that adults eat breakfast (although the agency does consider the meal essential for growing children). And it offers no guidelines on whether the meal should be light or heavy.

One thing is certain, however: A good breakfast can offer a jump on the day's nutritional needs. Government studies find that many Americans don't consume enough fiber, calcium, and complex carbohydrates. Breakfast foods provide a good chance to get all three. But a breakfast weighed down by too much fat or too many calories means you should watch what you eat the rest of the day.

To see how fast-food breakfasts measure up, Consumers Union sent shoppers to several Northeast outlets of the top three chains for multiple samples of the dishes on their menus. A chain's bestseller was always included. Back in the lab, we probed the food's nutritional value.

The Ratings are based on manufacturers' nutritional data, supplemented and spot-checked in our own labs and in an independent testing laboratory we commissioned. (We found the chains' data generally accurate.)

We focused mainly on calories, fat, cholesterol, and sodium because they are problem nutrients for many people. Protein is not, so it's not listed in the Ratings. Indeed, Americans as a group consume about the right amount of protein.

Fat, on the other hand, has proven itself such a dietary villain that public-health authorities recommend trimming fat consumption to just 30 percent or less of a day's calories. That's 67 grams of fat in a 2,000-calorie diet. (Since each gram of fat contains 9 calories, 67 grams contribute about 600 calories.) The average fat intake in the United States is closer to 37 percent of the calories consumed.

The Ratings separate the foods we tested into five categories: pancake platters and French toast sticks, egg sandwiches, no-egg sandwiches, scrambled-egg platters, and baked goods. We consider fat so important that, within each category, we've ranked the menu items by the percentage of calories they get from fat. For each group, the foods with the lowest percentage of calories from fat are the most nutritious choices and head the group's Ratings.

Comparing the five groups—asking whether egg sandwiches are better or worse than pancake breakfasts—is difficult, since nutritional values can vary dramatically within each category. Any comparison also involves looking at several nutritional factors, including your own individual needs.

Government agencies and health authorities now advise limiting sodium to 3,300 milligrams or less a day, and cutting cholesterol to 300 milligrams or less. But while there's certainly no reason to want to eat *more* than those amounts, we believe that people with normal blood pressure and no risk factors for hypertension (family history, obesity, diabetes, being black) have no urgent reason to restrict salt. Likewise, healthy people with normal or low blood cholesterol can generally eat what they please, eggs included. Those people may even gain some benefit from eating a few high-cholesterol or high-sodium foods in moderation, when such foods also contain valuable nutrients such as calcium and iron.

Despite those complexities, the percentage of calories from fat overall is still a good yardstick for comparing the breakfast categories. So we've included a pie chart in each Ratings group showing the percentage of calories from fat, carbohydrate, and protein for a representative dish. A good breakdown for the overall diet, according to government guidelines, is to get no more than 30 percent of calories from fat, about 15 percent from protein, and 55 percent or more from carbohydrates (mostly complex).

The fattiest (and most calorific) items we sampled were scrambled-egg platters with all the trimmings: hash browns, a biscuit or croissant, and a sausage patty or bacon. Those meals deliver between 700 and 850 calories, about 60 percent of them from fat. Scrambled-egg platters are also rather high in sodium. And they're unavoidably high in cholesterol, given each egg's 200-plus milligrams and the 25 to 50 milligrams the sausage adds.

Hotcake platters are a better nutritional bet—and far less fatty, if you don't load them up with butter or margarine. Three Hardee's pancakes with bacon and one packet of syrup contain fewer than 500 calories, just 17 percent of them from fat, and virtually no cholesterol. The enriched flour in the hotcakes also provides a goodly amount of iron.

One dish we'd stay away from: **Burger King French Toast Sticks,** deep-fried sticks of bread you can dip in syrup and eat with your fingers. A 622-calorie serving packs 150 calories more than Hardee's pancakes and more than triple the fat. And it doesn't even come with bacon!

If you're on the run, sandwiches are easy to deal with. Maybe that's why, next to orange juice and coffee, sandwiches were the breakfast items readers in our survey ordered most often.

No-egg sandwiches pack only a little cholesterol. But they're made with biscuits, which, like croissants, are high in fat. And fat, mostly from the biscuits and the fatty breakfast meat, accounts for most of the sandwiches' 350 to 450 calories.

The egg sandwiches, of course, have cholesterol in the eggs themselves; they also typically have cheese, which adds to their fat and cholesterol counts. Even so, two stand out as lower in fat: the **Burger King Bagel with Egg and Cheese** and the **McDonald's Egg McMuffin.** Neither is extremely fatty. McDonald's manages to make its sandwich with fewer than 300 calories and yet delivers an unexpected dividend: calcium, about one-fourth of the day's need, from the enriched English muffin and the cheese.

The worst sandwich choice for those eschewing fat: **Burger King's Croissan'wich with Sausage, Egg, and Cheese.** At just over 530 calories—one-quarter of a day's total—it contains 40 grams of fat, close to two-thirds of a day's fat quota. That's about the amount of fat in 10 pats of margarine or butter.

Maybe you have time for just coffee and a baked snack. That might mean a sugary Danish—at 300 to 400 calories, more than some breakfast sandwiches supply and fattier than a couple of them. Or you might try the new **McDonald's Apple Bran Muffin,** a 190-calorie cupcake that lives up to its fat-free, cholesterol-free claim. It also turned out to pack the most dietary fiber of the baked goods tested: 5 grams, about one-fourth of an adult's daily need for fiber. The Danishes averaged 2 to 3 grams of fiber.

Professional tastings. When we asked our readers why they eat at fast-food places, convenience figured high on their list. Taste did not. That point was reinforced when we presented readers with a list of the big chains and posed a hypothetical question: Which chain would you visit at breakfast time, on a vacation, if you were on the road with all the chains before you? McDonald's, which garnered 37 percent of the vote, tied for first place with "None of the above."

We sent a sensory expert to three outlets of each chain to try their breakfast dishes and give us a professional evaluation. Our consultant tasted each dish immediately (when it was warm), dissected sandwiches to appraise the bread and fillings separately, and scored each dish's taste and texture.

The consultant reported similarities in quality across the different chains, reflected in the Ratings sensory comments. Fried potatoes everywhere tasted pretty good—crispy and salty, with a potato taste like French fries. Scrambled eggs tasted like eggs, though Hardee's were a bit greasier than the others'.

Sometimes a restaurant chain's servings were inconsistent. Burger King usually served two eggs on its platters (unlike its competitors)—except at one outlet, which served only one.

The Hardee's and McDonald's pancakes were gummy and a bit rubbery—you can't easily cut them with the side of a plastic fork—from steaming in the closed foam tray. McDonald's pancakes were a bit larger and had a little more wheaty taste. The syrups tasted like typical pancake syrup with no real maple.

The chains did differ on sausages: McDonald's were spiciest and a bit gristly. Burger King's were blandest. Hardee's were more like "country" sausage, seasoned with sage and black pepper; but their dull brown color wasn't too appealing.

Biscuits everywhere were tasty—they were crusty yet moist inside— and the English muffins were nicely toasted. Sometimes, though, the sandwiches were greasy and hard to handle.

Our taste expert didn't think much of Burger King's bagels or crois- sants. The bagels were more like bread in texture: tender rather than chewy, sweet, and with a musty off-taste. The croissants were on the dry side, not light and flaky as croissants should be. Burger King's Danish also tasted of its paperboard packaging.

If you order coffee, McDonald's pours the most consistent cup. We found its coffee and Hardee's typically had good roasted character, with no off-flavors. Burger King's sometimes tasted burned and bitter.

Recommendations. It's hard to deny the convenience of fast-food breakfasts—and hard to find another reason to buy them. Overall, we found the fare a little tastier at McDonald's and Hardee's than at Burger King.

The mediocre-tasting fast-food breakfasts we sampled can also be laden with fat, cholesterol, and calories. If you eat them often enough for that to be a concern, here are ways to minimize the damage:

- Order a small sandwich, not a big platter. The **McDonald's Egg McMuffin** and **Burger King's Bagel Sandwich with Egg and Cheese** aren't bad nutritional choices, unless you're watching cholesterol closely. The **Egg McMuffin** tastes better and has about 120 fewer calories, just 290 calories in all.

- Choose toast, English muffins, or bagels over biscuits and crois- sants, which are very fatty. Try to stay away from sugary, greasy Danishes. For more fiber and not even a gram of fat or milligram of cholesterol, try a **McDonald's Apple Bran Muffin.**

- Among platters, pancakes are a more nutritionally sound choice than scrambled eggs. They have far less fat and cholesterol, and they offer a good serving of complex carbohydrates.

- Go easy on butter or margarine on bread or pancakes. While margarine has less saturated fat, it has just as much fat overall and as many calories as butter (36 per pat). A little jelly is better, with about half the calories per teaspoon. Likewise, go easy on syrup. Each packet adds 80 to 120 calories.
- If you like meat, pick sandwiches with bacon over those with sausage patties—they add less fat.
- Skip the fried potatoes or leave some on the plate. They get half their calories or more from fat.
- Don't worry about getting enough protein. Eat a reasonably varied, balanced diet and your protein needs are almost certain to take care of themselves.

Ratings of Fast-Food Breakfasts

As published in the September 1991 issue of *Consumer Reports*

Listed by types; within types, listed in order of the percentage of calories from the fat in each menu item. Ties are listed in alphabetical order.

❶ **Price.** The average paid by CU shoppers in the Northeast.

❷ **Nutrient levels.** Data come from manufacturers' and CU's tests. Pancake platters include one packet of syrup but no butter or margarine. Each pat of butter or margarine adds about 36 calories; extra syrup packets add 80 to 120 calories.

❸ **Sensory comments.** Our sensory consultant's impressions after testing breakfasts at three outlets per chain.

Optimal calorie breakdown

Pie charts show the protein/fat/carbohydrate breakdown for five sample dishes. An optimal breakdown is shown at right.

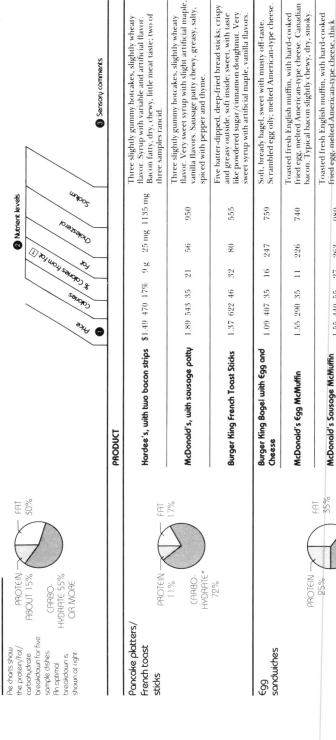

Optimal breakdown:
PROTEIN ABOUT 15% · FAT 30% · CARBOHYDRATE 55% OR MORE

Pancake platters/French toast sticks:
PROTEIN 11% · FAT 17% · CARBOHYDRATE* 72%

Egg sandwiches:
PROTEIN 25% · FAT 35% · CARBOHYDRATE 40%

PRODUCT	① Price	Calories	% Calories from fat ⚠	Fat	Cholesterol	Sodium	③ Sensory comments
Pancake platters/French toast sticks							
Hardee's, with two bacon strips	$1.49	470	17%	9 g	25 mg	1135 mg	Three slightly gummy hotcakes, slightly wheaty flavor. Syrup with variable and artificial flavor. Bacon fatty, dry, chewy, little meat taste; two of three samples rancid.
McDonald's, with sausage patty	1.89	543	35	21	56	950	Three slightly gummy hotcakes, slightly wheaty flavor. Very sweet syrup with slight artificial maple, vanilla flavors. Sausage patty chewy, greasy, salty, spiced with pepper and thyme.
Burger King French Toast Sticks	1.37	622	46	32	80	555	Five batter-dipped, deep-fried bread sticks; crispy and greasy outside, soft inside; sweet, with taste like powdered sugar/cinnamon doughnut. Very sweet syrup with artificial maple, vanilla flavors.
Egg sandwiches							
Burger King Bagel with Egg and Cheese	1.09	407	35	16	247	759	Soft, bready bagel, sweet with musty off-taste. Scrambled egg oily; melted American-type cheese.
McDonald's Egg McMuffin	1.55	290	35	11	226	740	Toasted fresh English muffin, with hard-cooked fried egg, melted American-type cheese. Canadian bacon. Typical bacon slightly chewy, dry, smoky.
McDonald's Sausage McMuffin with Egg	1.55	440	55	27	263	980	Toasted fresh English muffin, with hard-cooked fried egg, melted American-type cheese, thick sausage patty. Sausage chewy, a bit gristly, fatty, salty, spicy, with thyme, pepper.
Burger King Croissan'wich with Egg and Cheese	1.09	315	57	20	222	607	Bready croissant, with greasy scrambled egg, melted American-type cheese.
Hardee's Sausage and Egg Biscuit	1.25	490	57	31	170	1150	Biscuit crusty but moist inside, a bit salty, with fatty coating. Slightly greasy egg. Salty sausage patty, with sage, thyme, pepper.

② Nutrient levels

Item							Description
No-egg sandwiches							
McDonald's Biscuit with Sausage and Egg	1.51	520	60	35	275	1250	Crispy, crumbly biscuit with greasy surface, moist inside; salty with baking-powder, buttery tastes. Large scrambled egg. Chewy patty, salty and fatty, spicy with thyme and pepper.
Burger King Croissan'wich with Sausage, Egg, and Cheese	1.62	534	67	40	268	985	Toasted croissant, with greasy scrambled egg, melted American-type cheese. Sausage patty chewy, salty, and fatty, not too spicy.
Hardee's Bacon Biscuit	1.05	360	53	21	10	950	Biscuit crusty but moist inside, salty, with baking-powder, fatty tastes. Bacon dry, chewy, salty, and very fatty, with distinct rancid off-taste.
Hardee's Sausage Biscuit	1.05	440	57	28	25	1100	Biscuit crusty but moist, salty, with baking-powder, fatty taste and feel. Thick patty slightly chewy and fatty, sage, thyme, pepper spices.
McDonald's Biscuit with Sausage	1.32	440	59	29	49	1080	Crumbly biscuit with crunchy crust and greasy surface; moist inside, salty, with baking-powder, buttery tastes. Chewy patty, salty with fatty taste; spicy, with thyme and pepper.
Scrambled-egg platters							
McDonald's, with sausage, potatoes, and biscuit	2.18	710	58	46	457	1700	Large scrambled egg, not greasy. Biscuit crisp but moist inside, buttery. Patty chewy, fatty, salty, spicy. Slab of hash brown potatoes, crispy but tender inside; slightly greasy; taste like French fries.
Hardee's Big Country Breakfast, with sausage, potatoes, and biscuit	1.89	850	60	57	340	1980	Greasy egg. Buttered biscuit crisp but tender inside, with fatty crust. Two patties, not too greasy or salty, with pepper, sage. Diced fried potato disks, crispy but tender inside, with taste like French fries.
Burger King, with sausage, potatoes, and croissant	2.12	768	62	53	412	1271	Eggs varied but with fatty taste, one sample very salty. Toasted, dry croissant. Chewy patty, spicing varied. Deep-fried disks of diced potatoes, like French fries.
Baked goods							
McDonald's Apple Bran Muffin	.79	190	0	0	0	230	Small muffin with coarse texture but no fattiness; apple and cinnamon-candy flavors.
Burger King Apple Cinnamon Danish	.79	390	30	13	19	305	Sugar-iced pastry with moist cinnamon-apple filling. Tasted of cardboard packaging; not fresh-tasting.
McDonald's Apple Danish	.78	390	41	18	25	370	Pasty with cinnamon-apple filling, crumb topping, sugar icing; one sample without crumb topping.
Hardee's Cinnamon 'N' Raisin Biscuit	.62	320	48	17	0	510	Small biscuit with nice cinnamon, plump raisins, sugar icing; sweet, sticky, messy to eat.

No-egg sandwiches: FAT 59%, PROTEIN 12%, CARBOHYDRATE 29%

Scrambled-egg platters: FAT 62%, PROTEIN 14%, CARBOHYDRATE 24%

Baked goods: FAT 30%, PROTEIN 6%, CARBOHYDRATE* 64%

*Includes appreciable amount of sugar

[1] 1 gram of fat contains 9 calories.

WHAT'S IN A MEAL

Nutritionists analyze foods to answer a basic question: Given the number of calories a food or a meal provides, will it give you a decent amount of "good" nutrients without an overload of "bad" ones?

The following graphs show nutrient profiles for five sample fast-food breakfasts, one from each of the categories tested for this report. The top bar, for calories, shows the percentage of an average woman's daily caloric needs that the breakfast provides.

In a nutritionally optimal food, the next four bars—for fat, saturated fat, cholesterol, and sodium—would be *no longer* than the calorie bar. If a food gives you only 20 percent of the calories you need, but 40 percent of your daily fat allotment, for example, you'll have to eat with extra care for the rest of the day to balance it out.

Protein is a problem for very few Americans. Most people now get roughly 15 percent of their daily calories from protein, enough to meet the body's needs without the risk of excess.

Iron and calcium represent beneficial nutrients and should be *no shorter* than the calorie bar.

	CAUTION
	ADEQUATE
	INCREASE

Hardee's Three Pancakes with bacon, syrup		
Percentage of recommended daily intake		0 20 40 60 80 100
Calories	470	
Total fat	9 g	
Saturated fat	3 g	
Cholesterol	25 mg	
Sodium	1,135 mg	
Protein	13 g	
Iron	5 mg	
Calcium	66 mg	

Burger King Apple Cinnamon Danish		
Percentage of recommended daily intake		0 20 40 60 80 100
Calories	390	
Total fat	13 g	
Saturated fat	3 g	
Cholesterol	19 mg	
Sodium	305 mg	
Protein	6 g	
Iron	1 mg	
Calcium	60 mg	

McDonald's Biscuit with Sausage		
Percentage of recommended daily intake		0 20 40 60 80 100
Calories	440	
Total fat	29 g	
Saturated fat	9 g	
Cholesterol	49 mg	
Sodium	1,080 mg	
Protein	13 g	
Iron	2 mg	
Calcium	83 mg	

Burger King Scrambled-Egg Platter		
Percentage of recommended daily intake		0 20 40 60 80 100
Calories	768	
Total fat	53 g	
Saturated fat	15 g	
Cholesterol[1]	412 mg	
Sodium	1,271 mg	
Protein	26 g	
Iron	4 mg	
Calcium	120 mg	

[1]Platter contains 137% of recommended maximum cholesterol intake.

McDonald's Egg McMuffin		
Percentage of recommended daily intake		0 20 40 60 80 100
Calories	290	
Total fat	11 g	
Saturated fat	4 g	
Cholesterol	226 mg	
Sodium	740 mg	
Protein	18 g	
Iron	3 mg	
Calcium	256 mg	

Profiles are based on an average woman's recommended daily dietary intake, from government guidelines and the advice of CU's medical consultants: calories, 2,000; fat, 67 grams (30 percent of calories); saturated fat, 22 grams; cholesterol, 300 milligrams; sodium, 3,300 milligrams; protein, 45 grams; iron, 18 milligrams; calcium, 1,000 milligrams. Recommended amounts for an average man are lower for iron and higher for calories, protein, and fat; for young children, recommended amounts are lower overall. Data are from the fast-food chains.

Eating breakfast at home can be more nourishing and nearly as quick as eating out. And you can make the calories count by choosing foods rich in fiber, calcium, iron, and other vitamins and minerals, while limiting fat.

Below, we profile two sample do-it-yourself breakfasts to show how each meal's foods add up. Having coffee or tea won't alter the pattern much, if at all. The pie charts below illustrate the carbohydrate/protein/fat breakdown of the breakfasts. (The ideal breakdown is shown in the Ratings.) In addition to the nutrients shown, both breakfasts supply fiber: The cereal and toast provide about 9 grams, while the toast-and-yogurt combination gives you about 3 grams. Ideally, adults should consume about 20 grams per day.

☐ **Caution** (fat, saturated fat, cholesterol, sodium). Though these aren't all problems for everyone, government guidelines say our national intake levels are too high for optimal health.

▨ **Adequate** (protein). Most Americans now get just about as much protein as they should.

▩ **Increase** (carbohydrates, iron, calcium). Many people, especially women, take in too little iron and calcium. Carbohydrates should be mostly complex, not simple (sugars).

High-fiber cereal and toast	Yogurt, toast, and O.J.
• Large bowl raisin bran (2 ounces cereal, 8 ounces 1 percent milk) • One slice whole-wheat toast spread with 1 tablespoon peanut butter	• Orange juice (6 ounces) • Plain low-fat yogurt (8 ounces) • Two slices whole-wheat, 2 tablespoons fruit preserves

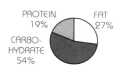

PROTEIN 19%   FAT 27%   CARBOHYDRATE 54%

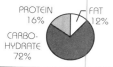

PROTEIN 16%   FAT 12%   CARBOHYDRATE 72%

Percentage of recommended daily intake		0 20 40 60 80 100
Calories	428	
Total fat	13 g	
Saturated fat	3 g	
Cholesterol	10 mg	
Sodium	763 mg	
Protein	20 g	
Iron	10 mg	
Calcium	352 mg	

Percentage of recommended daily intake		0 20 40 60 80 100
Calories	454	
Total fat	6 g	
Saturated fat	2 g	
Cholesterol	14 mg	
Sodium	471 mg	
Protein	18 g	
Iron	2 mg	
Calcium	474 mg	

Fast Food for Lunch or Dinner

As with fast-food breakfasts, fast-food lunches or dinners can be fairly well balanced if you keep an eye out for damage control. Here are some tactics that will help you and your family dine defensively:

- If you want beef, choose roast beef sandwiches. Roast beef is often leaner than a hamburger. An exception is McDonald's new McLean hamburger, which our 1991 tests showed had a lower percentage of calories from fat—a crucial dietary test—than every fast-food beef sandwich we tested and was as low or lower in calories than all but one chicken sandwich.
- Choose McLean or small plain burgers instead of the giant mouth-filling burgers with all the works. Skip the mayonnaise and cheese. You can save nearly 150 calories on a Burger King Whopper, for example, just by having them hold the mayo. Cheese, while a source of protein and calcium, also carries some fat.
- Choose regular fried chicken, not the "extra crispy" recipe. Extra fat adds the crispiness—up to 100 extra calories per piece for Kentucky Fried Chicken's extra crispy recipe.
- Order milk instead of a shake. Low-fat milk provides much more protein and calcium per calorie than the fast-food concoctions. Or order a diet soda.
- If you're looking to cut calories, go easy on the French fries. Split an order with someone else, or consider a plain baked potato, if it's available.
- Choose a boxed fast-food salad or one from the salad bar. If you try a boxed salad, one with chicken or shrimp will supply some protein along with the fiber, complex carbohydrates, vitamins, and minerals from the vegetables. At a salad bar, choose carrots, tomatoes, and dark green vegetables. And go easy on dressings, fatty croutons, taco chips, and mayonnaise-laden pasta and potato salads. The packet of Thousand Island dressing that comes with a McDonald's salad can give it more calories than a Big Mac.

Eating Right for Breakfast

Frozen Orange Juice: Tasty and Thrifty

It's hard to beat the flavor of fresh-squeezed orange juice. But to avoid the bother of squeezing, many people turn to juice that has been squeezed for them already. The main choices are juice in cans or boxes, frozen concentrates, and chilled juices.

Besides freshly squeezed juice, the best-tasting orange juices are frozen concentrates and chilled juices. Of the two, the frozen variety tastes better and often costs less. If you think you are buying a higher-quality product when you buy chilled juice, try switching to frozen concentrate and stop carrying home the extra water.

Orange juice packaged in a box (the juice boxes favored by children, not to be confused with cartons of chilled juice in the dairy case) is heated, quickly cooled, then packed in multilayer laminated cartons without any air space. The "aseptic" description of this packaging refers to the closed, germ-free environment in which the packing takes place. Like cans, aseptic cartons can be stored at room temperature and packed in a lunchbox or bought from a vending machine without fear of spoilage.

While boxed juice may be easy to store, its taste is just about on a par with canned juice, and it's apt to have the same metallic off-flavor. Consider it only for situations in which the package's convenience and portability demand that you put up with poor flavor.

If frozen and chilled juices aren't stored properly, their flavor—and their vitamin C content—can deteriorate. Use an airtight jar, because both the orange flavor and vitamin C degrade rapidly in the presence of air.

If you like the convenience of chilled juice, consider buying it by the quart, rather than in the half-gallon size. That will help to preserve freshness.

A morning glass of orange juice is a good way to meet your daily requirement of vitamin C. A 6-ounce serving of juice from frozen concentrate provides just about an adult's U.S. Recommended Daily Allowance (U.S. RDA) of 60 milligrams of vitamin C.

Orange juice is also a good source of potassium, as are many other common foods, such as meat, potatoes, bananas, and peanut butter. Since potassium is so abundant, healthy people rarely, if ever, develop a potassium deficiency. (Indeed, there is no Recommended Daily Allowance for potassium. Typical daily intakes range from 800 to 5,000 milligrams.) People who take potassium-depleting medication (some drugs used for treating hypertension, for example) may need extra potassium. That's something to discuss with your doctor.

While orange juice is a nutritious drink, it's not a diet drink. Ounce for ounce, orange juice has about as many calories as cola or beer— roughly 80 calories per 6-ounce serving. More than 10 percent of orange juice is fruit sugar. That's why people on a diet are advised to *eat* an orange rather than drink a glassful of juice, the equivalent of three or four oranges.

Saving Money on a Pancake Breakfast

The best pancakes come from a favorite do-it-yourself recipe or, failing that, from prepared mixes that require you to add fresh eggs, oil, and milk. You sacrifice some taste but save some time if you use a complete mix that requires only water or milk to complete the batter.

Dry mixes are the cheapest to use, usually costing less than a nickel per pancake. Pancakes made with frozen batter cost about a dime apiece, while frozen ready-made products cost as much as 18 cents each. Frozen batters also require advance planning because they take at least a day to thaw. You can't defrost them quickly in a microwave oven; doing so will cook the batter.

Pancake syrup. Real maple syrup tastes best, but it costs three to four times as much per ounce as products containing just a little maple syrup or none at all. Then again, genuine maple syrup is extremely sweet, so you'll probably use it more sparingly than the synthetic variety. Pure maple syrup is by far the best choice if you are watching your sodium intake.

Pancakes from a Bottle

The newest wrinkle in pancake mixes adds a dollop of convenience to an already convenient food by eliminating the need for a mixing bowl and spoon. **Aunt Jemima Pancake Express** and **Bisquick Shake 'n Pour** mixes consist of small plastic bottles part full of mix. You just add water, shake, and pour the batter onto the griddle.

For that extra convenience, you'll pay about 14 to 17 cents per pancake—three to four times the cost of pancakes made from mix in a box. Could it be that the new pancakes are three times better? Even a little bit better? No such luck.

We compared buttermilk versions of the shake-and-pour mixes with **Aunt Jemima Buttermilk Complete,** a mix that earned respectable notices in our last pancake test. That mix made slightly better pancakes.

Aunt Jemima Express batter is supposed to keep in the refrigerator for up to three days. We kept some that long, then cooked it. The flapjacks still tasted passable. It did beat the two-day-old **Aunt Jemima Complete** pancakes, which were virtually inedible—gummy and stale.

We paid a little less for **Aunt Jemima Pancake Express,** which makes 6 pancakes, than for **Bisquick Shake 'n Pour,** which yields up to 10 pancakes. The use-and-toss plastic bottle adds packaging waste, another cost of convenience.

Cereal and Milk: A Breakfast Bargain

Compared with other breakfasts, cereal and milk are an inexpensive way to start the day. Ready-to-eat cereals average about 19 cents a serving; hot cereals are a nickel cheaper. Even with milk and fresh fruit, breakfast cereal is still cheap. Here are more ways to economize:

- *Forgo fortification.* High-vitamin cereals usually cost considerably more than their less fortified counterparts.
- *Think big.* Larger packages are generally cheaper. So are bulk canisters of hot cereals, compared with single-serving packets.
- *Add your own toppings.* Generally, the more fruit and nuts the company adds, the more it charges—and the more the markup. The same goes for added sugar.
- *Try generics.* Generic and supermarket-label cereals are nutritionally equivalent to the big-name products, save for possible minor differences in fortification. The generics may even come from the same factory. Yet such cornflakes, bran flakes, shredded wheat, puffed wheat, and crisped rice cost much less than national brands.
- *Try a hot cereal.* Hot cereals generally cost a bit less than ready-to-eat brands and can be almost as convenient to prepare. Virtually all can be microwaved in a minute or two right in the bowl.

Eggs: Get the Most for Your Money

If you took a freshly laid egg and cracked it into a skillet, you'd see no distinct orange yolk. It would barely show through the center of a thick, opaque white. When you cooked it, the egg would have a mild aroma and a delicate flavor.

Eggs you buy in the supermarket, even the freshest AA grade, probably won't look—or taste—quite like that.

Although an egg may retain its nutritional value for several months, it starts to lose sensory quality from the moment it's laid. The white gradually becomes runnier, the yolk more likely to break. With each passing day the mild flavor gives way to a stronger, "eggier" taste.

The quality of an egg, as determined just before packing, is reflected in a letter grade. Top-quality eggs, Grade AA and A, are sold in supermarkets. Grade B eggs go to manufacturers to be used in other food products.

Skilled workers assess egg quality through a process called "candling." Eggs pass over a strong beam of light that illuminates defects both inside and outside the egg. The grader looks for eggs with clean, intact shells of proper shape and texture. Cracked eggs and those with blood spots are discarded. The grader also notes the visibility of the yolk. The fresher the egg, the less delineation between the yolk and the white.

Eggs that have been graded by a government inspector usually have a USDA shield on the carton. Government grading is a voluntary process, paid for by the egg producer. For the consumer, the USDA seal may offer some assurance of freshness. The government stipulates that eggs it grades be refrigerated before and after packing and that cartons bear a packing date. Eggs not graded by federal inspectors are subject to the grading laws of the state in which they are sold. Most states follow guidelines similar to those of the USDA.

Despite such grading procedures, there's no guarantee that a top-quality egg will still be Grade AA at the point of sale. After eggs leave the plant, the quality of care they receive depends on the shipper and the store that sells them. A change in temperature or humidity will adversely affect freshness.

Will you notice if a Grade AA egg has slipped a bit? Unless your palate is accustomed to the freshly laid variety, probably not. Chances are you won't even taste much difference between different grades of supermarket eggs, particularly if you scramble them or use them in recipes. White eggs and brown eggs also taste pretty much the same. Although brown eggs are often priced higher, the only real difference between the two is shell color.

Accordingly, unless you know that a store takes pains to ensure freshness, you're likely to get the most for your money if you simply shop for price. Eggs come in six sizes—jumbo, extra large, large, medium, small, and pee wee—with each size about 10 percent smaller than the one before. So if extra-large eggs are selling for $1.10, large eggs should be priced at about $1.00. If the larger ones are selling for less than that 10 percent difference, you've found a bargain.

Buying Coffee: Watch Those Deceptive Cans

Coffee prices, like those of other commodities, are affected by changes in politics as much as by the weather. Prices have been fairly steady recently, because a complex price-support system known as the International Coffee Agreement—actually a cartel of coffee producers—collapsed in 1989.

When *Consumer Reports* bought coffee for a January 1991 report, it cost an average of $4 a pound, about 45 percent higher than in 1987.

That "pound" of coffee is something of a misnomer, however. A few brands, such as **Brown Gold,** still put 16 ounces of coffee in the can. But 13 ounces seems to be the standard these days. The so-called high-yield coffees deliver as little as 11½ ounces per container, whether metal can or foil-and-plastic brick. Though the amount of coffee varies, most cans are the same size. So check unit prices at the supermarket to compare costs.

Saving on Lunch and Dinner

Tuna: Should You Buy a Premium Product?

What's the best tuna? Depending on what you're making, the best canned tuna may be the cheapest. If you plan to mix the tuna with mayonnaise and onion in a salad or with other ingredients in a casserole, any canned tuna should do.

If you want to eat tuna straight, you will probably be able to detect subtle differences between types and brands. You may prefer a moister, oil-packed tuna; you may also prefer the milder taste of albacore to the stronger taste of light-meat tuna. If you do, you'll usually have to pay extra for it.

Low-salt brands are the highest priced. If you are watching sodium intake, you can save money by buying regular tuna and rinsing it under running water. Rinsing the tuna may diminish the taste somewhat, but that shouldn't matter much in a tuna salad.

Next to the stacks of 6½- and 7-ounce cans of tuna on your grocer's shelves, you're likely to find some 12½- and 13-ounce cans. You may think that big cans mean big savings, but that's not always true.

You can usually save money by buying a store brand instead of a national brand. However, if you like your tuna straight and you prefer oil-packed tuna, stick to the national brands. They are apt to taste better than oil-packed store brands.

Tuna varieties. According to the Food and Drug Administration (FDA), 12 different fish can be called tuna. But only one, albacore, can be labeled "white-meat" tuna.

White tuna has light flesh and a characteristically mild flavor. Other tunas, such as yellowfin, bluefin, and skipjack, are darker and a bit more robust in flavor and are labeled "light-meat" tuna. The delicate taste of white tuna isn't necessarily better than light tuna; it's a matter of personal preference. They can be used interchangeably in many recipes.

Generally, white tuna comes in solid style and, less often, in chunk style. Light tuna comes most often in chunk, occasionally in solid style or—less expensively—in grated or flaked styles. The words *fancy* and *selected* simply tell you that the tuna is solid rather than chunk.

Nutrition. Canned tuna is high in a number of important vitamins and minerals. Like most fish, it's also a good source of protein, and it's relatively low in calories, fat, and cholesterol.

Tuna's average protein content is about 24 grams per 3-ounce serving. That's a little more than you'd find in a cooked 3-ounce hamburger.

Water-packed tuna has fewer calories than oil-packed. A water-packed brand has approximately 105 calories per serving, compared with undrained oil-packed tuna's 240 calories per serving. However, if you prefer the taste of oil-packed tuna, drain the oil. This reduces the caloric difference between the two types to only 75.

Water-packed tuna averages 1.5 grams of fat per serving. The average fat content of undrained, oil-packed tuna is about 16 grams—or 10 grams if the oil is drained off.

Excluding low-salt brands, tuna's sodium content is quite high—averaging 400 milligrams per half-can serving. (Draining an oil-packed brand should reduce its sodium content by about 15 percent.)

Hot Dogs: Nutritionally They're No Budget Stretcher

If you think of hot dogs as a thrifty source of protein, think again. Nutritionally, the hot dog is no bargain. Americans love hot dogs—they wolf down some 19 billion each year. But this popular fare consists largely of water and fat. Hot dogs are made of odds and ends of meat ground with water and spices; these ingredients are pumped into casings, cooked, cured, and packaged. Currently the USDA allows manufacturers to add up to 10 percent more water than is normally found in meat. This water is mostly in the form of ice, which is meant to keep the meat cool while it is being ground.

The USDA also allows manufacturers to make hot dogs with up to 30 percent fat, the amount found in a well-marbled steak. With so much water and fat, there's not much room for protein in a hot dog—it averages only 13 percent, while cooked steak and hamburger are almost 25 percent protein by weight. This means you can pay more for a pound of protein in a hot dog than you would for a pound of protein in a sirloin steak.

Preservatives and other ingredients. Processors can also add up to 3.5 percent other ingredients, which are usually binders, such as skim milk. Preservatives and flavorings are also added, including salt; sweeteners, such as corn syrup and dextrose; ascorbic acid (vitamin C) or one of its derivatives, such as sodium erythorbate or sodium ascorbate; and nitrite.

Nitrite is by far the most controversial. It preserves meat and gives it its characteristic color; it also inhibits the growth of the bacterium that causes botulism, a form of food poisoning that's often fatal. The controversy centers on whether nitrite poses a cancer hazard in the quantities consumed. The FDA and the USDA have permitted the use of lowered amounts of nitrite but have not banned it, mainly because no substitute has been developed that matches its preservative effects. Many scientists also consider any risks posed by nitrite to be minimal and preferable to the risks of doing without it in cured meats.

Most hot dogs are high in sodium as well; a good-tasting wiener may contain 400 milligrams or more of sodium.

Obviously, hot dogs do not bring joy to the heart of a nutritionist or a prudent dieter. But if you insist on eating them occasionally, buy the best-tasting ones and enjoy them. On an ideal hot dog, the outer "skin" should resist slightly when you bite into it. Breaking through this outer layer, you should be rewarded with a spurt of meaty juice. The meat at the center should be moist and firm.

Canned Beans: Cheap, Nutritious, and Easily Fixed

Eat beans: They're inexpensive, easy to fix, and a good source of several key nutrients. They are good in a weight-loss regimen because they are low in calories and very filling. You can always dress up a can of beans with catsup, Worcestershire sauce, or wieners.

Beans are the basis for many simple heat-and-eat dishes that can be quickly made ready for the table.

The most common canned bean varieties consist of navy beans, also called small white beans. But there are also products made from pinto beans, pink beans, and Great Northern beans (a common white bean, two to three times as big as a navy bean but with about the same taste). No matter what the variety, once beans are cooked in sauce, their distinctive characteristics become too submerged for any differences in flavor to come through.

Although not a perfect food, beans are a surprisingly good source of protein, fiber, and iron. The small amounts of meat, usually bacon, in many canned beans help round out the plentiful plant protein.

Some brands of canned beans have a meaty taste; others lean toward the sweet, spicy, or smoky. These are trivial departures from a balanced bean flavor. Defects that aren't so trivial include bitter and burned flavors and strong, uncharacteristic spices. Regardless of the sauce, beans should be moist and moderately firm, about as resistant to the bite as sliced American cheese.

Overall, canned beans tend to be soft and a bit dry—texture problems possibly attributable in part to the canning. A slight metallic flavor may be present in the beans; that seems to be characteristic of canned beans in sauce, whether packaged in cans or glass.

Here's how the types taste:

Pork and beans. This Southern cousin to baked beans should have a meaty flavor related to the pork and pork fat it contains. It may have moderate tomato, smoke, onion, or "brown spice" accents (brown spices come from the cinnamon/clove/allspice family).

Baked beans. A sweet flavor is what you should expect.

Barbecue beans. Southwest-style spiciness and barbecue-sauce sweetness are characteristic for this type. Some meat or smoke flavors (or both) are common. Meat flavor is not an infallible clue that meat was part of the recipe; yeast (extract or torula yeast) or hydrolyzed vegetable protein (HVP) can add a "meaty" flavor.

Vegetarian beans. Several companies put out a type called vegetarian. Some brands may suffer from flavors that shouldn't be there— untypical or unbalanced spices and bitter or scorched flavors.

Saving on Spreads

Margarine: Savings Plus Possible Health Benefits

Americans eat more than twice as much margarine as butter—10.5 pounds of margarine a year to every 4.6 pounds of butter. One reason may be cost; margarine typically costs less than half as much as butter.

Federal regulations require margarine, like butter, to be at least 80 percent fat. But butterfat (the real, the natural) is a highly saturated fat. Margarines, made from vegetable oil, are usually much less saturated. Consumption of saturated fat, of course, has been heavily implicated in heart disease.

Then there are the margarine substitutes. Products containing less than 80 percent fat—typically, 45 to 75 percent fat overall—are called "spreads." (Food manufacturers reduce the percentage of overall fat by adding water.) "Diet" margarines generally have even less fat.

In 1988, the Surgeon General urged Americans to cut down on cholesterol and fat, especially saturated fat. A year later, a committee of the National Research Council (NRC) echoed the theme and gave specific advice: Consume fewer than 300 milligrams of cholesterol daily and cut fat intake to no more than 30 percent of all calories. (Most Americans get closer to 37 percent of their calories from fat.) No more than one-third of the fat eaten should be saturated fat, the NRC committee added.

Margarine, derived from vegetable sources, has no cholesterol. Only animal products—meat, dairy, eggs, and fish and seafood—contain cholesterol. A tablespoon of butter contains 25 to 30 milligrams of cholesterol—about one-tenth of the daily quota.

Saturated fats tend to raise the body's blood cholesterol level more than cholesterol-rich foods (eggs) do. Here, the picture is more troubling for butter lovers. About 65 percent of the fat in butter is saturated. By contrast, the saturated-fat level in margarine ranges from 9 to 27 percent of total fat, depending on the oil used and how hydrogenated, or hardened, the oil is. Assuming the same oil is used, soft margarines (in tubs) or semiliquid margarines (in squeeze bottles) tend to be less hydrogenated—and thus less saturated—than regular margarines.

Following the NRC committee's recommendations, a woman who consumes 2,000 calories daily should have no more saturated fat over an entire day—and from all sources—than the amount in about 3 tablespoons of butter. A man who consumes 2,700 calories a day would nearly reach his daily saturated-fat quota with about 4 tablespoons of butter.

Note that merely eating a product low in saturated fat doesn't guarantee you'll eat less than the quota. If you eat enough of a regular margarine that's high in unsaturates, you could wind up consuming more saturated fat than you would by eating less of a lower-fat, more highly saturated product.

Nevertheless, margarine typically has less than one-third the saturated fat of butter. High-quality margarine tastes quite good, with some dairy flavor, an appropriate hint of oil flavor, and a texture that's a bit softer than butter's. Both products contain 100 calories per tablespoon.

Strawberry Jam—Forget the Gourmet Labels

If you're fond of strawberry jams and preserves, forget the fancy labels and prices. In our tests of jams, the more expensive "gourmet" jams did not distinguish themselves from the average jam.

Flavor. A strawberry jam should taste and smell like strawberries. But some of the flavor of the fresh berry is lost in processing, even when fresh fruit is used.

When you start with frozen fruit, as the commercial makers usually do, a lot of the fresh berry flavor is lost. A commercial strawberry jam, then, can't be expected to match a good homemade jam.

Strawberry is the most popular flavor in jams and preserves. (The distinction between "jams" and "preserves" has been blurred. Historically, preserves usually contained larger pieces of fruit and were made with more sugar than jams. Now, the terms seem to be used interchangeably.)

Jam may or may not contain large pieces of strawberry. Whatever their size, the fruit pieces should be relatively firm, and the gel around the fruit should be soft yet cohesive. The jam should also be easy to spread, and it shouldn't have the caramel flavor of overcooked strawberries, the flavor of any berry or fruit other than strawberry, or any bitter, artificial, or off-flavor taste.

Sugar content. A quality jam should be sweet, but not *overwhelmingly* sweet. Sugars show up on the ingredients lists in several guises—sucrose, corn syrup, cane sugar, and even honey. Jams are usually composed of 60 to 65 percent sugars, the level that retards spoilage. That much sugar translates into many calories. Most regular jams contain about 65 calories per 1-tablespoon serving.

For the calorie conscious or for those cutting down on sugar, low-calorie "light" jams may contain only half the calories of the regular jams and still taste good.

Low-calorie jam uses less sugar or sometimes substitutes saccharin.

Instead of using a lot of sugar to prevent spoilage, the low-calorie jams contain harmless preservatives such as ascorbic acid, sorbates, and propionates.

Peanut Butter: Nutritious, Tasty, and Cheap

Every day, about one out of six Americans eats peanut butter. By year's end, we've gobbled enough of the stuff to make 10 billion peanut-butter-and-jelly sandwiches. And we don't just tuck it between slices of bread. Some people dip into peanut butter with celery, apple slices, spoons, even an unadorned finger. Peanut butter is included in recipes for Senegalese sweet potatoes and cabbage, Thai noodle sauce, and Ghanaian chicken-and-okra stew.

Although peanuts alone are a good source of protein, that protein is incomplete because some essential amino acids are present in proportions that don't match the ones people need for good nutrition. Add the spread to a slice of bread, however, and you improve the quality of the protein. Peanut butter also contains fiber and B vitamins. It has a lot of fat, but most of the fat is unsaturated.

In addition to being nutritious, peanut butter is tasty and inexpensive. Whether you prefer creamy or chunky, there are a number of very good products from which to choose. Brands we like best in creamy form— **Jif, Smucker's, Deaf Smith Arrowhead Mills, Adams,** and **Skippy,** for instance—also head the chunky list.

The top product overall, chunky **Smucker's Natural** (no salt added), would satisfy not only people looking for an intense taste of peanuts but also those who want to avoid salt, sweetener, and stabilizer.

If you want to save a few pennies, choose **Jif** or **Skippy,** both a bit less expensive than most other high-rated peanut butters. A note to people concerned about aflatoxin, a natural poison sometimes found in peanut butter in small amounts: Samples of **Jif, Peter Pan, Skippy,** and **Smucker's** all showed substantially lower levels than did most other brands.

Unwelcome additions. For people who can't leave well enough alone, there's **Trombly's,** a brand of peanut butter laced with honey cinnamon, chocolate, chocolate raspberry, or banana crunch. It's sold by mail and in some supermarket chains and other large stores. Our trained sensory panelists tried all four varieties. The only one with more than a hint of peanut flavor was the banana crunch; the peanut flavor in the others was overpowered by the added ingredients.

The honey cinnamon, very sweet, had a fudgelike texture; the chocolate had a bitter aftertaste, and two of the four samples were laden with lumps of cocoa butter; the chocolate raspberry had the flavor of over-cooked preserves and tasted, our tasters said, like a Tootsie Roll; and the sticky banana crunch sported brittle chips of dried banana—"disconcerting to bite down on," the tasters pointed out.

Trombly's peanut butters cost per serving about double the highest-priced product in our regular-brand group. If you'd like to try peanut butter combinations, think about doing your own mixing.

Hot Pockets: Worth the Money?

A heat-and-eat food known as **Hot Pockets**—meat and vegetables swaddled in pastry—caught our eye for a 1990 report.

We tried two varieties of **Hot Pockets,** beef and cheddar and pepperoni pizza. We also tested the beef-and-broccoli and pizza varieties of the reduced-calorie version, **Lean Pockets.**

The pockets heated in a microwave oven with their "crisping sleeve" left a mess behind. Some of their filling bubbled out onto the oven floor. Even with the crisping sleeve, the crust became soggy. Pockets cooked in a regular oven had a crisper crust, and most of the filling stayed in place.

The pockets weren't necessarily neat to eat. The thin gravy in the beef and broccoli **Lean Pockets** dribbled or squirted out each time we took a bite.

Our expert tasters did not care for the salty taste of any of the pockets. The crusts tended to be slightly hard and tough, the tasters said. And all the pockets except the **Lean Pockets Pizza Deluxe** had an unappealing thin layer of paste on the crust's inner surface that tasted like raw dough.

Both the **Lean Pockets** beef and broccoli and the **Hot Pockets** beef and cheddar use "restructured" beef—meat that has been chunked, mixed with a binder, then extruded into new shapes. It was moderately tough and chewy, with a stale, warmed-over flavor.

The cheese in the beef-and-cheddar pocket was slightly stringy. And the small chunks of vegetables in the beef-and-broccoli pocket were slightly tough and spongelike, according to our tasters.

The two pizza varieties weren't much tastier. The **Hot Pockets** pizza had slightly spongy pepperoni and stringy cheese blobs. Sausage balls and pepperoni in the **Lean Pockets** were spongy. The **Lean Pockets** sauce was spicy—too spicy, perhaps, for some people.

Both **Hot Pockets** varieties were high in fat and sodium relative to the calories they provide (about 400 calories per pocket). The **Lean Pockets** pizza provided about 300 calories. The **Lean Pockets** beef and broccoli had the lowest amount of fat and calories.

We suggest that you pocket the money and put it toward some tastier, and more nutritious, meal.

Buying Hamburger—Fat Really Doesn't Matter

The varieties of ground beef available at supermarkets vary substantially in price because price and fat content have a close relationship. The cheaper the hamburger meat, the higher the fat content. Sometimes the package label states fat content; sometimes it doesn't. Packages labeled "ground beef" (with a maximum percentage of fat or a minimum amount of lean stated on the label) are generally the cheapest per pound and contain the highest percentage of fat.

The next cheapest type may be labeled "ground chuck," "lean beef," "ground beef, 80 percent lean," or "ground beef, does not exceed 22 percent fat."

More expensive ground beef will be labeled "ground round," "extra-lean beef," or "ground beef, 16 percent fat." The most expensive is usually "ground sirloin."

"Hamburger meat" and "ground beef" are designations one tends to use interchangeably, but there is a difference. "Hamburger meat" is ground beef to which seasonings and beef fat may have been added while the meat was being ground. "Ground beef" is just that, without any extras (but seasonings may be present if they are identified on the label).

A cooked quarter-pound patty ground from sirloin contains about 15 percent fat. Ground round and ground chuck have more fat, about 17 to 18 percent. "Ground beef" contains the most fat, about 20 percent.

The calorie count doesn't vary much from one kind of beef to the next. After cooking, a quarter pound of ground raw meat runs 200 to 210 calories. Ground sirloin's protein content (about 22 grams) isn't much higher than the 19 grams in a ground beef burger.

It makes sense to buy hamburger by price. When you pay extra to get ground round or sirloin, you don't necessarily get significantly leaner beef. Nor do you get much more cooked yield or protein for your money. And you don't save calories in any significant way.

The only circumstance in which it might be wiser to pay extra for leaner meat is when the dish you're cooking will contain the fat that would be rendered out if you were cooking burgers. For ordinary baking and grilling, buy either low-priced ground beef or, if you find that a bit chewy or too bland, ground chuck. And note that if a burger is going to be "dressed" with ketchup or other condiments, and if a meat loaf will be doused with sauce, the cheapest meat isn't likely to taste noticeably different from the next cheapest.

Freshness. When you buy ground beef, make sure the plastic film on the package isn't torn. Choose a package that feels cold, and make it one of the last items you select before going to the checkout counter.

Prepackaged ground beef is often red on the outside and a grayish shade inside. That's the result of the oxymyoglobin in meat. This natural pigment combines with oxygen when exposed to air and turns red.

Refrigerate ground beef as soon as possible after you buy it. Store the meat in the coldest part of the refrigerator, in its original transparent plastic film wrapping. If the meat has been wrapped in butcher paper, rewrap it in plastic film. If you don't plan on cooking the beef within a couple of days, freeze the package. It should keep for a couple of weeks. For longer storage, wrap the meat tightly in aluminum foil, freezer paper, or a plastic bag. If your freezer operates at 0°F, the meat should keep quite well for as long as three months. You can keep track of storage time by marking each package with the date it was placed in the freezer.

When you get around to thawing frozen ground beef, move the package from the freezer to the refrigerator. That will result in slow but safe thawing, because the meat will remain cold. For quick thawing, place the meat in a watertight wrapper in cold water or defrost it in a microwave oven; then cook it as soon as it is thawed.

Safety. Authorities advise against eating or tasting raw ground beef because of the possibility of bacterial contamination. As for eating rare hamburgers, the inside shouldn't be raw; it should be at least brownish pink in color.

Turkey Rolls:
Pricey Stand-in for a Whole Bird

Love turkey but hate to deal with it? Turkey rolls and roasts look appealing because of their easy preparation—no thawing, basting, stuffing, or disguising the leftovers. But they are not very good. These rolls can be gristly, salty, oily, and wet instead of juicy, and they may taste heavily of broth and processing—and usually they don't have much turkey flavor.

So far as nutrition goes, a serving of turkey roll has about the same number of calories as a serving of turkey breast. But the roll derives fewer of those calories from protein and more from fat. The rolls also contain a lot of sodium—about 600 milligrams in a 3.5-ounce serving. Turkey breast, by contrast, contains about one-third as much sodium.

Finally, turkey rolls are much more expensive, pound for pound, than whole turkeys.

Chicken: A Thrifty Meat If You Buy with Care

Chicken is wholesome and (if you don't eat the skin) low in fat. These factors probably helped poultry surpass beef in popularity. Chicken's reputation as a cheap meat has helped its popularity, too. In the supermarket, whole chicken and some cut-up parts are cheaper per pound than beef.

But despite its reputation, chicken isn't necessarily all that cheap when you consider cooking losses and inedible parts. Chicken breasts lose about 20 percent of their raw weight in cooking and almost 20 percent more when you discard the bones from the cooked meat. With thighs, you get only about 50 percent of the original weight. So the cost per pound of chicken you can actually eat is roughly twice the cost of the raw breasts or thighs. As a result, chicken often turns out to be no cheaper than hamburger.

Hamburger, too, slims down in cooking—by almost one-third of its raw weight. Even so, it's often considerably cheaper on your plate than chicken breasts or thighs. Only whole chicken or store-brand thighs beat hamburger in cost per serving; you often pay a premium for cut-up chicken. Brand-name chicken parts generally command a price premium over supermarket brands. And there isn't always more edible meat on brand-name bones to justify the extra money.

Some brand-name chicken parts, notably **Perdue** and **Empire** breasts, are indeed meatier than some supermarket parts, *Consumer Reports* noted in a February 1989 report. But certain supermarket brands provide more cooked meat than some brand-name parts. In any event, buxomness alone doesn't make a chicken a good buy; the meatiest parts are neither the cheapest per portion nor the tastiest.

Free-range chicken, dear to the nostalgic memories of gourmets, is likely to prove quite flavorful. But the breasts may be no tastier than some brand-name and supermarket breasts. And free-range breasts are stunningly expensive—more than double to triple the price of other breasts.

When you shop. Buying a brand-name bird doesn't guarantee superior taste or even consistent quality. But you're apt to pay a premium price for the brand name.

When you shop for chicken, just compare the purchase price of your alternatives. Once you've identified the cheapest brand per pound, select the breasts or thighs that look plump.

To find the freshest chicken, select the package with the latest sell-by date. If you're going to freeze the bird, be sure to rewrap it tightly in aluminum foil, freezer wrap, or a plastic bag. Chicken will then keep in the freezer for about six months without much loss in quality.

Don't rely on a grade level to help you find the best chicken. Any chicken parts you buy are likely to be Grade A, whether the label says so or not. Grade B and C chickens usually end up as frozen pot pies, chicken-noodle soup, and the like. In any event, a Grade A sticker simply means that the chicken meets federal standards for looks and fleshiness; it's no guarantee of tenderness or tastiness.

Rice Mixes: Save by Doing It Yourself

Rice-A-Roni, the front-runner in prepared rice mixes, has long called itself "the San Francisco treat." Apparently a lot of people agree that mixes are a treat—they represent the fastest-growing segment of the rice marketplace. But the products are no boon to those concerned about sodium. A typical cup of cooked mix packs more than 800 milligrams, about a quarter of what's recommended as an adult's daily intake. And it can cost 10 times as much as regular white rice. That's a lot to pay for a sprinkling of dried herbs, spices, or cheese.

You can prepare a better-tasting and cheaper dish with little effort. The amount of fat and calories may be similar, but you can cut down on the salt or leave it out. First, choose a good white or brown rice. Sauté it in butter or margarine with the desired combination of chopped onion, garlic, and vegetables, add herbs or spices, then add hot water or broth and cook in the usual way.

Don't Pay for Packaging

New Food Packaging: Today, Pasta. Tomorrow, the Main Course?

The **Contadina Fresh** pasta fetching a premium price at the supermarket is noteworthy more for the packaging than the product. Carnation Company, which markets the **Contadina Fresh** line, was one of the first companies in the United States to use the "modified-atmosphere" packaging process. Some of the air in the package is replaced with other gases, such as nitrogen and carbon dioxide, when the food is packaged. The packages are then refrigerated.

This kind of packaging holds considerable promise. The modified atmosphere makes the food less perishable, so it can remain on sale longer than milk, meat, and other refrigerated foods. (**Contadina Fresh** pasta, for example, has a 30-day shelf life and a clear expiration date to tell you when time's up.) Further, the food gains its shelf life without suffering the damage to flavor caused by freezing or canning.

But the modified-atmosphere packaging also holds some hazards. If the food isn't packaged properly and refrigerated constantly, it may spoil. Food processors in the United States, aware of the risk of spoilage, say they are maintaining scrupulous quality control. In Europe, where this kind of packaging is more widely used, problems with it reportedly have been minimal.

The **Contadina Fresh** fettuccine we tested, though packaged in an intriguing new way, isn't very different in quality from ordinary dried fettuccine in a box. **Contadina Fresh** and **Ronzoni** dried both tasted, well, like fettuccine. **Contadina** tasted eggier than **Ronzoni**; the **Ronzoni** tasted more of grain.

Nutritionally, **Contadina** and **Ronzoni** fettuccine were comparable. A 10-ounce serving of **Contadina** contained slightly higher amounts of fat, protein, and cholesterol.

The main difference between **Contadina** fresh and **Ronzoni** dried? The fresh pasta in the new package costs much more than the dry.

Mail-Order Food: Often Overpriced

The high prices charged by mail-order food companies often buy you fancy packaging and trimmings: Filet mignon may be delivered in a Styrofoam cooler packed with dry ice; fruit comes wrapped in tissue paper and foil and packed in a carton stuffed with protective "grass." But do fancy prices buy better quality than you can get from a local store?

Filet mignon. Most people who buy mail-order steak buy it as a gift for someone else. The best mail-order steaks are tender and flavorful, with no off-flavors or visible fat or gristle. But consumers who order by mail for themselves, assuming they are getting a superior product, should first check out a local butcher shop. Prime filet mignon could turn out to be as good there as the best mail-order steak, and a lot less expensive.

Smoked salmon. If you're buying mail-order salmon as a gift, don't expect top quality. Buy the least expensive brand you can, and hope the fancy wrapping pleases the gift's recipient enough to compensate for what's inside. If you're buying for yourself, you may get better salmon by shopping in your neighborhood.

Cheddar cheese. You may find a good, fresh cheddar locally, one as good as the best you can get by mail. Look for cheese that's creamy yellow, with no color change or dryness at the edges. There should be a slight crumbliness at the cut edge, and the cheese should be wrapped tightly.

Coffee beans. Coffee beans would appear to be an ideal mail-order food. They require no special packaging or handling and they're not heavy. An unusual variety of coffee can be a nice present for someone who doesn't have a specialty shop nearby. And it can be fun for you, since you can experiment conveniently with various types that may not be available in your area.

Be warned, however, before you decide to make mail-order coffee your gift of choice for friends and relatives. In our 1991 tests, we were disappointed with the quality of most of the "gourmet" coffee beans being hyped by mail-order gourmet and specialty outlets. As a rule, our tasters found them either "underroasted" and "weak" or "overroasted" and "bitter." A bright spot were the beans sold through humbler outfits such as grocery chains. In particular, A & P's Eight O'Clock 100% Colombian beans faired well. The grocery chain brands were also far less expensive, as a rule, than the gourmet and mail-order brands.

Still, even if you pay $12 per pound, an exotic gourmet coffee costs less than 20 cents per cup—far less than a soft drink. At these prices you can afford to shop around until you find a gourmet coffee that suits your taste.

In most cases, it should take a week or two for a mail-order company to deliver your order. If the package spoils during shipping or the person you sent it to is not satisfied when it arrives, most mail-order companies will refund your money or reship the order.

Planning Meatless Meals? Consider Cottage Cheese

Nutrition. Cottage cheese is a reasonable protein substitute for meat. The protein in a 4-ounce portion, generally about 14 grams, provides about one-quarter of an adult's recommended daily intake (44 to 65 grams). Furthermore, the cheese delivers its protein without the load of calories found in meat. Creamed cottage cheese averages about 108 calories per half-cup serving—half the calories in a cooked hamburger patty, some two-thirds of the calories in a typical serving of tuna. Low-fat cottage cheese is only slightly lower in calories than the creamed type, ranging from about 75 to 85 calories per serving in 1-percent-fat cheese to 85 to 110 calories in 2-percent-fat cheese.

You also get more calcium in cottage cheese than you do in most fish or red meat. On the average, cottage cheese provides a respectable 74 milligrams of calcium in a half-cup portion. However, a typical serving of tuna or cooked hamburger supplies more of certain important nutrients. You should include bread or crackers, fruit, or a vegetable with cottage cheese to make a well-balanced meal.

Frozen Pot Pies: Some Are Fairly Cheap and Very Good

You *can* find a pot pie that's reasonably inexpensive and very good. We did when we tested frozen ones for a January 1990 report. But others were merely cheap.

We tested four varieties: beef, chicken, turkey, and vegetable with beef. Most weighed only 7 or 8 ounces, although the heftiest, **Swanson Hungry-Man** pies, were a pound apiece.

What's in them. USDA regulations govern the minimum amounts of meat in today's frozen pot pies. For beef pies, processors must provide a mere 25 percent by weight in raw beef; for poultry pies 14 percent

cooked flesh is the minimum (the discrepancy between those percentages presumably being counterbalanced by weight lost as the beef
cooks). For pies categorized as vegetable with beef, processors need contribute only 12 percent raw beef by weight.

None of the pot pies we tested could muster all the favorable attributes necessary to earn a judgment of excellent. But **Stouffer's** and
Swanson products time and again proved themselves superior to the rest
of the field. They fell down on only a few points: by missing distinctive
flavors in the vegetables (typically peas, potatoes, and carrots), by lacking
sufficiently firm vegetables, and by lacking enough flavor in the crust. All
the **Stouffer's** pies were judged very good, as were the **Swanson Hungry-
Man** turkey pie and all three **Swanson** chicken pies that we tested
(**Homestyle Recipe, Hungry-Man,** and **Original Style**). The beef in the
Swanson pies (**Hungry-Man** and **Original Style**) was chewy and a little
stringy.

At around 20 cents an ounce, though, the **Stouffer's** and **Swanson
Homestyle Recipe** pies were relatively expensive. Two other **Swanson**
variants, **Hungry-Man** and **Original Style** pies, cost 11 to 14 cents per
ounce. Overall, considering taste and nutrition as well as cost, we'd say
that a 16-ounce **Hungry-Man** might provide the best deal for someone
seeking a full pot-pie meal. Those **Swanson** pies cost about $1.75 to
$2.20 apiece, depending on the meat type. Any of them is generally
superior, nutritionally, to any two of the 8-ounce or smaller pies we
tested, with fewer calories and less fat and sodium.

The best thing that the less palatable pies had going for them was
price. Many of them cost only five to seven cents an ounce.

Saving Money on Snacks

Popcorn: As Snacks Go, Not Very Sinful

Popcorn is fairly nutritious—low in calories, reasonably high in fiber.
And it's cheaper than most snacks for munching. Without oil or added
butter, a 3-cup serving can cost as little as three cents.

The microwave products on supermarket shelves come in numerous
varieties, including "natural," "butter," and other flavors. Natural flavor more or less means plain, unbuttered popcorn, though some natural
products come with *added* "natural flavor"—an essence of corn, presumably. Any added flavoring is contained in the product's oil, a solidi-
fied mass packed with the corn in the disposable cooking bag.

The way you cook popcorn probably affects taste more than the brand. Microwave popcorns are better than the corns cooked in hot oil, and those are better than the same products cooked in a hot-air popper.

By and large, popcorn popped in hot oil is less crisp and a little tougher than microwave popcorn—telltale signs of too much moisture in the cooking. Apparently, microwave cooking allows moisture to escape better than hot-oil poppery.

Hot-air popping perhaps allows moisture to escape too well. It makes the corn pop into the biggest blossoms, but they tend to be tougher and less crisp than kernels popped either in a microwave oven or in hot oil. With popcorn, bigger (and fluffier) is not necessarily better. Hot-air-popped corn also tends to leave more particles stuck in your teeth.

Varieties that come in their own pan pose problems of a different sort. They are among the most troublesome to make because you have to keep the pan moving in a vigorous motion on the stove (and you still end up with burned corn at the bottom).

Inevitably, not all the kernels pop successfully. Down at the bottom of the bowl or the bag one finds unpopped and partly popped kernels. Microwaving generally leaves a bit more unpopped corn than other methods.

If you decide on buying bagged, prepopped popcorn, you can expect a lack of crispiness and an overly chewy texture.

You pay a considerable premium for the convenience of microwave popcorn. A typical price for a 3-cup serving is about double that of oil-popped corn (including the price of the oil) and five times more than air-popped corn.

One factor that can affect the price per serving is the size of the popped kernels. Other things being equal, popping with air tends to puff a bigger bloom of popcorn out of each kernel, so it takes fewer kernels to make 3 cups. A typical serving of air-popped corn weighs about two-thirds of an ounce, whereas most microwave and hot-oil varieties weigh a full ounce, plus or minus a small fraction.

Chocolate Bars: Pricey Isn't Necessarily Better

Candy isn't just kids' stuff anymore. Adults buy more than half of it these days, and what they buy, mostly, is chocolate candy. Not necessarily the familiar chocolate bar of childhood, but fancier stuff, with a fancier price.

Do you buy something superior when you peel off bills for an expensive imported bar of chocolate instead of spending loose change for a domestic brand? To find out, we evaluated more than four dozen brands and varieties of chocolate bar—dark bittersweet chocolates, milk chocolates, white chocolates, and chocolates with added nuts, fruits, or crisped rice. The selection included imports from Switzerland, the Netherlands, Germany, Belgium, and Italy, as well as a broad range of domestic bars.

The results of the taste tests may throw chocolate fanciers into disarray. The high-priced brands weren't necessarily the best. And when it came to milk chocolates and chocolates with nuts or fruits, a number of moderately priced American brands did better than the imports.

Occasionally, you may come across a chocolate bar with a whitish or grayish film on the surface. The discoloration, called "bloom," can occur if chocolate is exposed to warmth; fat or sugar then migrates to the surface of the bar. Fat bloom is greasy and can be rubbed off; sugar bloom is crystalline. Bloom doesn't affect flavor or make chocolate unsafe. Don't worry about it.

Avoid Unnecessary Products

Vitamin Supplements: Don't Overspend for "Insurance"

The best way to get vitamins is from the foods in a balanced diet. Vitamin supplementation may be appropriate for children up to two years old and for people with certain illnesses.

Rather than take vitamins for "insurance," evaluate your diet to determine whether you are eating a variety of foods from the basic groups. If you have trouble figuring that out by yourself, record what you eat for a week and ask a registered dietician or a physician whether you are missing anything. If you are, the best course of action is probably to improve your eating habits, not to supplement your diet with vitamins.

As a rule, don't take more than the RDA amounts (the Recommended Dietary Allowances published by the Food and Nutrition Board of the National Research Council/National Academy of Sciences), and avoid doctors or nutrition consultants who recommend vitamins as cure-alls. Furthermore, if you must take vitamins, note that synthetic vitamins are just as effective as "natural" vitamins.

It's possible to overdose on some vitamins. Fat-soluble vitamins (A, D, E, and K) are not excreted efficiently—generally stored in the body until used up, they can accumulate to toxic levels. For example, prolonged excessive intake of vitamin A can cause headache, increased pressure on the brain, bone pain, and damage to the liver. Excessive vitamin-D dosage can cause high blood calcium levels and kidney damage.

Though the water-soluble vitamins are generally excreted quickly when taken to excess, some of them can cause trouble. Large doses of niacin can cause severe flushes, skin rash, and abnormal liver-function tests. High doses of vitamin C can cause diarrhea. And high doses of vitamin B-6 over long periods can cause permanent damage to the peripheral nervous system.

Bottled Water

Bulk bottled water—sold in jugs or delivered to kitchen coolers—need meet no standard higher than prevailing government standards for tap water.

Some bottled waters that we've tested in the past are actually drawn from municipal water systems, though they *may* undergo additional filtering, distillation, or other treatment. No federal rule obligates bottlers to disclose the location of their water's source. California, Connecticut, Florida, New York, and Texas have more stringent rules. In addition, all water bottlers are expected to follow "good manufacturing practices" for cleanliness.

Saving on Cookware
Who Needs Cookware in a Matched Set?

There's no practical reason to buy cookware in a matching set. If, for example, you buy a set of pots and pans with metal handles so you can use the skillet for broiling, you are stuck with several hot-handled saucepans. Half a dozen pieces of well-designed cookware made from appropriate materials will see you through most recipes. Here's the basic range-top cookware every kitchen should have:

• *Saucepans.* You'll need a minimum of two—a 2-quart and a 3-quart pan—both with lids. Look for sturdy stainless-steel saucepans with copper or aluminum embedded in the bottom and with comfortable, plastic handles. A nonstick saucepan is optional but handy for cooking oatmeal, puddings, or sticky sauces that can make a conventional pan hard to clean.

• *Frypans.* You'll need a 10-inch skillet that heats very evenly and a 7-

to 10-inch "gourmet" pan with a nonstick coating. As a rule, skillets have steep sides, and gourmet, sauté, or omelet pans have shallow, curved sides. Steep-sided pans usually hold more and are good for frying or cooking food items in liquid. The sloped sides of a gourmet pan make it easier to slide a spatula in when turning an omelet, for example.

Like a saucepan, the skillet should be made of stainless steel with an aluminum or copper bottom. Cast aluminum is an acceptable substitute, but if the pans have an anodized aluminum surface, don't put them in a dishwasher.

• *Dutch oven.* A Dutch oven is used for baking and braising—that is, browning the meat on top of the stove and then transferring it to the oven to cook. A Dutch oven should be made of thick aluminum or cast iron to hold the heat. The handles should be metal and able to withstand even a hot oven.

• *Stockpot.* Stockpots rely on the liquid in the pot to distribute heat. In a process called convection, the heated liquid rises, while the colder, slightly heavier liquid sinks. A stockpot is designed with a relatively narrow bottom and high sides so that it can distribute heat quickly and evenly without much evaporation. For this type of pot, it doesn't matter what metal you use. You can save money by buying a pot made from plain aluminum, stainless steel, or porcelain-coated steel. If you choose aluminum, make sure the bottom is thick enough to resist dents.

You may want to add a double boiler for cooking delicate sauces; a large, inexpensive pot for boiling pasta and corn; and a cast-iron skillet for pan broiling.

Taking care of cookware. Here are a few simple rules for prolonging the life of your pans:

• Always match the pan size to the burner and use the lowest possible heat for whatever dish you are cooking.

• If you overheat a metal pan, don't plunge it into cold water. And don't heat a pan you just took from the freezer. Subjecting a pan to temperature extremes can "craze" a porcelain surface and cause metal to warp.

• Don't chop or slice anything in a pan. Scratches can mar a pan's looks and make it difficult to clean. Always use plastic or wooden utensils with nonstick pans.

• When cleaning, soak before you scrub. And never scour stainless steel with abrasive cleansers.

Microwave Cookware

Once you start using a microwave oven, you'll find yourself changing old habits. One of them is what you cook in. You'll make hot chocolate in the same cup you drink from. You'll heat dinner right on your plate. And your stainless-steel cookware will be left hanging on the wall. Metal reflects microwave energy—use a metal pot in a microwave oven and you'll get either a cold meal or a damaged oven.

Many common kitchen items are fine for microwave cooking. Bacon cooks well on paper towels. You can defrost foods right in their plastic freezer containers (with the cover off), so long as you're careful not to heat the food enough to melt the plastic. You can even heat food in straw serving baskets.

Most ceramic or glass casseroles and baking dishes for use in a regular oven also work in a microwave oven. Such utensils cost a lot less than many dishes designed for microwave use. An old-fashioned glass dish may suit your needs just fine. Still, if you use a microwave a lot, you may want some cookware made specifically for the purpose.

A utensil's shape affects its performance in a microwave oven. Round pans are superior for casseroles and meat loaf; in rectangular ones, food in the corners tends to overcook. Food also cooks more evenly when spread out in a shallow pan. Most glass and ceramic microwave utensils can also be used in a regular oven, if it's no hotter than 375°F to 400°F. Few, if any, microwave pots and pans can be used on a range top. Plastic microwave utensils may also be used in a regular oven, but they may give off an unpleasant odor.

Clever design gives many microwave utensils versatility. Casserole lids, for example, can be used as cooking vessels. Some open roasting racks double as baking trays. Others come with a trivet to use when roasting and remove when baking. A few racks come with a cover to help keep food from drying out and spattering during cooking.

Food browns better in a microwave oven when you use a special browning dish but still not as appetizingly as when cooked the traditional way. Grilled cheese sandwiches turn out pale and unevenly cooked—the cheese melts before the bread shows much color. If you don't like microwaved roasts, you don't need a special roasting rack. Microwave ovens also don't bake well, so baking utensils aren't essential.

To see if one of your nonmetal dishes or utensils is usable in the microwave, set the oven on High and put the dish inside for about eight minutes. If the dish stays fairly cool to the touch, it's probably all right for microwave use. But don't use good china or dishes with a decorative metal trim in a microwave. Be careful of pottery, which may have metal in the glaze or impurities in the clay.

Cutting Costs by Careful Storage and Recycling

Store Food Wisely to Preserve Eating Quality

Spoiled foods can't (or shouldn't) be eaten. So good food storage has budgetary as well as safety implications.

Some people leave hot foods uncovered to cool before storing them in the refrigerator. Prompt refrigeration, however, is a good safety precaution. The danger is that if any bacteria survive the cooking process, they'll proliferate much faster if the food is allowed to cool at room temperature for an hour or two before being refrigerated.

But food poisoning is not often a problem in home cooking; it's more common in commercial or institutional facilities, where food is handled in bulk quantities. So allowing small portions of food to cool for a while, the old-fashioned way, is unlikely to pose a threat—unless it sits there too long.

Whether you refrigerate the food or not (we suggest you do), be sure to cover it. Leaving food uncovered can hasten spoilage by exposing it to microorganisms in the air. In fact, cover any food you intend to store, whether or not you let it cool. A pot cover or paper towel can help protect it. Covering food can also prevent it from picking up other cooking odors; a hint of garlic won't enhance your custard pie or chocolate pudding.

If you want to seal hot food in plastic wrap or foil, wait until it has cooled; this will help prevent excessive moisture condensation.

Save by Recycling Your Cooking Oil

Many people discard cooking oil after each session of deep-frying. High-quality oil should remain fit for more frying if it's filtered through cheesecloth or a fine sieve to remove burned food particles that might speed its deterioration. Since the used oil has undoubtedly suffered some degradation anyway, infuse it, by one-quarter to one-third, with fresh oil at each new use. This infusion will minimize the tendency of an oil to begin smoking at an ever lower temperature as it decomposes with use.

TWO

Lowering Your Home Expenses

Overpaying on any single purchase of paint, cleaning products, garbage bags, or the like won't send you to the poorhouse. But it's surprising how the extra nickels and dimes mount up over time. Here are some budget-gentle ways to keep your household stocked with life's little necessities.

Save on Soaps and Detergents

Your Best Buy in Laundry Detergents

You don't have to pay extra for performance, we found when we tested laundry detergents for a February 1991 report. Indeed, there is little correlation between price and cleaning ability. You pay more for the convenience of liquids or the premeasured packets of **Fab 1 Shot.** The addition of bleach adds a few pennies per wash, too, as do phosphate-free or biodegradable products. Interestingly, detergents containing fabric softener don't cost any more than the detergent products alone. They also don't work very well, either as detergents or as softeners.

When we published our test findings, the powders cost us 16 to 94 cents per wash; the liquids, 30 to 53 cents. Our cost-per-wash estimates are based on the amount of detergent needed to do a large or heavily soiled load. You'll spend less to launder a regular wash. Penny-pinchers can reap savings by forgetting brand loyalty: Clip coupons and stock up on whatever satisfactory product is on sale.

Good performers. Overall, the phosphorus version of **Tide With Bleach** did best. Parents will appreciate its prowess on chocolate, grass, and grape juice. At 35 cents per use, it was midpriced among the tested detergents. Nearly as good and 11 cents cheaper was **New System Surf,** a nonbleach phosphorus powder. It brightened as well as the top-rated **Tide.**

Among nonphosphorus brands, **Tide With Bleach** led again; it almost matched its phosphorus twin. (The difference: Nonphosphorus **Tide With Bleach** was not quite as good at brightening and at treating a tea stain.) Regular **Tide** powder, at 29 cents a wash, came in second.

Liquids can now clean nearly as well as the leading powders. **New System Surf** and **Advanced Action Wisk** were the best liquids. **Wisk** was better at brightening, **Surf** at removing makeup and grape juice. Washing costs for both products ran a little over 40 cents a load.

Fab Ultra ranked above **Ultra Tide** and **Wisk Power Scoop,** the two other superconcentrated powders we tested, and among the top detergents overall.

Stay away from the detergent–fabric softener combinations, which were only moderately successful at either task. The optimal softener is a liquid you add during the rinse cycle.

What if . . . ? Because people don't wash laundry under the same conditions, we ran a series of special tests on three detergents: a powder with phosphorus (regular **Tide**), a phosphorus-free powder **(Purex),** and a liquid **(Advanced Action Wisk).**

We washed some stained cotton/polyester swatches in hard water, others in cold water. We tinkered with the dosage recommended for a large-capacity washer, lowering it and raising it by 50 percent. Finally, we presoaked some swatches.

Hard water: All three products lost some cleaning power here. The **Tide** was affected least; its phosphates softened water effectively and protected the detergent against a loss of stain-cleaning ability.

Cold water: Only **Tide** did much worse when we dropped the water temperature. **Wisk** showed no significant change in performance; **Purex** improved slightly.

Different dose: You can't get away with using a lot less detergent. Halving the recommended dose generally depressed cleaning scores. On the other hand, none of the swatches came out looking much better when we raised the dose by 50 percent.

Presoaking: Allowing the swatches to soak for 15 minutes in a detergent-and-water solution didn't help **Tide** or **Wisk** much. But it gave a big boost to **Purex,** a marginal cleaner.

Ways to Shave Costs of fabric Softeners

While we were testing laundry detergents, we were also evaluating fabric softeners. There are three basic types of fabric softener. *Rinse liquids* are added to the wash during the rinse cycle; many washing machines add them automatically from a dispenser atop the agitator. *Dryer sheets* of fiber or foam are impregnated with softener. You throw a sheet into the dryer along with the laundry, and heat releases the softener. *Detergent-softeners* contain both products. The softener is present during the wash cycle, and the manufacturer has to use chemical tricks to make sure that it sticks around for the rinse cycle. A variation of the detergent-softener is the **Fab 1 Shot** single-use packet, which looks like a big teabag. The bag contains detergent, which dissolves during the wash; the fibers of the bag hold the softener. When the washing machine has done its work, you transfer the empty bag to the dryer along with the laundry.

Pinching pennies. The better rinse liquids cost us between 11 and 16 cents per use. The price of a dryer sheet ranged from 4 to 8 cents. The most effective detergent-softeners cost us between 13 and 23 cents per use. If you consider that you also get your laundry cleaned for that price, the combination products look like the best deal, but they're not: They neither clean nor soften as well as single-purpose products.

You can save money by buying whatever is on sale or using the coupons that come with your Sunday newspaper. You might also try using a little less than the recommended amount of a softener—cutting a dryer sheet in half, for example. (We didn't test them that way, but we'd guess that the practice would work with small washloads.)

How to Pick a Good Bleach

Chlorine bleach, when used properly, is the most effective way to whiten clothes, including many synthetics. It's ideal for the occasional whitening your wash may need. But knowing how to use chlorine bleach is essential: Improper or long-term use will take its toll on colors and fabric life.

Using chlorine bleach may be tricky, but buying it is simple. The only real difference among chlorine bleaches is apt to be price. **Clorox** and **Purex,** the best-selling brands, sell for considerably more than supermarket brands.

All-fabric powdered bleaches have the advantage of being safe with most fabrics and dyes, even over the long term. But they're a lot more expensive to use than chlorine bleaches, and they aren't as good at whitening.

You can get extra whitening performance out of powdered all-fabric bleaches, if you prefer them. When we doubled the recommended dose in bleach tests, some all-fabric brands approached chlorine bleach in whitening ability. Of course, that maneuver doubles their cost per use.

A more reasonable and less costly approach might be to incorporate both chlorine and all-fabric bleach into your laundry routine. For chlorine-safe white fabrics, occasional and cautious use of chlorine bleach will deliver the whitening you need. Use all-fabric bleach to brighten colors without fading, whiten fabrics that aren't safe with chlorine bleach, and remove greasy stains.

When you do use chlorine bleach, follow these guidelines:

1. Bleach only when necessary, or you will get color fading and fabric deterioration.

2. Before you bleach, read the garment's care label.

3. Don't use chlorine bleach on wool, silk, mohair, or noncolorfast fabrics or dyes. If you're unsure about a garment's fabric content, experiment with a slightly diluted solution of bleach on an inside seam. Any discoloration should appear in a minute or so.

4. If your washer has a bleach dispenser, use it according to the manufacturer's directions. If there's no dispenser, you can add the bleach full strength to the wash water *before* you add the laundary or dilute the bleach with a generous amount of water and add it to laundry that is already immersed in wash water.

5. *Never* use chlorine bleach with ammonia or toilet cleaners. That combination can produce deadly fumes.

Who Needs Special Hand-Laundry Detergents?

Sometimes what makes a garment more difficult to clean is the fiber itself. Woolens can shrink or lose their shape. Silks can shrink, pucker, or fade. Some cottons can shrink or fade, too.

Sometimes the finish makes for difficult laundering. Rayon, for instance, needs a finish to give it body, a finish that harsh treatment can wash away. A garment's weave, its dyes, or construction (linings, edgings, interface) can conspire to make cleaning an all-but-impossible job.

Your best guide on how to clean a fabric is the care label, which by law must be sewn into virtually all articles of clothing. If that label says a garment must be dry-cleaned, take the advice. If the label permits hand washing, you have to decide how to wash it.

On supermarket shelves, next to the **Tide** and **Cheer,** stands **Woolite,** the product that originally persuaded shoppers they need special hand-washing detergents. **Woolite,** as the name implies, began with a special claim for cleaning wool. Competitors in the specialization game include **Softball Cot'nwash** for cotton sweaters and **Silk'n Wash,** which touts its "Special Formula Enriched with Silk Protein."

Specialization as a selling tool can cut both ways. Make a detergent *too* specialized, and shoppers may pass it up for something that can tackle a wider variety of garments. So these cleaners also claim to work on other "fine washables," too.

But do you really need a special detergent? To find out, we tested for a May 1989 report not only the specialized detergents but some ordinary laundry detergents—and even dishwashing liquids, many of which claim to double as detergents for fine washables.

For our main test we used white silk crepe turned a mousy gray with a standard concoction of dust and simulated sebum (skin oil), the kind of ring-around-the-collar dirt that a silk blouse or shirt might easily pick up.

We used a special machine to simulate very gentle hand washing and always washed in hard water at 70°F, water warm enough to be comfortable to hands but cool enough to prevent shrinkage. And we kept the wash and rinse to four minutes each. The less time delicate fabrics soak, the better.

We also tested the detergents' prowess at fighting stains on wool gabardine, nylon, rayon, and silk. We stained large fabric swatches with red wine, spaghetti sauce, and strong tea; let the stains set for a week; and then gave the swatches the same gentle-wash treatment as in the main test.

Our tests indicated that you can hand wash delicate fabrics for mere pennies or for substantially more, depending on which detergent you choose. Since there was little difference in overall cleaning ability among the better products, whether specialized detergent, laundry detergent, or dishwashing liquid, we see no reason to buy one of the specialized brands. Use a dishwashing liquid (1 teaspoon per 2-quart wash). All they lack are the optical brighteners that regular detergents and most hand-washing products contain to give whites extra dazzle.

Saving Money on Hand Soap

We recruited a score of staffers to visit our chemistry lab twice a day to get their hands dirty, then wash them with one of the 42 brands we were testing for a January 1991 report. In their morning visits, the panelists wore a surgical glove on their right hand and soiled their left with a gooey smear of finely powdered clay mixed with light mineral oil. In the afternoon, they reversed hands.

Panelists used as much soap and took as much time washing as they needed. We carefully removed or covered the name of each product so as not to prejudice our hand washers.

Panelists judged how well the soaps cleaned and how their hands felt after soaping. They also assessed how well the soaps lathered up. We weighed soaps before and after use to gauge how long they lasted and how much they actually cost to use.

None of the soaps was judged less than good in cleaning or in the way they left the hands feeling. But some clearly performed better than others. **Dove Unscented White,** a bar containing moisturizing cream, won the panel's highest marks for both cleaning and feel—and for its lathering and ease of rinsing.

Save on Kitchen Aids

Dishwasher Detergents: Savings for Some

If you have a good dishwasher and soft water, you can save money and detergent: Buy the cheapest dishwasher detergent you can find. (A brand name on sale can cost less than a supermarket's own brand.) However, with hard water, a so-so machine, or other dishwashing problems, it's best to use the most effective detergent possible.

Powdered detergents have been standard for a long time, even though they are imperfect. They can cake up in the box or in a dishwasher's dispenser cup. Or they may leave gritty deposits of undissolved detergent on dishes and glassware. That is more likely to happen if you pour the detergent into the machine and don't start the dishwasher immediately, thereby permitting the detergent powder to pick up moisture, which diminishes its solubility.

Liquid dishwasher detergents are supposed to solve the problems of the powdered products. These detergents are actually gels that contain a lot of fine, powdered clay and other suspended solids. They're thick enough to stay put in the dispenser cup when you close the dishwasher door. Despite the new form, liquid products resemble powders quite closely in makeup. In troublesome situations, the best performer is still apt to be a powder.

In general, a name-brand product cleans better than a store brand and is less likely to leave glass plates and tumblers cloudy or spotted. The liquids aren't as good as the best powders at keeping glasses free of water spots and food debris. And liquids can leave an unsightly film on glasses, instead of the powders' annoying grit.

Some dishwashing detergents can harm the decoration on fine china. Overglaze (the colored, somewhat dull decoration on china) is applied after the main glaze. It's fired at a lower temperature than the main glaze and thus is less durable. The same is true of gilding and other metallic decorations. We recommend that you hand wash your fine china.

How to Buy Paper Towels Wisely

The strongest, most absorbent towels tend to be among the premium-priced brands. But that doesn't make those towels the best value. For simple spills or small mop-ups, keep a roll of cheap paper towels handy.

To get the best price, check unit prices at the supermarket or take a pocket calculator to compute the price per square foot (or per 100 square feet) yourself. It's true that towels are perforated and that the price per square foot is affected in a practical way by how much towel you have to tear off the roll each time you use one. Nevertheless, the careful shopper may find some satisfaction in trying to "beat the game," at least once in a while.

A cents-off coupon or a special store sale may make an otherwise expensive brand a good buy. But towels in two-roll or three-roll packs don't necessarily give you a price break; a multiple-roll pack may be no cheaper per 100 towels or per 100 square feet than single rolls of the same brand.

Garbage Bags: Check Out the Cheapies

Plastic garbage bags come in many varieties—trash, rubbish, scrap, kitchen, wastebasket, and lawn and leaf. The name, along with some fine print on the package, is supposed to help you pick the right size bag for your needs. But what about the time you bought "26-gallon" bags that barely fit the 26-gallon can? Some manufacturers measure a bag's capacity when it is filled to the brim; others measure with the bag tied closed. Without industry-wide standards, some bags won't fit some garbage cans, even though the gallonage is the same for both.

You might think that the thickness of the plastic or the number of plies, as given on the label, would be a good guide to the quality of a bag. That's not so. A bag 2 mils (or .002 inch) thick may be weaker than a bag 1.3 mil thick. Paying more to buy the thickest bags you can find is no guarantee you'll get a strong bag.

If a cheaper bag turns out to meet your needs and is strong enough most of the time but not for an occasional heavy load, try double-bagging for those challenging occasions.

Cleaning Drains Without Chemicals

A little forethought can spare you the expense of a chemical drain cleaner. The best way to keep a drain flowing is to pour some boiling water down it about once a week. Heat about a gallon, pour in half, wait a few minutes, then pour in the rest. Be careful to pour the water directly down into the drain rather than in the basin—boiling water may crack porcelain fixtures.

If a drain becomes clogged despite the boiling-water treatment, there are chemical drain cleaners you can use. But those cleaners are among the most hazardous of consumer products. Most of them are strongly corrosive alkalies or concentrated acids: They open a blocked drain by eating and boiling their way through the clog. Such chemicals can severely damage your eyes, lungs, and skin. Accidentally swallowing even a small amount of drain opener can result in injury or even death. It is far safer and no less effective to use a mechanical device to clear a clogged drain.

Try a rubber plunger first. It's cheap and easy to use, and it usually works. A second alternative is a product that uses pressurized air or gas to push an obstruction around the bend in the drainpipe and into the clear. But beware of the pressure if you have old, corroded drain lines.

Stubborn clogs call for the services of a licensed plumber.

Let Your Oven Do the Cleaning

Both self-cleaning ovens and chemical oven cleaners will get rid of baked-on grime. But self-cleaning ovens do the dirty work with less fuss, less expense, and less hazard to you and the world around you.

The ovens basically incinerate what's spilled or splattered inside. When you activate the self-cleaning cycle, the oven heats to between

800°F and 1,000°F or so, and encrusted food turns to ash. When the cycle is complete, you just wipe the ashy residue away with a damp sponge.

Because such ovens are well insulated, they use on average only about 40 to 70 cents' worth of electricity during a 3½-hour cleaning. Letting the oven do the job is cheaper than using an aerosol oven cleaner, which costs around $2 for a 16-ounce can, good for two cleanings.

One drawback: Ovens that are especially dirty can release smoke from a back vent or burner for up to 30 minutes while they're cleaning. So long as you self-clean the oven before it becomes encrusted and keep the kitchen well ventilated, smoke should not be a problem.

Most oven cleaners contain lye (sodium or potassium hydroxide), which turns burned-on fats and sugars into soapy compounds that can be washed away. One of the most dangerous substances sold for household use, lye can burn your skin and eyes. Even if you can manage not to spray it on yourself, it's hard to avoid breathing the fumes, airborne droplets of lye that can sear your throat and lungs. People with asthma, bronchitis, and other respiratory problems are particularly likely to be harmed.

If you don't have a self-cleaning oven, use a cleaner without lye, such as **Easy-Off Non-Caustic Formula.** Another alternative: scouring cleanser, water, and elbow grease.

Plastic Containers: A Food-Storage Alternative

Sometimes, the best way to keep food fresh is to stash it in a plastic container, rather than wrap it or bag it.

Containers stack neatly, they survive inside a dishwasher, and some are right at home in a microwave oven. Best of all, containers are reusable and therefore economical. The best value may be recycled containers from the deli or the supermarket freezer case.

We tested a small sample of popular brands—**Tupperware, Rubbermaid, Ingrid**—as well as containers that once held **Cool Whip** and **Kraft La Creme** frozen whipped topping. Some samples were better than others; lids didn't always fit with the same degree of snugness. But overall, the containers were as good as the best wraps and bags for keeping in moisture.

The prices we paid ranged from $1.09 for a **Rubbermaid** 1-cup container to $9.49 for a three-piece set of **Tupperware Classic Sheer Servalier Bowls.** Once we'd eaten the **Cool Whip** and the **La Creme,** those containers were free.

Get More Mileage from Your Bedsheets

You can add to a sheet's longevity by caring for it properly. Reverse a sheet (top to bottom or inside out if that won't affect the color or pattern) each time you put it on the bed. That distributes wear.

Wash dark sheets separately, at least for the first few times, because they tend to run. If you feel you must use bleach on white sheets, do so sparingly, and don't use it every time.

Sheets vary widely in price. But in our judgment, you'll sleep just as soundly on an inexpensive set of sheets as you will on a pricey set. In fact, according to a *Consumer Reports* panel test, you're likely to sleep better on a moderately priced set of polyester/cotton sheets than on the highest-priced satin sheets. Even if you're willing to pay extra for a particular pattern or color, it still pays to shop around. One of CU's shoppers bought a package of pillowcases in one store, then found the identical pillowcases in another store at less than half the price.

White sales are held in January and July, when stores want to clear their stockrooms to make way for the new lines. There are sales at other times of the year, but they're generally limited to just a couple of patterns or colors or to irregulars. Irregulars can be a very good buy if the flaw is cosmetic rather than functional. An off-color, an oil stain, or a few thick threads won't affect a sheet's durability; frayed edges, slight tears, or missing threads will. Inspect irregulars carefully before using them. If you find a functional flaw, return the sheet to the store.

Don't Buy More Than You Need

Buying Wall-to-Wall Carpet Thriftily

It's easy to overspend on wall-to-wall carpet if you don't do a bit of homework first. Here are some things to do *before* you go shopping.

Measure the area to be carpeted. To get a rough idea of the square yardage you'll need, divide the square footage by nine. Keep that figure in mind as a multiplier when you're considering the square-yard prices. The store will send someone to your home to measure more precisely.

Don't be surprised if the yardage you are quoted is higher than the yardage you calculated. Most carpeting is 12 feet wide, so it has to be pieced when installed in large rooms and trimmed when installed in small rooms. That "waste" can add to the yardage required. Closets and doorway insets can also add yardage, as do allowances for matching pattern or pile direction.

Ask to see the installer's plan, so you know where seams will be located. By doing that, you can satisfy yourself that you aren't buying more carpet than you need. By living with one more seam, for instance, you may be able to buy less carpet.

Determine traffic patterns. You can get better performance from a carpet by matching the carpet to its use.

• *Kitchen and bathroom.* To resist moisture and mildew, a carpet needs a synthetic face fiber and a fully synthetic backing. Polypropylene resists water-based stains, so it's a good choice. Use a thin, dense foam-rubber or urethane pad underneath. A kitchen carpet should also have a low, very dense pile that will keep crumbs on top so they can be vacuumed up. In the bathroom, consider a washable carpet, the kind you can cut and fit yourself.

• *Living room.* Smooth plushes or Saxonies look luxurious and give a formal feel to a room. Remember, these textures show footprints, especially in light, bright colors.

• *Dining room and family room.* For well-traveled areas where food is likely to be spilled, consider the latest nylon varieties with built-in stain resistance. Stay away from light colors that will show stains and traffic wear and tear. Textured constructions such as frieze and cut-and-loop help hide signs of use; level-loop or low cut-pile are easiest to vacuum. A dense hair-and-jute pad underneath will help the carpet to wear well.

• *Bedrooms.* Carpets of almost any construction will do where there's little traffic. Here you can indulge in light colors, deep pile, and thick padding. A carpet that is soft to the feet will be appreciated in an area where you often go barefoot, so consider fibers that have a good "hand." Conversely, if you have to scrimp on carpet, it will matter least here.

• *Stairs and halls.* For high-traffic areas, low level-loop or low, dense cut-pile carpets give the best wear. Deep pile on stairs not only won't wear as well, it can be slippery. Medium solid colors or multicolors such as tweeds or Berbers show dirt least. Use firm padding such as felted hair-and-jute; use a double layer on stairs. Foam-rubber and urethane pads can be too bouncy to use safely on stairs.

Ask about face weight. This is the number of ounces of pile yarn in a square yard. Architects and decorators routinely use face weight when specifying "contract" carpet for offices and other commercial buildings. The minimum they would specify for a heavily traveled lobby, for instance, is 26-ounce carpet. More luxurious carpets have a face weight of 30 to 40 ounces or more.

Although face weight and other carpet specifications are not usually revealed to the ordinary shopper on labels, the store should have the information, since a store's carpet buyer orders carpets from the mills in those terms. So ask.

Once you've settled on a carpet, make sure you know exactly what the total price includes. Find out if you have to pay extra if the installers have to move furniture, remove door saddles and floor moldings, and take up the old carpet and padding and haul it away. Stairs and other tricky installations will probably entail an extra charge.

Telephones: Do You Need a Full-Feature Model?

Before you rush out to buy a phone loaded with features, ask yourself whether you really need all the electronic talents that come with a top-of-the-line model. The 32-number memory bank and speakerphone that are so useful at the office may be silly to have on a bedside phone and excessive even for a study desk. A traditional no-frills model for desk or wall lists for about $50 and may be found on sale for less. You can find small phones selling for much less—of uncertain quality, perhaps, but worth considering as a spare.

Here are some other considerations:

• There are features for special needs in today's phones—compatibility with hearing aids, lighted buttons, and volume that can be turned up or down. Ask your dealer for information on those types of accessories.

• Try holding the receiver to your ear before you make a final decision to buy. A poorly shaped earpiece can make the phone painful to press against the ear.

• Whichever model you buy, be sure you can return it if it doesn't work on your line.

Figure Your Needs Before You Paint

Painting the outside of a house calls for a bit of forethought. You'll waste money if you buy the wrong product or tools for the job. Here are some factors to consider:

Paint versus stain. Paint isn't the only option for sprucing up a home's exterior. Stain offers a mellow, weathered look that may be appropriate on some surfaces, for some styles of house, and in certain settings.

Stain is meant to soak into wood, leaving at most a very thin film on the surface. That's an advantage if you want the texture of the wood to show through the color.

Like paint, stain comes in water- and oil-based formulations. Stain comes in transparent, semitransparent, and opaque varieties (the last essentially a thin paint).

Most people own a house with existing painted or stained siding made of a natural wood or manufactured wood product such as hardboard or plywood. If the house was stained years ago, the exterior may just look shabby. If it was painted, the exterior may look faded and show signs of cracking and peeling.

Many stain manufacturers advise against using a stain over a painted or otherwise sealed surface. If a stain can't soak into the wood, it may be more difficult to apply, may not cover well, and may erode prematurely.

Latex versus oil. For the outside of a house, latex paint or stain is simpler to use than an oil-based product. It's easy to apply and adheres well to damp surfaces. It dries quickly. Spills and spatters as well as tools and hands clean up with plain water.

Oil-based (also called alkyd) products dry faster than they used to— so fast that you can probably apply two coats in as many days. But you still can't apply an alkyd to a damp surface, and you still need solvent to clean your hands and everything else after painting.

The convenience of a latex product may tempt you to rule out oil-based paint and stain right from the start. But you should consider the surface you intend to cover. An alkyd product is often the solution to common painting problems.

Peeling and flaking paint is probably the most frequent problem encountered on an exterior surface. Peeling seems to occur most often after several layers of paint have built up or when latex paint has been used over alkyd. Solution: Don't switch formulations. Paint latex over latex, alkyd over alkyd.

Figuring your paint needs. Estimate the distance in feet from the top of the foundation to the eaves (add 2 feet if the roof is pitched) and measure the distance around the foundation. Multiply the two numbers and divide the total by the coverage on the paint can label. That's how many gallons you will need for one coat. You'll need only about half as much for a second coat.

Be sure that all the cans you buy for the job have the same batch number, or the color may vary from can to can.

Tools. Using a roller may seem like a good way to speed up the job. It is. But only a brush will get under the bottom edge of clapboard siding or shingles. And only a brush will work the paint into the textured surface of rough-cut shingles. With water-based paints and stains, use a brush with synthetic bristles.

Do It Yourself

Why Spend Money to Clean Your Windows?

Do your windows when they're only lightly soiled and it will cost you almost nothing. Put plain water or one of our homemade brews in an old pump container, whip out a squeegee, and you can clean a 32-by-40-inch window for less than one cent—or for free.

To make an inexpensive homemade cleaner, top up the active ingredients with enough water to make a gallon: *vinegar,* ½ cup white vinegar; *vinegar homebrew,* ½ cup vinegar, 1 pint rubbing alcohol, 1 teaspoon dishwashing liquid; *ammonia,* ½ cup sudsy ammonia; *ammonia homebrew,* ½ cup sudsy ammonia, 1 pint rubbing alcohol, 1 teaspoon dishwashing detergent.

Remove Paint Yourself and Save

The toughest part of most painting projects isn't slapping on a new coat, it's stripping off the old one—or two or three. It's tempting merely to add a new layer, but when a finish is cracked or peeling, the only way to prevent further deterioration is to take it down to the bare surface. You can hire a professional to do that for you, but it's a lot cheaper to do it yourself. Professional paint removers have one big advantage over do-it-yourselfers: the tank. By immersing items in a vat of chemicals, the pros can get the last traces of paint out of nooks and crannies.

"Dip" stripping systems differ significantly. Some rely on corrosive lye, others on solvents. When you approach a company, it's a good idea to ask about the method used.

Lye not only dissolves paint, it can also stain wood fibers, raise their grain (leaving it feeling "fuzzy"), and extract natural resins. In addition, immersion can dissolve glues and swell wood so badly that it warps or falls apart. That won't happen if the operator snatches an item from the tank as soon as the paint is softened. In practice, such care isn't always possible.

With pros, we suggest the solvent method. Oversoaking is less likely to produce ruinous results. Still, because some dealers who use solvents rinse the articles in water, wood grain may rise and iron parts may rust. Fortunately, there are solvent systems that avoid the use of water.

We took old chairs and shutters to two pros. Both stripped with solvents: One used methylene chloride, hand scraping, and a water wash-down; the other, a Chem-Clean franchise, used xylol and dimethylfor-mamide (DMF), first as a bath and then in a spray that dislodged the softened paint.

DMF did very well. The methylene chloride cleaning was a bit less satisfactory: The shutter had some raised grain and mild rust on its fittings; the chair retained patches of paint and showed signs of too much scraping.

Both companies charged $75 for our two items: a large, flat shutter and a kitchen chair. Stripping the shutter yourself with the cheapest chemical (for instance, **Parks No Drip Strip**) would cost $12 and a lot of effort; the **Parks** is also flammable, produces toxic vapors, and can irritate skin. With **Peel Away 6,** a relatively safe product we top-rated in a May 1991 report, the job could set you back $40.

Which Glue for Which Job?

If you're profligate, you can always throw away that oak chair with the dislodged rung, the sneaker with the loose sole, or the cup with the broken handle. If you're thrifty, however, you reach for the glue. But which glue? If you believe the labels, many glues can handle practically any household repair. That's not necessarily so. Some are so rigid they may break loose under heavy stress. Some shrink enough to make them unsuitable for gluing a worn chair rung back into its slot. Some are good for wood but not plastic or metal. Some don't resist water well. Some demand clamping; others bond almost instantly. And so it goes. The key to a successful repair is to match a glue to the job it must do.

Epoxy adhesives come in two parts, a resin and a hardener. These glues are strong, hard, and water-resistant, with fine gap-filling abilities.

Catalyzed acrylic glues are strong, stick to oily surfaces, and can glue almost any material except flexible plastic.

Silicone rubber glues can take a very wide range of temperatures and can be used on most surfaces, but they can't be painted. Their elasticity, water-resistance, and gap-filling properties let them serve as sealants and caulks as well as adhesives.

"Instant" glues, the *cyanoacrylates,* are fast-setting, although they have been reformulated to slow down their bonding speed to a manageable minute or so. The quick bonding is a cyanoacrylate glue's biggest advantage, because it lets you glue hard-to-clamp objects, provided that the mating surfaces are hard and smooth.

Contact cements are flexible adhesives used most often for gluing plastic laminate to a countertop, resetting a loose wall tile, or reattaching a shoe sole. Their big advantage is that they bond on contact the instant the coated surfaces are brought together (you must first let the glue dry a bit). Because contact cements bond so quickly, they can't be used for gluing joints that must be slid together for final assembly.

Plastic cements are clear adhesives in small squeeze tubes and are commonly used in building model airplanes, model ships, and the like. They shrink as they dry, so they don't work well in loose joints.

White glues are inexpensive, water-based, strong, paintable, and not very flexible. They take a while to harden and can be cleaned up with water before they set.

Aliphatics, also called carpenter's glues, grab faster than white glues, so they require a shorter clamping time. They also shrink less than white glues.

Because of their water-resistance, *resin glues* are often used in construction or marine applications. They are toxic and irritating. Although inconvenient to use, resin glues clasp wood powerfully and resist water well.

You should be able to handle most repairs and do-it-yourself projects with an epoxy glue for very strong bonds on a variety of materials, a white glue or an aliphatic for ease of use and strength on wood, and a cyanoacrylate for quick bonding of hard-to-mend items.

For repairs that need flexibility, you might want to use a contact adhesive or a plastic cement.

THREE

Saving Energy and Water

Saving energy around the house can be as simple as caulking around windows; saving water can be as easy as installing a new shower head. Here are some tips on saving money by reducing your home energy and water use—all the while staying warm in the winter, cool in the summer.

Energy Labels:
Your Clue to Thrifty Major Appliances

Energy-cost labels are now attached to many major appliances. Required under the Energy Policy and Conservation Act of 1975, they appear on refrigerators, refrigerator-freezers, freezers, dishwashers, clothes washers, water heaters, and air conditioners.

The labels for a class of products—refrigerator-freezers, say—show how the estimated annual running cost of a given model compares with that of other models of a comparable size. The label does not, however, indicate the brand and model number of those other models. You can obtain that type of information for a small fee—$1 for room air conditioners and refrigerator-freezers, 25 cents for humidifiers and dehumidifiers—by contacting the Association of Home Appliance Manufacturers, 20 North Wacker Drive, Chicago, IL 60606 (telephone: 312-984-5800) and requesting AHAM's latest directories of certified appliances.

The federally mandated labels greatly simplify comparison shopping by energy cost. Each label highlights an estimate, based on the national average energy rate, of the yearly operating cost of the unit to which it's affixed. A table giving yearly costs at other rates is also prominently displayed on the label, as is the range of operating costs for models in the same product category.

Note that the labeled estimates for appliances may not be identical with those published in *Consumer Reports* as part of CU's test reports. Differences in test methods and different assumptions about how an appliance will be used account for the variations. That said, cost differences between models should be proportionate.

Also remember that energy use is just one criterion to consider when shopping. CU's engineers take many other factors into account in testing products and in determining the Ratings. In fact, some highly energy-efficient appliances may be deficient in other important aspects.

Choosing a Refrigerator-Freezer That's Thrifty to Run

With a refrigerating product, your first energy-saving decision can be made right in the store. Refrigerator-freezers come in various configurations: Some have the freezer on the bottom, some have it on the side, and some have it on top.

Top-freezer models are the most popular. The two competing styles do have their advantages, however. Side-by-side freezers usually provide more freezer space than top-freezers, as well as multiple freezer shelves arranged for orderly storage and easy access. Bottom-freezers, for their part, put the more frequently used refrigerator section at eye level and the freezer below—a logical and handy arrangement.

But to get those niceties, you pay and pay. Bottom-freezers and side-by-side models both command a premium price. They're also more expensive to run. The cost factors, we think, make a top-freezer your best choice.

Refrigerator-freezers typically supply heat to areas around the freezer door to keep moisture from condensing there in humid weather. Most of today's units use an electric heater that draws additional power when switched on (and so "saves" energy when switched off).

You must, of course, remember to turn the heater off at the end of the summer; you won't have to switch it back on until you notice condensation on the outer surface of the freezer's door. Typically, switching on the electric heater adds $1 or so to the monthly operating cost of a refrigerator-freezer.

When you buy a refrigerator-freezer, equip yourself with a refrigerator-freezer thermometer as well. It will help you set the appliance for the best balance between performance and economy. A freezer should be set to hold foods at 0°F. Colder than that, and energy costs rise; a few degrees warmer, and the storage life of food may be cut in half. The refrigerator section, for its part, should be set to store food at 37°F. That's a reasonable compromise between near-freezing, at which meats and most fruits and vegetables do best, and the 40°F or more that's appropriate for other foods. Because a change of control setting for one compartment may affect the temperature of the other one, it may take some trial-and-error adjustment to achieve that 0°/37°F balance between the two compartments.

You may have to repeat that balancing act several times a year. When seasons change, a refrigerator may have to cope with swings in kitchen temperature of as much as 20°F, which could affect interior temperatures by as much as 5°F. Such a change calls for an adjustment of the controls.

Freezers:
Chests Versus Uprights

With freezers, as with refrigerators, the type you buy has some effect on performance and energy efficiency. CU's tests suggest that chest freezers have an edge over uprights.

The design of the chests helps explain why they tend to have slightly lower energy costs. When you open the lid of a chest freezer, cold air tends to stay put. But when you open the door of an upright, the colder air at the bottom spills out and warmer air moves in to take its place.

As in refrigerators, the internal temperature of a freezer may change with the seasons. In spring and fall, use a refrigerator-freezer thermometer to help you to reset the controls to maintain 0°F.

Dishwashers:
As Efficient as Washing by Hand

A dishwasher may not leap to mind when you think of ways to cut energy costs. But some machines can match or better a human dishwasher in saving energy while washing dishes.

People who wash dishes under a steady stream of water, we have found, are apt to use more hot water, and hence more energy, than a machine would. For such people, buying a dishwasher could bring about an energy saving.

Washers consume only a bit of energy directly. Those we tested for a 1990 report consumed between 0.6 and 1.1 kilowatt-hours of electricity when supplied with 140°F water. That works out to between five and nine cents of electricity at average power rates.

The major energy cost of a machine dishwasher lies in the expense of heating the water it uses. An electric water heater uses about 19 cents worth of electricity to provide the 11 gallons of 140°F water the typical dishwasher uses for one load; the total comes to about $95 a year, assuming you run the dishwasher once a day. The hot water cost for a gas- or oil-fired heater is about 6 cents a load, or a total of about $45 a year. Setting the water heater's thermostat to 120°F should cut those totals by a few dollars a year. Using the cooler water also cuts the household's overall hot-water costs by about $11 to $32 a year.

You can't, however, get away with supplying any dishwasher with water at only 120°F; the machine's performance might suffer. You need a model designed to boost its water temperature internally. The boost feature lets you lower your water heater's thermostat setting by 20°F, saving 10 percent in water-heating costs.

At that, you're apt to save with a booster-heat dishwasher only if you heat water with electricity. If you have a gas water heater, you would be trading off a reduction in the use of a relatively inexpensive source of energy for an increase in the use of costly electricity. You might easily find that with a gas water heater it did not pay to use a booster-heat dishwasher.

You can save a bit of energy with any dishwasher if you don't use heat to dry your dishes. Dishwashers commonly offer a no-heat drying feature. (With machines lacking that feature you have to remember to open the door as the dry cycle starts.) No-heat drying should save you a penny or so on every dishwasher load.

Two minor features also affect a dishwasher's energy use. A short-wash setting lets you bypass the first one or two parts of the machine's regular cycle to handle loads that are only slightly soiled. You thereby make a small saving in water and electricity (as well as in time and detergent). A plate-warm cycle, however, merely applies dry heat to a load of clean plates, so you can serve food on warm plates. That may be a nice touch, but using electricity to do it seems frivolous.

Clothes Washers and Dryers: Cutting Running Costs

The main energy cost in a clothes washer lies, once again, in the hot water it uses. So prudent use of the machine offers an opportunity for a saving. Virtually any modern washing machine lets you control the amount of water you use. If you have a large load of laundry, set the water control for maximum fill. To save water, energy, and detergent, use a smaller fill for smaller loads. In most models with a large tub capacity, the difference between the maximum and minimum fill is from 20 to 30 gallons. For best economy, note that washing a few large loads is more efficient than washing the same amount of clothes in many small loads.

Water-temperature selection provides another opportunity to save on energy. Most machines give you several ways to combine temperatures for wash and rinse water—typically, hot/warm, hot/cold, warm/cold, and cold/cold. It makes sense to use as little hot water as possible. And always use a cold rinse: Warm water doesn't rinse any better—and it may increase wrinkling of permanent-press fabrics.

When filling a clothes washer, you can save some bother, and some money on hot water, with a simple approach that still gives a clean wash. Sort out the obviously troublesome items—oily overalls and brand-new blue jeans. Then wash everything else together in warm or cold water. If clothes aren't heavily soiled and your laundry needs freshening more than scouring, you'll probably lose nothing in cleaning, and you'll have spared yourself the traditional chore of sorting whites from colored items and cottons from synthetics, washing some items in hot water, bleaching some things, and so forth.

However, you may still want to do a special load now and then. To do a load that's all colorfast cottons, for instance, use a hot wash/cold rinse; if the dirt is really bad, first let the load soak awhile.

Some washing machines may offer a hidden energy saving if you machine-dry your laundry. A washer that extracts water particularly efficiently yields loads that shorten the running time of a dryer—and reduces operating cost. Unfortunately, how well a washer spin-dries is not apparent to the shopper's eye.

As in a clothes washer, the larger the load to be dried, the more efficient the energy use. Try waiting until you have enough laundry to fill the washer and dryer close to capacity, but not beyond. Overloading can prevent adequate washing in the washer and air circulation in the dryer.

Dryer control arrangements are worth considering. The longer a dryer runs after the laundry is dry, the more energy it wastes. All dryers have some sort of mechanism that tells them when to turn off. It's easy to go wrong with the simplest device, a timer. Overestimating drying time wastes energy, yields harsh-feeling laundry, and may result in damage to some fabrics; underestimating means damp laundry. An automatic dryness control can overcome those problems.

To save energy, set a dryer's automatic control for as low a dryness setting as will provide proper drying; with a timer control, be careful to avoid oversetting. Both those methods require you to experiment a bit. Another way to cut energy costs is to use a clothesline or drying rack to dry such items as bath mats, which hold considerable moisture. In fact, for maximum energy saving, use a clothesline or drying rack for as much of your wash as is convenient.

If you have a choice of either a gas or an electric dryer, pick the gas dryer: It should cost you less to run. Where energy is billed at national average rates, an electric dryer costs more than twice as much to run as a gas model. At those rates you'll probably make back the extra cost of a typical gas dryer within a year or less.

Here's a rule of thumb for those whose rates differ from the national average: A gas dryer costs as much to run as an electric dryer when the cost per 100 cubic feet is about 25 times the cost per kilowatt-hour of electricity. When the cost per 100 cubic feet is less than 25 times the cost per kilowatt-hour, gas is cheaper; more than 25 times, electricity is cheaper.

Water Heater Insulation Kits: Wrap Up a Saving

Want to cut your hot-water bills? Wrap an extra layer of insulation around your water heater's tank.

A water heater can lose a considerable amount of heat while it's standing by. At average fuel rates, even a well-insulated energy-saver storing 140°F water in a 70°F room over a year's time can accumulate about $62 worth of storage losses (for an electric water heater) or $32 (for a gas one); older water heaters or standard models, which are less well insulated, could lose twice as much.

Insulation kits for water heaters typically consist of a fiberglass blanket, about 1½ inches thick, to be wrapped around the heater and secured with tape. Some kits also have an insulating lid, or top plate, to cover the top of an electric water heater. (The top of a gas-fired water heater should not be insulated; the insulation would interfere with the flue and create a safety hazard.)

You can usually install a kit in less than an hour. Kits with a top plate may take a little more time. The job is generally easy, and the only tool you're apt to need is a pair of scissors. When installing a kit, be sure to keep insulation away from the heater's controls and wiring.

When handling fiberglass, wear a dust mask, gloves, and long-sleeved shirt. Wash your clothes separately so the fibers aren't transferred to other clothing.

It Pays to Switch to a Low-Flush Toilet

Toilet-flushing represents the greatest demand on this country's residential water supply, accounting for about 38 percent of all the water used indoors. For decades the conventional American toilet used 5 gallons of water per flush. In the late 1970s, manufacturers introduced the so-called water-conserving toilet, which uses 3.5 gallons per flush.

The newest low-flush toilets are even more sparing: They use only 1.6 gallons or less. For a report in 1990, we tested 11 low-flush toilets, priced from $100 to $285. All were acceptable performers, and 3 were excellent.

Water and sewer rates vary so widely from city to city, even within the same region of the country, that it's not always meaningful to speak of average dollar savings from water-conserving measures. The table on page 65 focuses on 13 representative cities and estimates the savings in combined water and sewer costs that a family might expect each year if it switched from an old-fashioned 5-gallon toilet to a low-flow model.

If the new toilet costs $200, including installation, it will pay for itself in about 3 years if you live in a high-cost area such as Houston and in just over 12 years in moderately priced Dayton. A toilet typically has at least a 20-year life expectancy, so it might pay to change over even if your own water costs are low.

In our calculations, we assume a three-person family whose members each flush the toilet at home four times a day. The savings are based on switching from an older, 5-gallon toilet to a 1.6-gallon toilet. Switching from a 3.5-gallon to a 1.6-gallon saves only about half as much.

If you have more than three people in your household, or if your water rates go up significantly, you'd get your money back faster. Installing more than one toilet, of course, would extend the payback period proportionately.

SAVINGS WITH A LOW-FLUSH TOILET

City	Water and sewer cost per 1,000 gal.*	Annual saving
Houston	$4.19	$62
Atlanta	3.64	54
Peoria, Ill.	3.58	53
Dallas	3.56	53
St. Petersburg, Fla.	3.24	48
San Francisco	2.78	41
Cincinnati	2.60	39
Boston	2.54	38
Los Angeles	1.95	29
New York City	1.84	27
Chicago	1.15	27
Fresno, Calif.	1.11	17
Dayton, Ohio	1.11	16

*Source: Arthur Young & Co.

Low-Flow Shower Heads for Energy Savings

Showers consume more than one-fifth of all the water used indoors and more hot water than any other fixture or appliance. Installing a low-flow shower head is a simple and inexpensive way to cut down on that water use.

For $10 or so per shower installation, the average family can save 5,000 to 10,000 gallons of water each year, plus the energy it takes to heat half that water, a total of perhaps $20 to $50. (As the saying goes, your mileage may vary. Savings depend, among other things, on how long and how often your family members shower, what kind of shower heads you currently own, and how much you pay for heating water.)

Before 1980, shower heads generally delivered 5 to 8 gallons of water per minute. Manufacturers have gradually scaled back the flow rates of new shower heads while trying to maintain the quality of the shower.

Heads designed for low flow usually have a narrower spray area so less water misses the showerer; they may also entrain air with the water to create a turbulent flow. Most new shower heads are low-flow heads that deliver 3 gallons per minute or less.

Installing a new shower head is a simple task. Follow the directions that come with the head. That usually means removing the old shower head with large pliers or an adjustable wrench. If it doesn't come off easily, steady the inlet pipe with a pipe wrench. Then simply screw the new head into place, using the appropriate tool.

Unless the instructions specify otherwise, it's usually a good idea to wind the pipe threads with a few turns of pipe-joint tape, available at hardware stores. And put a rag between the plier jaws to avoid marring the fixture's finish.

Scald hazard? A few manufacturers of low-flow heads have cautioned that low-flow shower heads may scald the user unless the plumbing is fitted with special antiscald devices. The theory is that if someone flushes a toilet connected to the same cold-water line as the shower, a low-flow shower head will deliver hot water straight from the hot-water lines.

When we tested shower heads using ½-inch supply lines and a quick-opening valve that simulated a toilet's flushing, there was indeed a scald hazard. But the problem shouldn't occur in bathrooms that are properly plumbed to begin with. Good plumbing practice specifies that ¾-inch supply pipes should serve bathrooms, which tends to minimize the problem. Further, major national plumbing codes call for the installation of thermostatic mixing valves, pressure-balancing valves, or antiscald valves in showers, any of which should also obviate the problem.

It would be wise to make sure your bathroom is properly plumbed. Try running your shower (on your hand) and have someone flush the toilet. If there is a significant temperature rise in your shower with your present shower head when the toilet is flushed, chances are you'd risk a scald using a low-flow head. Either have an antiscald valve installed (a job for a plumber), set your water heater lower (to 120°F or so), or make sure the door is locked when you shower.

Should You Change That Light Bulb?

The lion's share of lighting costs—some 80 to 90 percent—is for electricity used, not bulbs. Among regular incandescent bulbs, differences in efficiency are not large.

Energy-saving bulbs save a few watts but not much money. The five watts of power conserved by an energy-saving bulb translates into less than 40 cents annually, at the national average of 8.2 cents per kilowatt-hour. Since you pay a premium of up to 25 cents for those bulbs, the net savings is small indeed.

Regular incandescent bulbs are generally cheapest. The energy-saving kind saves a few watts, but the payoff is on the order of dimes, not dollars, and you're apt to get a dimmer bulb.

If you want long life and energy savings, look beyond the usual incandescent. The real long-life power misers are to be found among other types of bulbs, especially fluorescents. The energy they save can easily more than offset their higher price.

Fluorescent tubes. These are incredibly efficient. They use only one-fifth to one-third the electricity of incandescents of comparable brightness, yet they last 10 to 20 times as long. "Cool white" models give off an unflattering cast, but new "warm whites" are closer to incandescent light in color. Newer bulbs are more compact—thinner tubes, only 5 to 7 inches long, for instance. Fluorescent fixtures are especially suited to area lighting.

Fluorescent adapters. In recent years, fluorescent bulbs have been marketed with adapters that are designed to screw into ordinary household lamps and light fixtures. General Electric's **Circlite,** for instance, comes in two parts: a 10-inch-diameter circular bulb and an adapter shaped like a space module, with socket threads on the nose-cone end. It can work in a ceiling fixture or table lamp with a wide shade.

Other makers produce other variants; a compact fluorescent stick and adapter can work in many home fixtures. The fluorescent-within-a-bulb (inside is a U-shaped fluorescent tube) fits an ordinary incandescent socket.

The initial high cost of such specialized bulbs ($10 to $25) is more than offset by their long life—around 10,000 hours—and greater efficiency. And the adapters are reusable.

Keeping Cool for Less

High-Efficiency Air Conditioners

Over the years, it's become axiomatic to choose an air conditioner with a high energy-efficiency rating, or EER, to save both energy and money.

An 8,000 Btu unit, say, with an EER of 9.5 uses about 5 percent less electricity than a comparable unit with an EER of 9.0.

But greater efficiency can also mean a reduced ability to dehumidify the air. Manufacturers wring extra efficiency from their units in part by designing the cooling coils to run warmer. That hampers the coils' ability to condense moisture from the air.

These measures can help you overcome this inherent problem with high-efficiency air-conditioners:

- Buy a unit that's properly sized. An oversized unit will cycle on only for brief periods and so won't dehumidify the air much at all. Use the worksheet below to figure out what size you need.
- Run the air conditioner at a low or medium fan speed. That will move the air across the cooling coils more slowly, enhancing dehumidification.
- Don't set the controls to make the room cooler just to compensate for high humidity. Studies have shown that people are usually just as comfortable in a room at 77°F and 60 percent humidity as they are in a room at 75°F and 40 percent humidity.

How Powerful an Air Conditioner Do You Need?

This worksheet, adapted from one published by the Association of Home Appliance Manufacturers, can help you estimate how much cooling capacity you need. (As published in *Consumer Reports,* June 1991.)

Preliminaries

1. Measure the length of each wall in the room.

2. Determine the area (length times width, in feet) of the floor and the ceiling.

3. Measure the area (width times height, in feet) of each window.

4. Measure the width of all permanently open doors. Rooms connected by a door or archway more than 5 feet wide should be considered one area. Take measurements for both rooms.

Calculations

Multiply the appropriate measurement by the factor given. Use factors in parentheses if the air conditioner will be used only at night.

1. _____ × 300(200) = ... _____
   width of permanently open doors, ft.

2. _____ × 14 = ... _____
   area of all windows, sq. ft. (multiply by 7, not 14, for double glass or block)

3. Use only the line that's appropriate for your house.
Uninsulated ceiling, no space above: _____ × 19(5) = ... _____
ceiling area, sq. ft.
Uninsulated ceiling, attic above: _____ × 12(7) = ... _____
ceiling area, sq. ft.
Insulated ceiling, no space above: _____ × 8(3) = ... _____
ceiling area, sq. ft.
Insulated attic above: _____ × 5(4) = ... _____
ceiling area, sq. ft.
Occupied space above: _____ × 3(3) = ... _____
ceiling area, sq. ft.

4. Enter length of all walls, in feet, as directed, and multiply by appropriate factor. Consider walls shaded by adjacent buildings as facing north.

Wall facing	Uninsulated frame or masonry up to 8 in. thick		Insulated frame or masonry over 8 in. thick
Outside, north _____	× 30(30)	or	× 20(20) = ... _____
Outside, other _____	× 60(30)	or	× 30(20) = ... _____
Inside _____	× 30(30)	or	× 20(20) = ... _____

5. If floor is on ground or over basement, omit this step and go to step 6.
_____ × 3 = ... _____
floor area, sq. ft.

6. If air conditioner will be used only at night or if all windows in the room face north, omit this step and go to step 7. Otherwise, enter the total area for all windows on any one side of the room on the appropriate line. Do the multiplication. Multiply factor by 0.5 for any window with glass block; by 0.8 for double glass or storm window.

Window facing	Window area		No shades			Inside shades	Outside awnings	
Northeast	_____	×	60	or ×		25	or × 20 =	_____
East	_____	×	80	or ×		40	or × 25 =	_____
Southeast	_____	×	75	or ×		30	or × 20 =	_____
South	_____	×	75	or ×		35	or × 20 =	_____
Southwest	_____	×	110	or ×		45	or × 30 =	_____
West	_____	×	150	or ×		65	or × 45 =	_____
Northwest	_____	×	120	or ×		50	or × 35 =	_____

Enter largest number from above _____

7. Subtotal. Add lines 1 through 6. Enter sum here: . . . . _____

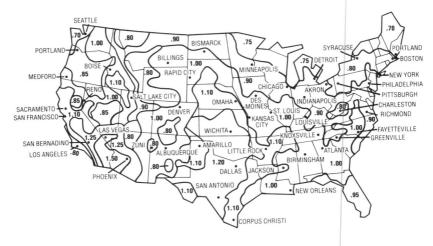

8. Climate correction

    _____ × _____ = ... _____
    figure from line 7   factor from map

9. _____ × 600 = ... _____
   people in room (minus 2)

10. _____ × 3 = ... _____
    wattage of all lights and appliances in room (not including air conditioner)

11. **Total cooling load.** Add lines 8 to 10. Enter sum: _____
    This number tells you how many Btu of heat build up in the room each
    hour. The air conditioner's cooling capacity (Btu/hour) should nearly
    match the heat buildup you calculated. A difference of about 5 percent
    between the number you calculate and the air conditioner's capacity
    shouldn't be significant.

Radiant Barriers: Help for Your Air Conditioner?

Air-conditioning, expensive as it can be, often provides the only effective
relief in hot, humid summer weather. But is there any relief for the cost
of air-conditioning?

A number of companies have been touting such relief in the form of
a radiant barrier—a sheet of foil tacked to the attic floor or roof. The
shiny foil is supposed to reflect radiant heat away from the house, thus
easing the load on the air conditioner.

Companies selling radiant barriers work primarily in the Sunbelt
states, charging hundreds of dollars for a product that's cheap to buy
and simple to install. Extravagant claims abound. Until Texas authorities
sued to stop exaggerated claims, one marketer was claiming its barrier

could cut utility bills by 30 to 50 percent and make cooling systems last longer.

That's a dubious claim. A radiant barrier might block half the heat coming in through the roof. But not very much heat enters the house that way if the attic is insulated. Most of the heat gets in through walls and windows. Further, a radiant barrier does nothing to lower humidity—the problem that makes many people turn on the air conditioner in the first place.

The Texas attorney general's office maintains that a radiant barrier can lower utility bills only by 3 to 8 percent a year, at best. (The Florida Solar Energy Center estimates a saving of 190 to 15 percent. Radiant barriers are required in some new construction in that state.)

Jerold W. Jones, a professor at the University of Texas who researches energy-saving materials, reckons that a radiant barrier priced at 15 cents a square foot and installed by the homeowner is cost-effective, given prevailing utility rates in the Southwest. But the prices we've seen are much higher than that—as much as 70 cents per square foot, plus installation.

Fans: Other Ways to Cool Your House

In areas where humidity isn't high and nights are cool, a fan or two may be enough to keep you comfortable. While a fan doesn't cool air, it can refresh you by drawing air through the house.

For a fan to cool a house, the outdoor air it draws in has to be cooler than that indoors. When you turn on the fan at night, the house will retain some coolness in daytime if you close windows and draw shades or drapes. (The effect may not keep you comfortable all day, but at least you'll reduce the load on your air conditioner and so cut its running costs.) Fans can also provide a breeze that makes you feel cooler, even if the temperature remains unchanged.

Whole-House Fans

These large air movers, with blades typically 24 to 42 inches in diameter, are usually mounted in an attic. They're not as cheap as their $200 to $400 price tags might suggest. Installation and such accessories as louvers, shutters, and remote switches can easily double their initial cost. On the other hand, a big fan working under the right conditions can cool and ventilate an entire house for about the energy cost of running an air conditioner in one room.

If you merely open your windows in the evening, your house won't cool off very quickly. If the outdoor temperature drops from, say, 85°F to 75°F in two hours, the house will take about four hours to cool that much. A whole-house fan, however, replaces indoor air with outdoor air every minute or two, so the house will cool off in a little more than two hours.

To know what size fan to buy, figure the air-moving capacity you need. Multiply length by width by height of each room, hallway, and stairwell to be ventilated. Don't include closets, pantries, storage rooms, or the attic. Adding the results tells you the cubic feet of space you need to cool.

Use that total house volume to determine the air-moving capacity (expressed in cubic feet per minute, or cfm) your fan should have. If your summers are generally hot, you want a fan that can change house air completely every minute. Therefore, a house with 6,000 cubic feet of living space calls for a 6,000-cfm fan. Where summer temperatures usually aren't extreme, a fan with a capacity of half the house volume will do.

Manufacturers sometimes rate their fans for *free air delivery,* the breeze a fan produces when nothing restricts air flow. That figure isn't very helpful. Look for another, more useful rating that tells you the fan's air delivery when working against a standard resistance (usually stated as .1 inch of water). If that rating isn't given, take 80 to 85 percent of the free-delivery rating as a reasonable approximation of real-life performance.

If the fan you want has only one or two speeds, house volume and fan capacity at maximum speed should match fairly closely. A variable-speed model can be a bit oversized, since you can always turn it down.

Window and Box Fans

A window fan is little more than a scaled-down—and much cheaper—version of a whole-house ventilator. Expect to pay from $20 to $80. A typical 20-inch fan blowing out a window can move about 2,000 cfm of air. That's enough to change indoor air once a minute in a two-room apartment.

Twenty-inch fans come in two common formats. Window fans, designed strictly for window mounting, work only as ventilators. Box fans can be moved from a window and set where you like to stir up the air in a room.

A window fan with blades that reverse direction can, at the flip of a switch, change from blowing air out of a room to blowing air in. That's useful for immediate spot cooling, if you don't mind the draft. It also

cools the room in which the fan is located first—when the fan is exhaust-
ing air, the fan room is the last to be cooled, unless that room has another
window opened enough to bleed in a little air.

Multiple speeds are also a convenience, especially if you are bothered
by noise.

A built-in thermostat saves you the trouble of shutting off the fan
should the room get chilly. Fans equipped with a thermostat often have
arbitrary numbers on the control to help you identify appropriate settings. Whenever you set the thermostat at night, remember to turn off
the fan in the morning. Otherwise, the fan will restart when the temperature rises, drawing in hot daytime air if it's window-mounted. An indicator light that reminds you that the fan is still on when the thermostat
suspends fan operations is a handy feature.

Ceiling Fans

The ceiling fan does have its virtues. While not portable, it doesn't take
up floor space. It's out of the ready reach of children. And it can move
a lot of air.

The most common size is 52 inches (that's the sweep of the blades),
though smaller models are available. Major manufacturers offer an
extensive choice of styles, from classic to contemporary. Built-in lighting
kits are also available.

Big fans move more air than smaller ones. That truism aside, you don't
have much to go on if you want to compare the performance of competing models. Some makers don't state the air-moving capacity of their
fans. Others may recommend a particular fan size for a given room size,
but those guidelines tend to differ from brand to brand. If you don't
know what you need, it might be wiser to depend on the know-how of an
established dealer, rather than shoot for a better price at a discount
outlet.

In a typical room, a ceiling fan keeps you cool by delivering a fairly
vigorous downdraft with a slower spot—or "eye"—in the middle. If the
fan is reasonably close to the room's center, the air column disperses as
it nears the floor, moves toward the walls, and turns upward.

You're pretty well stuck with that air pattern. If you don't like it, your
main alternative (short of moving yourself and perhaps your furniture)
is a change of fan speed. For that reason, even some of the cheapest
models offer two speeds. You get more flexibility, of course, with a three-
speed model.

Better yet is a variable-speed control. It lets you fine-tune the air flow—up to a point, anyway. But the slowest setting of a variable or multispeed control may still be too fast if you want a ceiling fan for charm as much as for comfort. If a languid spin is important to you, check manufacturers' specifications for minimum revolutions per minute. Fifty rpm should be low enough.

Ceiling fans are also touted as winter energy savers, moving warm air from on high down to people level. We weren't impressed, however, when we checked that claim some years ago. Indeed, the fan's breeze is likely to cool you off rather than improve the distribution of warm air, unless the fan is in a room with a high or vaulted ceiling or in a room heated with a wood stove.

Keeping Warm

Furnaces: Home Heating for Less

New developments in home heating units can cut your fuel bills substantially. Over a heating season, your present furnace may misdirect as much as half of the heat you've paid for. But modern, high-efficiency designs deliver nearly all the heat content of their fuel to your living spaces. Even a furnace costing $2,000 or more can pay for itself rather quickly.

A new, high-efficiency furnace isn't for everyone. Unless you live in a particularly cold area or have unusually high energy costs, it probably doesn't pay to discard a recently purchased functioning furnace for a high-efficiency model. But if your furnace is more than 15 years old, an investment in a new high-efficiency unit can make sense.

Efficiency. Combustion efficiency (CE), or steady-state efficiency (SSE), is the percentage of a fuel's energy that's converted into usable heat when a furnace operates continually. CE is what a technician tests when tuning your furnace. CE measures only operating (or on-time) losses, so it doesn't tell you much about overall fuel use (there are also losses when a furnace cycles off). A better measure is the annual fuel utilization efficiency (AFUE), the percentage of the fuel's energy converted to usable heat over a full year's operation. The AFUE takes into account both on-time and off-time losses; it provides a good basis for comparing furnaces.

High-efficiency furnaces with an AFUE of 90 percent and above are available. If you now own a 15-year-old furnace, its AFUE is probably about 55 percent (if gas-fueled) or about 60 percent (if oil-fueled). You can boost these figures—but only a bit—by modifying the furnace. We tell you how below.

Use the worksheet on page 76 to figure your possible fuel savings in replacing your present gas or oil furnace with a high-efficiency one. There's a sample set of figures (for a home with an annual gas use of 1,600 therms or an oil use of 1,600 gallons) to show how it's done. The worksheet can't be used if you plan to switch fuels.

Upgrading an existing furnace. To get more efficiency from an old but still serviceable oil furnace, consider *derating*—that is, using a smaller nozzle, which is likely to boost the AFUE by about 5 percent. Have the derating done as part of your furnace's annual tune-up, which should include a nozzle replacement anyway. If your oil furnace is fairly old, install a flame-retention burner. It may cost as much as $600 to install but can save you 15 to 20 percent a year on fuel.

Derating a gas furnace is not as easy. If you install a smaller nozzle or orifice, you'll also have to modify the flue to restrict the flow of air, which your local building code may not allow.

Replace the pilot light of a gas furnace with an electronic ignition system (which costs perhaps $200 for hardware and labor). You should save about 5 percent on your annual gas bill.

Automatic-Setback Thermostats

The simplest way to lower your heating bills is to turn down the thermostat. Begin by lowering your normal daytime thermostat setting to the coolest comfortable temperature. If you set back the temperature further at night or when the house is empty, you add to your saving. The greater the setback and the longer the setback period, the greater your saving will be. A computer simulation prepared at the Oak Ridge National Laboratory showed the approximate saving that could be expected in a house that switched from a constant temperature of 68°F to two kinds of nighttime setbacks: from 68°F during the day to 60°F between 10:00 P.M. and 6:00 A.M. and from 68°F to 55°F in the same time period. If, for example, there are about 4,000 heating degree days in your area and you use a 68°F to 60°F setback, you could save roughly $17 on every $100 you now spend for heating your home. And if you use a 68°F to 55°F setback, you might expect to save $22 per $100 of your heating costs.

Calculating Savings with a High-Efficiency Furnace

Amount of fuel used now	Example	Your House
1. Number of units of fuel (therms of gas or gallons of oil) used per year.	1,600	_____
2. If some of that fuel is used to produce hot water, put .8 here. If none of the fuel is used for hot-water heating, put a 1 here.	✕ .8	_____
3. Multiply line 1 by line 2.	1,280	_____

Amount of fuel used by new furnace		
4. Copy the number on line 3 here.	1,280	_____
5. Write the AFUE of your present furnace here. If you don't know what it is, use 55 for gas, 60 for oil.	✕ 55	_____
6. Multiply line 4 by line 5.	70,400	_____
7. Write the AFUE of the new furnace here.	90	_____
8. Divide line 6 by line 7. The result is the number of units of fuel you'll have to buy to heat your home with the new furnace for a year.	782	_____

Annual saving in dollars		
9. Copy the number on line 3 here.	1,280	_____
10. Copy the number on line 8 here.	− 782	_____
11. Subtract line 10 from line 9. The result is the number of units of fuel you can save with the new furnace.	498	_____
12. Write the most recent price you paid for a unit of fuel.	✕ $ .62	_____
13. Multiply line 11 by line 12. The result is the amount you might save per year with the new furnace.	$309	_____

SAVING PER $100 OF
PRESENT FUEL BILL
(NIGHTTIME SETBACK)

Degree days	68°F to 60°F	68°F to 55°F
2,000	$23	$30
3,000	20	25
4,000	17	22
5,000	14	20
6,000	12	18
7,000	10	16
8,000	9	14

As the above table shows, the greater the setback on your thermostat, the greater the saving. The warmer your locality is, the higher the *percentage* of saving, though probably not the *total* saving. Don't be misled by the "saving per $100" figure. Homeowners who face cold winters run up very high fuel bills, and thus their overall dollar saving will probably be higher than for people living in warmer climates. In other words, it's more helpful for people in Chicago to save 20 percent of their fuel bill than for people in Los Angeles to save 80 percent of theirs.

By lowering a conventional thermostat manually, you can save money without any additional expense. But that can be a nuisance. You can do away with the nuisance by installing a thermostat that controls two temperatures so that the heat is automatically turned down at night and up again before you get out of bed the next morning.

For do-it-yourselfers, the simplest automatic-setback thermostat is probably a "two-wire" model, needing no new wiring to replace an existing manual thermostat. (Some thermostats, particularly those that control central air-conditioning as well as heating, require four or more connections.) Any reasonably handy person should be able to install a two-wire unit.

You may find a two-wire "clock-timer" thermostat handy. These have a timer dial with movable pins that switch the unit between normal and setback temperatures. By moving the pins, you control the duration of the setback periods. You then set the units for the normal and setback temperature desired.

Once set, the thermostats work automatically. The built-in, battery-operated clock keeps time. With a self-recharging battery, it requires little or no attention in normal use.

Portable Electric Heaters Can Lower Heat Bills

An electric heater, used wisely, can lower your heating bill. True, such appliances can draw a lot of power (portables are commonly rated at 1,500 watts), and electricity is expensive in some areas. But the cost of running one—typically 12 to 18 cents per hour—pales beside the cost of fueling a central heating system, which can run well over a dollar per hour.

The opportunity for energy saving, at no sacrifice in comfort, arises when you need to heat only one room or part of a room. At that point, use the portable heater and lower the setting on the central system's thermostat. You're thereby apt to save energy (and money) in the long run.

Thus, you might use a portable heater to warm the kitchen during breakfast while leaving the central system's thermostat at a low nighttime temperature for an extra hour or so. Or you might use a heater to take the chill off an early spring day, if you've turned off the central heating as soon as possible after winter.

A good electric heater can be bought for well under $50, set to work at the flick of a switch, and moved from room to room as needs dictate. Portables come in several basic types:

Radiant/convection heaters are made in upright and baseboard versions. They heat by a combination of radiation (a reflector beams out heat from the heating elements without heating the air itself) and convection (the heated air rises, aided by a fan, creating a flow of warm air).

In general, a radiant/convection heater is good for spot heating—to warm someone sitting at a desk, say—but not quite as good for heating a room evenly. But they make a fan noise and a visible glow that cycles on and off, possible annoyances in a bedroom at night.

Convection-only models heat by convection alone. They're generally better than radiant/convection models at distributing heat evenly through a room, but not as good at spot heating. Convection-only units can be bought in either the upright or baseboard format. The typical design affords a distinct advantage for bedroom use—the heating element is concealed, so no light is emitted when the element is working. And many models do not use a fan, so there's no fan noise.

Radiant models are apt to be the best at spot heating. These commonly use a quartz tube to radiate heat. One common design is about a yard high, with a shaft-on-a-stand shape that lets the heater beam "line-of-sight" heat at a person who is standing or sitting. That arrangement can boost a localized temperature about 10 degrees in as little as 5 minutes and hold it remarkably stable. But a quartz heater is apt to be only fair at spreading heat throughout a room.

Having no fan, quartz models are much quieter than many other heaters. Their tubes, however, may tend to rattle when someone walks by, and their glow might disturb a light sleeper.

Will a Fireplace Cut Your Fuel Bills?

If you have a fireplace and think you can save energy by building a fire in it, take note: An open fire can draw more heat from the rest of the house than it supplies to the room it's in. Even in that room, the fire's heat contribution may be rather minor; about 90 percent of the heat from wood burned in an open fireplace escapes up the chimney. For every cord of wood you buy, only about 10 percent of it will actually go to warming the room.

With every working fireplace comes a working draft. The rush of heated air up the chimney pulls in air from the room around the fireplace—much more air than is needed to keep a flame alive. Strictly speaking, a fireplace doesn't heat the air in a room directly, as a central heating system does. Rather, the open fireplace heats by direct radiation that warms whatever is in the hearth's line of "sight." The closer you are to the fireplace, the more heat you get.

A fireplace, then, directly warms only the side you present to the fire. While one side of your body is receiving heat radiated from the fire, your other side is losing body heat to the room. In colonial times, keeping comfortable often depended on sticking close to the fire and turning oneself around from time to time like a goose on a spit. (Eventually, though, the fire warmed the walls facing the fire, in turn heating the air in the room.) In a modern house, you usually rely on the central heating system to keep the rooms warm. Unlike a fireplace, that system works primarily by heating the air, which in turn heats you and the walls.

A working fireplace in a house with central heating creates an economic problem. The heat radiated by the fire may not be enough to off-set the loss up the chimney of room air, which has been preheated by your furnace at considerable expense. Turn off the furnace and the fireplace will indeed heat the immediate surroundings, but the rest of the house is apt to freeze. And most of the heat will go up the chimney in any case.

Exterior Caulking Saves Fuel Dollars

In a less energy-conscious age, houses were caulked mainly to protect the structure against water and to cut drafts. But caulking is also a key to saving fuel dollars.

A surprising amount of cold air can find its way through chinks in siding, open seams between house and foundation, or crevices around door and window frames and on into the house through even such unlikely inlets as electrical receptacles. That cold air is not only an extra burden for your heating system but can also make a home uncomfortably drafty. Warm indoor air escapes by the same routes.

Only a few kinds of caulk are marketed much to do-it-yourselfers: latex-based, silicone-based, and latex-silicone hybrids. All are viscous polymers that cure to a rubbery solid that expands and contracts with changes in temperature.

If a caulk doesn't cure with a dry skin, it may pick up dirt and wind-blown grit. Clear caulks usually resist dirt very well, and their neutral color tends to mask the dirt they do pick up. Most white caulks, if left untreated, will eventually look at least a little the worse for wear.

Painting a caulk also helps it shed dirt. Latex and acrylic latex caulks generally hold a coat of paint well. Most silicone-based caulks are not paintable; paint just beads on them. But some "paintable" silicone caulks now can hold a coat of paint, though not necessarily very well.

Most exterior caulk comes in cylindrical cartridges about a foot long. Most people use a simple, hand-operated caulking gun to squeeze a bead of the stuff out of the cartridge and a putty knife to remove any excess. Latex- based products clean up with water, a marked convenience when putting away tools and policing your working area. Some caulks, particularly the solvent-based products and the silicones, can be stringy, sticky, or so stiff to gun that they are fatiguingly hard to work with.

All in all, you'll probably do best with a latex caulk. Latexes run only about one-third the price of silicones, yet a latex will probably hold up just as well as a silicone. If you are going to paint the caulk, the choice is clear: Use a latex-based caulk rather than a "paintable" silicone.

Don't buy a "clear" caulk and expect an invisible bead. It may cure colorless, but it won't usually be more transparent than, say, petroleum jelly. You may want to consider a colored, or pigmented, caulk, tinted to match popular colors of siding, which might be more unobtrusive when in place.

Another kind of caulk worth considering isn't packed in a cartridge. Instead, the caulk is applied to a paper backing and sold in rolls. To use the caulk, you cut off the length you need, press it into the space you want to fill, and peel off the backing. The caulk works by bridging the surface of a crack; standard caulk is forced into the crack to seal it.

Caulk sold in rolls can take the place of standard caulk in many instances. In fact, it may be preferable to standard caulk for bridging extra-wide gaps. But it does have its limitations. You can't adjust the width of the applied caulk, as you can when using standard caulk.

Weather Stripping Plugs Heat Leaks

Money in the form of heated air escapes through loose windows and doors. You can block that escape with weather stripping, sold in lumber yards and in hardware, discount, paint, department, and variety stores in a dozen or so types. Many of the products come in long rolls, designed to be cut into lengths to fit into place. With few exceptions, all can be used on doors as well as windows. All allow doors and windows to operate normally. The products can be applied from the inside or the outside. Some can be tacked on, some stuck on with their own adhesive. Some are nearly invisible when in place; others are all too visible.

Double-hung windows should have weather stripping around the entire frame and where the two sashes meet. Casement windows and doors should have weather stripping all around the frame. (Bottoms of doors present a special problem and need special treatment. See page 83.)

Here's what's available.

Nonreinforced, self-adhesive foam. These floppy, nonreinforced strips are usually inexpensive. Some are polyurethane ("open-cell") foams, soft and lightweight. Some are vinyl ("closed-cell"), a somewhat denser, firmer material. Some are black sponge rubber, of even greater density and available in a larger selection of thicknesses. There is also a relatively new foam, known as EPDM rubber, which has a firm, nonporous surface, sometimes ribbed. It's more expensive than the other types.

Self-adhesive foam is easy to install. It should be applied to a smooth, dry, dust-free surface that isn't too cold. Don't stretch the foam as you put it on, lest it pop off as it shrinks back to size.

The foam strips are invisible when they're installed at the tops and bottoms of window sashes. Along a doorjamb, they're visible only when the door is open. Don't install foams between sliding parts, where friction may abrade them. Foams should not be placed where the two sashes of double-hung windows meet, for example.

Nonreinforced felt. Inexpensive, nonreinforced felt strips come in polyester or wool in a variety of widths and are not self-adhesive; the strips have to be nailed, stapled, or glued in place. Felt can be used in much the same manner as foam; unlike foam, however, it can resist abrasion. Because felt tends to hold moisture, it's a good idea to use it only where it isn't exposed to the weather.

Reinforced vinyl, felt, and foam. Usually reinforced with a fairly stiff strip of aluminum or plastic, reinforced stripping is butted up against closed windows or doors, inside or out, and stapled, nailed, or glued to the frame. It can be used with all types of doors and windows. If the window is one you want to open, reinforced vinyl or felt makes an especially useful seal because it can be fastened firmly to the window frame; reinforced foam is less durable in this application.

Tubular gaskets. Some are hollow and flexible; others are foam-filled and rather firm. They're often made of vinyl or EPDM rubber. Like the other reinforced strips, gaskets are installed in full view. The tubular section of the gasket butts against the closed door or window. The flat lip, or flange, is nailed or stapled to the frame.

Tension strips. These are thin, flexible products that bend or fold in place to form a tension seal. Most are metal, generally packaged with nails for installation. A newer type is made of self-adhesive plastic. If invisibility is important, tension strips are usually your best bet. These strips fit into the side channels of a window and at the tops and bottoms of both sashes (or into the woodwork around a door), where they're completely out of sight when the window or door is shut.

Special-Purpose Weather Stripping

The most common kinds of weather stripping are meant for windows or the sides and tops of doors. There are also special-purpose materials for specific problem areas.

Door sweeps, door bottoms, and thresholds. Gaps at the bottom of a door are often a major source of heat loss. Door sweeps are attached to the inside face of an in-swinging door (or to the outside face of an out-swinging door) with just enough overlap at the bottom to seal the gap. Most sweeps contain a felt, vinyl, or brush strip reinforced with aluminum or wood. They are easy to install: Most screw on, though you may also find self-adhesive models. Ordinary door sweeps work well, unless there is interference because the door has to swing open over exceptionally deep carpeting. There are automatic sweeps that solve that problem—they rise automatically when the door is opened, lower when it is shut.

Door bottoms attach to the bottom of a door to fill the gap between door and threshold. Most are vinyl gaskets held in place by an aluminum or wood channel that screws onto the door. There are two types, one far easier to install than the other. The easy version is an L- or U-shaped channel that fits over the bottom of the door but can be screwed into the face of the door. This type generally has slotted screw holes, allowing you to adjust the height after the device is installed. The channel holds a vinyl or other pliable gasket that meets the sill when the door is closed. This type is somewhat visible when in place. More difficult to install but less visible is a gasket that requires removing the door, because it attaches to the bottom edge.

Thresholds are attached to the sill beneath the door, replacing the existing threshold. Typically, they are aluminum or wood, with a channel containing a rubber or vinyl gasket. The only drawback to the threshold type of weather stripping is that the gasket can be quickly worn down if the doorway is in constant use. A gasket can be replaced, so you don't have to buy a whole new threshold (but gaskets may be difficult to find in local stores).

Gaskets for wall outlets. Electric wall outlets and wall switches can be an unexpected avenue of air leakage to and from the outdoors. Even those mounted on interior walls are often connected to an unheated area via a hollow wall that lets drafts circulate. These leaks account for a surprisingly high percentage of a house's total air leakage. You can buy special gaskets that quickly and inexpensively block the air that sneaks around electric outlets and light switches.

FOUR

Bringing Up Baby Economically

In the flush of new or oncoming parenthood, many couples feel impelled to go out and buy, buy, buy for the new arrival. But you can get almost everything you need for a baby for less than top dollar without stinting or scrimping. Here's a dollarwise guide.

What You Need and Don't Need

Magazines and makers of baby products often tell parents that they need a lot more things for their baby than they really do. Here's a list of items we think you need and others that are luxuries or unneeded extras. Prices can vary widely among stores, so shop around. The easiest way to comparison shop is by telephone. Be sure to know the specific brands and models of the products about which you inquire.

Before Your Baby Comes

Child restraint for traveling in car

Crib with mattress

Bedding
  bumper pad
  4 waterproof pads

4 fitted sheets
quilt or comforter
lightweight blanket
2 to 3 receiving blankets

Diapers
  48 cloth diapers
  6 diaper pins
  4 pair waterproof pants
  or 4 cases newborn-size disposable diapers and 12 cloth diapers

Toiletries
  cotton balls
  rectal or digital thermometer
  baby soap (optional)

Feeding equipment (if bottle-feeding)
  four 8-ounce bottles; four 4-ounce bottles
  extra nipples and caps
  bottle and nipple brushes
  sterilizer kit (optional)
  bottle warmer (optional)

Feeding equipment (if breast-feeding)
  four 4-ounce bottles for water, juice, or expressed breast milk
  bottle and nipple brushes
  manual breast pump (optional)

Clothing
  6 to 8 snap or tie-front T-shirts (6-months size)
  3 to 4 nightgowns (6-months size)
  (Note: The 6-months size, although it may seem to swallow your new-
    born, will give your baby a longer wearing time than the tiny shirts
    and gowns that are useful for only a month or two.)
  3 pair booties or bootielike socks
  2 small sweaters
  knitted, tie-on cap (winter) or small tie-on brimmed hat (summer)
  bunting or hooded jacket (winter)

After Your Baby Comes

A safe high chair (for use after your baby is eating solid foods and can
  sit up unaided)

A safe stroller or carriage-stroller

Optional Purchases

Soft carrier and/or backpack

Bassinet, carrycot, or cradle for the first months after birth

Baby bathtub

Changing table

Soft washcloths and hooded towels

Expensive Options (but Possibly Worth It)

Automatic baby swing (especially if your baby is fussy)

Playpen

**Expensive Option
(but a Safety Hazard and Not Worth It)**

Walker

Furniture and Equipment

Bassinets, Carrycots, and Cradles

Should you invest in a bassinet, carrycot, or cradle? The *bassinet,* with its enclosed sides, wheels, and small dimensions, is probably the most useful. Most parents want their baby near them in the early months so that the child can be monitored. A bassinet can easily be wheeled from room to room and takes up little space.

There are safety hazards associated with bassinets, however. According to the U.S. Consumer Product Safety Commission, a number of children have been injured by falling, either when the bottom of a bassinet broke or when it tipped over or collapsed. There were similar accidents with cradles.

When you shop for a bassinet or cradle, look for a model with a sturdy bottom and a wide base. Follow the manufacturer's weight guidelines. Avoid using a pillow in a bassinet and be careful that the cushioning you use is firm enough that your baby's face can't get buried in it. As a rule of thumb, discontinue using the unit when your baby begins to roll over or pull up—usually at age four or five months.

When buying a bassinet, check to see that its folding legs have locks so that the unit won't fold during use. Periodically check screws and bolts, especially on the base, to be sure they're tight.

Bassinets offer an alternative to putting your newborn into a large crib. But despite the bassinet's old-fashioned charm, it's probably more economical to buy a new crib in the first place.

Carrycots are small baby beds with handles designed for carrying very young babies from place to place. They can be useful, especially for daytime naps while away from home, but a stroller or a fabric front carrier could serve the same purpose.

Carrycots come in two basic styles: those made of fabric that fold down for storage and those made like woven baskets. Woven basket carrycots have handles that are scratchy and uncomfortable to carry for any length of time. These handles also tend to fray and break and may allow a baby to fall. If you do opt for a woven carrycot, look under the fancy lace and fabric for sturdy construction, especially in the handle attachments. Also check that the basket is well balanced while the baby is in it.

Safety is a critical issue with carrycots. They may tip if the handles are placed too close to each other, and handles may snap loose, causing the baby to fall. Be sure that the attachment points for each handle are widely spaced so that when your baby shifts position, the carrier won't tilt from head to toe. Inadequately reinforced handles may eventually pull loose and break. Models that rely on cardboard sewn inside the fabric for backing may warp or deteriorate if the material gets wet.

Cradles have a romantic, old-fashioned air, but we suggest that you resist buying one. Should the baby's weight cause the cradle bed to shift to one side, the cradle's side-to-side motion can roll a tiny baby back and forth until he or she ends up helplessly pressed against one of the wooden sides. If you want to provide your baby with soothing, rhythmical motion, invest in a cushiony rocker-recliner or a baby carriage with a springy suspension system.

Cradles can be quite an expensive investment (several hundred dollars) for the four or five months that a baby can use one. Most aren't portable. And they may pose hazards similar to those of bassinets. Our suggestion? Buy a less expensive, sturdy bassinet or a portable crib instead.

Cribs and Mattresses

Cribs can range from under $100 for a Spartan-looking model to over $500 for a crib that later transforms into a youth bed and chest. But happily, a crib is not an inevitable purchase. Consider purchasing a safe, sturdy portable crib rather than a more expensive full-sized model and keeping it in the low, play-yard position on the floor for increased safety.

Combination crib-beds are widely available. They are bulky pieces of furniture that, when taken apart, convert into a junior bed with a small table, desk, or dresser. They're quite expensive, often exceeding $400. Since you'll have to buy a regular-sized bed sooner or later for your growing child, CU thinks a standard crib is a better buy.

All full-sized cribs are now covered by a federal safety standard. So the kind of crib you purchase—if new—need not be selected strictly in terms of safety. Whatever your taste or budget, buy a crib without fancy cutouts or cornerpost protrusions, which can result in harm to your baby. At the store, try out the drop sides to be sure they operate without a hitch, run your hand along the wood to see that the finish is smooth, and make sure all hardware and components are securely attached. In particular, check the plastic sleeve, or "teething rail," that runs along the top railings of the crib sides. It should firmly adhere to the rails so that your toddler won't be able to pull it off, possibly breaking it into plastic shards or exposing splintery wood underneath. Never allow your child to sleep in a malfunctioning crib, since most crib-related fatalities happen with them.

Making Sure Your Crib Is Safe

Hand-me-down cribs or yard-sale finds may not be safe, since they may predate mandatory safety standards, in effect only since 1973. You can judge a crib's safety yourself if you know what to look for. In some cases, you can alter an older crib to make it reasonably safe. To check an older crib, you'll need a tape measure.

Sides. When fully raised, sides should measure at least 26 inches from their upper edge to the top of the mattress support in its lowest position. When lowered, the top of the side should be at least 9 inches above the mattress support in its highest position.

End panels. Check that they extend below the mattress support in its lowest position so there's no space for the child's head, arms, or legs to become trapped.

Slats. Terrible accidents have occurred when widely spaced crib slats allowed a child's legs, arms, and torso to slip through but then caught the head. Check that there's no more than 2⅜ inches between slats, spindles, crib rods, or any other such openings.

Decorative end panels. These have sometimes proved to be a hazard. As early as 1984, we reported problems with specific discontinued crib models made by Bassett Furniture Industries. The "Early American" design of the cut-out headboard left a gap in which a child's head could be trapped, and at least nine strangulation deaths occurred. Although those models are no longer manufactured (they were made from 1974 to 1977) and Bassett has tried to recall them, people are apparently obtaining them secondhand. Recalled are the **Candelite** pine finish model **5127** and maple finish **5028** and the **Mandalay** maple finish models **5126** and **5621** and the white finish model **5225** (the model numbers are stamped in ink near the bottom of the inside of the headboard). Consumers are asked to call Bassett to report such cribs. A free modification kit is available by calling 800-366-3324 (in Virginia: 703-629-7511).

There has also been a recall of all 900,000 **Questor Baby Line** cribs manufactured between 1970 and 1982. Hangers that attach the crib springs to the mattress frame can break or bend, allowing the mattress and springs to drop slightly, possibly resulting in injury to babies. The cribs have slotted, rather than smooth, hangers to attach the springs and tubular, rather than flat, mattress supports. The cribs can be identified by the Questor label located under the mattress on the headboard or footboard. Free replacement hangers and brackets are available (even for cribs in storage) by calling 800-543-8954 (Ohio: 800-762-8926).

Corner posts. Corner posts that protrude above a crib's end panels can snag a ribbon, pacifier string, or necklace a child may wear (but shouldn't), and even loose-fitting clothing such as "football shirts," resulting in possible strangulation. Since 1973, the Consumer Product Safety Commission has recorded nearly 40 strangulation deaths associated with protruding corner posts.

As a result, CU argued in 1983, when this hazard became known, that there should not be any protrusion at the corners, or that the posts be so high that the tops would be inaccessible to the child. Industry argued that 0.59 inch with a bevel would protect against strangulation. As that standard came up for review in 1989 and after several more deaths (including one that was within the 0.59-inch limitation), we argued again that the protrusion be reduced. This time most of the manufacturers concluded that they could make cribs with a protrusion of not more than .625 inch at any point 3 inches from the outer edge. Cribs built to that standard have been on the market since the beginning of 1991.

Paint. Cribs made before 1978, and especially those made before 1970, may be coated with paint or varnish that contains lead. That crib of an uncertain age you're considering could be a toxic hazard to a child who might chew on the crib's parts.

Though the odds are slim, it's a chance we'd suggest not taking. To be safe, be prepared to strip and refinish all chewable surfaces, as well as any cracked, peeling, or chipped areas of the crib's coating. Use paint designated for baby products, which is required by law to be lead-free.

Mattresses. You may not object to using an old crib so long as you can buy a new mattress for it. Crib mattresses don't vary much in size— they're usually 27¼ inches wide by 51⅝ inches long by 6 inches thick. Measure the crib carefully: Any mattress you buy should fit snugly. Gaps between the mattress and the sides or ends of the crib could allow a child's head, arms, legs, or torso to become trapped. Some children have managed to lodge themselves in such gaps and have suffocated. If you plan to use an existing mattress, make sure it fits the crib tightly. The plastic mattress cover should be clean and free of tears.

When you buy a new crib, the mattress is normally a separate purchase, costing $60 or more. Like adult mattresses, the baby units come with names that imply that they affect a baby's physical development and posture. However, the difference in the surface cushioning of models is often minimal. Generally, thin vinyl upholstery is more likely to snag, tear, and stretch than materials that are a combination of fabric and a plastic laminate.

High-quality innerspring models are a good choice if you're willing to pay the price and do not mind the extra few pounds of weight. The number of coils in a mattress isn't a sure indication of quality. However, in the past, CU tests have shown that the more coils a mattress had, the better it tended to perform. Check that the mattress has good edge firmness.

Polyurethane foam mattresses are normally lighter than innerspring units, which can make bed making easier. They are also less expensive than innerspring models. If foam is your choice, go for the high-density variety. Low-density polyurethane foam units are less expensive than high-density ones, but the low-density variety may not provide adequate support around the mattress edges. This could allow a baby to get trapped between the metal mattress support that accidentally dislodged and the crib sides, in our judgment.

The mattress should fit snugly next to the crib's side so that there is no gap that could entrap your baby. If you can place two fingers between the mattress and the sides, the mattress should be replaced.

It's a good practice to turn the crib's mattress over and rotate it occasionally in order to prevent sagging. A crib-mattress protector can be bought to help protect the mattress from being torn by the crib's sharp, metal springs.

We do not suggest purchasing "baby waterbeds." While we know of no injury or death of a baby on a crib water mattress, we do know of suffocation deaths of infants on adult water beds.

Nursery Decor and Accessories

Salespersons may try to sell you a coordinated suite of nursery furniture, or perhaps a fancy brass crib or one with an arched canopy. But a crib or a diaper table will be outgrown in only two years. Plan ahead for the preschool years: Purchase open shelves that can store diapers and shirts now and toys later and small chests with easy-to-open drawers for your self-dressing preschooler.

Used baby equipment can save you money. But be careful to select only items that are safe and in good condition.

Cribs, playpens, high chairs, and other nursery items that are broken are likely to cause serious accidents. If furniture has been painted, consider removing the paint, just in case it is lead-based, and repainting it with a nontoxic finish.

Special touches in the nursery can help make the room cheerful and inviting. Babies spend a lot of time on their backs looking around. Bare ceilings can be made more interesting with suspended fabric kites or billowing fabric draped through rings on the ceiling. Even if you're not interested in wallpapering your baby's entire room, you may want to think about patterned borders, many of which are designed just for babies' and children's rooms. You can usually hang them yourself in only a few hours.

Many babies are fascinated by the contrasts of light and dark, such as the pattern created by leaves fluttering outside the nursery window. Press-apply vinyl prisms, available in some science centers and toy stores, break up light into colorful beams that are projected across the room onto the wall. An aquarium with a light and pump, stationed out of a baby's reach, can provide an interesting visual scene, although it can be an expensive and time-consuming investment. You may find that the pump is too noisy, but the monotonous sound may be soothing to some babies.

Drapes in bright patterns can serve to capture a baby's gaze, while more subtle fabrics can be used to create a more restful mood. Since diapering will be an oft-repeated activity, pay special attention to the wall and ceiling area near the diaper-changing table. An unbreakable mirror behind the table will interest baby. A suspended mobile of birds or butterflies or a Japanese lantern hung well out of baby's reach can be something to look at. A shelf installed on the wall far from baby's reach can be useful for storing diapering toiletries and other items that your baby shouldn't get to. Create an indoor tree by painting a large branch, securing it in a bucket of plaster of Paris, and hanging toys with bows on it. Be sure to remove the decorations when baby begins to pull up and crawl.

You can paint a used chest, rocker, and table in coordinated colors as a part of your decorating scheme. A closet can be turned into a nursery nook by removing the door and installing a padded, plywood changing platform. Shelves are also useful in the closet during the first few years, since only a few items of baby's clothing will need to be hung up and they will take up only a few feet of hanging space. (Note: Older toy chests are dangerous—the lids often fall shut suddenly—and have caused numerous deaths. Newer versions should be safe, but we think open shelves are a better way to store toys.)

Instead of using a night-light, consider installing a dimmer switch on the nursery's switchplate (and in your bedroom, as well) that can lower the fixture's brightness when you check your sleeping baby. Or use a lamp with a three-way brightness switch. If you do purchase a night-light, check to be sure that it is UL approved.

Think about your own comfort when you plan such special space. You are apt to be awakened by your child several times a night in the early months and periodically for several years thereafter. A comfortable rocking chair will help as you feed or comfort your baby. Look for one with flat armrests for support during breast- or bottle-feeding.

A footstool or hassock will give you a place to put your feet up. A small table beside the chair can be used to hold late-night extras: a book, a reading lamp, a container for drinking water, and a radio or tape recorder for soft music.

If baby is sharing a room with an older brother or sister, consider buying or making a room divider or hanging bright, patterned sheets that can be slid back and forth on a dowel and shower curtain hooks. Or you can construct a semipermanent room divider from plywood. Blackboard paint, available from some hardware stores, will allow big brother or sister to draw pictures and to scribble on the divider.

Playpens

Ask yourself whether you really *need* a playpen. Some parents would answer a definite yes; their babies don't appear to mind being in one and it temporarily frees the parents to do chores. Others would give a qualified yes, perhaps because their babies don't tolerate one for very long, but they find it useful when dinner's being cooked or a floor's being mopped. Still other parents would confess that their playpens have become cumbersome and rather costly toy containers that take up valuable floor space or against which their babies protest vigorously.

Today's playpens look more like bins than pens. They can be folded up for storage. While there are still a few wooden pens on the market, mesh playpens with tubular metal frames are now the standard design. The top rail is vinyl covered and often padded. Typically, the top rail is hinged so that one side or the other can be lowered to make it easier to lift the baby in or out of the pen. That's called a drop side, and it creates a hazard.

When a side is left down, very young babies can roll into the "suffocation pocket" of loose mesh and vinyl around the bottom and the rigid floor, where they can become trapped and suffocate. As of this writing, nearly 20 babies have died in this kind of accident in the United States.

For that reason, never leave the drop side down! You might consider purchasing a model with sides that lower only as a part of the folding-away process. And never leave a child in a playpen unattended.

When you shop for a mesh playpen, look for a model certified by the American Society for Testing and Materials, with thick vinyl on the side railings and the floor pad. Since 1983, the vinyl on these models has had to meet minimum thickness requirements. Babies can and do bite or pinch holes in thin-gauge vinyl. They can then pick out pieces of the foam padding underneath and perhaps choke on it. They can also choke on pieces of the vinyl itself. You can test the relative thickness of vinyl on different models by pinching it. If the vinyl comes up into your fingers readily and shows pock marks from stretching, it is probably too thin.

Prices of mesh playpens can vary according to the thickness of the vinyl and padding on the railings and mattress. Other deluxe features include wheels, larger floor area, and more heavyweight tubing. The bottom-of-the-line models may lack side padding or railing cushioning, have thin mattress pads (½ inch thick), and have no wheels, but they usually offer a center-leg support to keep the floorboard from giving way during a tot's jumping. More costly models have firm foam padding under thick vinyl on the top railing and side supports, come with a thicker (¾-inch) pad, and have wider dimensions on all sides.

Choose a model with well-protected hinges and hardware that doesn't have a scissoring action, so that there's no danger of a baby's or sibling's fingers getting caught as you fold or open the pen. The floorboards should be thick and have some type of support underneath, such as crossbars, to assure that they can withstand a baby's jumping. Wheels, even if they are just on two legs of the pen, are a nice extra.

Many newer mesh models are being made with colorful fabric railing covers and floor pads that often don't stay in place. A baby may slip and fall when the pad shifts, exposing the hard floorboard. To solve that problem, secure the pad firmly to the floorboard, perhaps by stitching Velcro-type strips near the edges, or replace the fabric pad with a firmer, vinyl-covered version (available at most nursery goods stores). Be cautious about using tape or tacks, which could be ingested by your baby.

Wooden playpens are superior, in some respects, to mesh models. Their bars allow a baby to see clearly out into the world, and they give solid support for sitting and pulling up. The floors generally hold up better. And you won't have to concern yourself with the scissoring action of hinges, the snagging potential of mesh, or the question of whether the railing vinyl will hold up to your baby's gnawing. Nor is there the possibility of a suffocation pocket. It's possible, however, for a child to stick a foot out between the spindles of a wooden playpen. In a fall, the foot or leg could be caught or twisted.

Many people use hand-me-down playpens or buy one at a yard sale. Inspect a prospective acquisition carefully. Make sure it's structurally sound (and don't alter its structures). Be cautious: It may have been painted with lead-based paint. Make sure the pen's flooring is intact and isn't splitting. The pen's vertical bars should be no more than 2⅜ inches apart, to prevent your baby's being strangled if his body slips through and his head becomes stuck. Run your hand along the wood's surface to be sure that it is splinter-free. Most wooden pens have a plastic sheath or teething rail that runs along the top railing. Be sure it's intact and not cracked or broken. The unit should have a firm vinyl pad; if it does not, consider purchasing a new one from a baby-goods store. Clean the playpen thoroughly before putting your baby in it.

Babies who have participated in our tests seemed to have more fun in playpens with large play areas. Those models generally weigh more, take up more storage space, and may cost more than the smaller ones. But we recommend them as a first choice.

Strollers

Should you buy a combination carriage-stroller, a lightweight stroller, or both? Prices are a major consideration. Accessories (except canopy or hood) to make the stroller more comfortable and climate-protected usually cost extra. To cut costs, you may want to consider buying a safe used stroller at a yard sale. Wherever you buy, take your baby with you and try out a stroller first. That way, you can judge for yourself how well the restraining belts operate and fit and how easily the stroller can be maneuvered.

If your baby is very young, you will probably want a unit that reclines almost completely. Look for adequate side and rear protection from the stroller's frame or for upholstery siding that will prevent the child from accidentally rolling out, being hit from the side, or being injured should the stroller tip over backward.

The following features are also important:

A sturdy, reliable seat belt. Look for a seat belt that makes positive contact around the sides and front of your child's waist and provides direct crotch restraint to prevent the child from climbing out, standing up, or slipping out of the stroller. Some seat belt buckles may be difficult to release, and others may require double-threading, which is time-consuming and may not be done right. Some units have belts that fasten across the stroller rather than around the baby, leaving a gap on the sides that might let a toddler get out.

Stability. Look for a unit with a wide, long wheelbase and a seat that is mounted low and deep within the frame. The stroller should resist tipping over backward when you press downward lightly on the handles. (If your baby's in the seat, be sure to strap the child in securely first.)

Brakes. Look for brakes that lock both rear wheels positively by engaging the wheels, rather than those that rely solely upon pressure into the tire. Tire pressure brakes are generally unreliable because they can be inadvertently released by rolling the stroller forward to backward.

Steering ease. Try steering the unit to see if it can be pushed in a straight line without veering when you use one hand. Wheels should be aligned, and in the case of double wheels, all eight tires should contact the floor and rotate when the stroller is in motion. Generally, the larger the wheel diameter, the easier it is to negotiate curbs and sidewalk irregularities. Some units have front wheels that can be locked into a forward-facing position or unlocked to swivel or rotate freely. Swivel front wheels make a stroller more maneuverable for turns, while stationary wheels or locked swivel wheels may function better on rough surfaces such as cobblestones and brick walkways.

Backup safety locks. The stroller frame should have a backup to the regular locking mechanism. Some units offer a primary lock plus an automatic safety catch, which means it takes two release actions to fold the unit. In that way, if the main lock fails, the backup latch prevents further collapse after the stroller has folded only a short distance. Children who are caught in strollers that accidentally collapse commonly suffer fractured or lacerated hands and fingers from the shearing side frame members; the stroller's handles may also flip forward and hit or trap the child. More severe injuries have also resulted. Some strollers, especially older designs, have unsatisfactory metal slip rings that slide down over the overlapping edges of the frame's tubing to hold the handle erect, but they can easily become mispositioned or slide out of place, causing collapse.

Frame safety. Look for a stroller frame that has no hazardous sharp edges or protrusions. A child's fingers and hands are the most likely to be hurt by the folding and opening of the frame, so keep the child or an older sibling well away when you fold or set up the unit. Small fingers and toes can get caught, cut, or mashed in the holes in tubes, in the gaps between metal parts, and in coils of springs if they are uncovered, so examine the unit you are considering very carefully. Include the backrest reclining mechanism, especially the bracket at the hinge points, in your inspection. This bracket should have a cover or it should be inaccessible to the child. X-joints, where two frame tubes fasten together, are especially hazardous because they can act like a large pair of scissors, cutting or shearing a child's fingers. Plastic caps on the ends of tubes should be securely fastened so that a baby cannot remove and choke on them.

Handlebar height and folding length. The stroller's handlebars should be at a comfortable height for the parent. An ideal height is at waist level or a little below. The plastic covering of handles should be securely attached so that it does not slip or shift. If you have a subcompact car, you may want to consider the bulk and length of the folded stroller and whether it will fit into your car trunk.

Child's Safety Gates

Here's a juvenile product on which you shouldn't spend a nickel: The old-fashioned accordion-style wooden gates that open to form diamond-shaped spaces with wide Vs at the top. Such gates have entrapped the head or neck of several children, causing death by strangulation. (U.S. Consumer Product Safety Commission files show that accordion "safety" gates have been responsible for more than 20 serious accidents, including 8 fatalities, to children between the ages of 9 months and 30 months.)

Gates of that potentially lethal design are no longer made. Unfortunately, many of these gates are still in use, and some are still available in retail outlets. We strongly recommend against buying a gate of this type. If you already have one, replace it with one of the newer models that is free of head/neck entrapments. The latest gates have straight edges and either a flexible mesh screen, plastic grids, or vertical slats.

We recommend the hardware-mounted models over the pressure-mounted gates, so long as the hardware-mounted model is properly installed. But none of these gates is perfect. Active toddlers can, and do, attempt to climb over them and may be injured as a result. There's no substitute for parental supervision at all times.

Do You Need a Changing Table?

When baby needs a change of clothes, a waist-high flat surface is handy for the job. You needn't spend money for a special table, though. You can install a sturdy wall-to-wall shelf at a comfortable height in baby's closet. Or simply plan to change baby on a waterproof pad placed on your bed or on the floor. (Always keep one hand on your baby.)

If you do opt for a special changing table, there are three kinds—wheeled, folding ones; railed, wooden versions; and hinged chest adapters. The first two are the most acceptable. Fold-down wooden adapters have been known to cause the entire chest to topple when a baby's weight is placed on the outer edge. The major safety concern with changing tables is that babies can fall off them. The higher the protective guardrail around the table, the better; some tables offer only a few inches of protection. However, never rely on the guardrail. For your baby's safety, always keep one hand on a baby on the table, and never walk away and leave your baby there. Open shelves that run the entire length of the changing table are far more convenient for storing items than small, high-sided basket containers.

Baby Bathtubs and Bathing Accessories

Parents sometimes dread bathing a baby, especially a tiny baby who howls. We recommend "damp mopping" a baby during the first weeks. Eventually, though, the baby has to be bathed.

As a practical strategy for saving money, you can use the kitchen sink, lined with a towel, or carefully bring the baby into the tub with you. But baby bathtubs are helpful—they provide a comfortable, secure environment for bathing. We recommend a tub that offers a semireclined seat, slip-resistant backing, and a drain hole with an attached plug. Look for a sturdy tub that has a smooth, rounded lip to make carrying easier and that is made of thick plastic that won't fold in the center from the weight of the water. Never carry the baby in the tub, especially in a tub with water in it, since the baby can get hurt if the tub slips out of your hands.

Certain products are unsafe to use as bath aids: Beware of flotation devices claimed to float babies up to six months in the bath; some may flip over. Suctioned seats without restraining belts may lead to drowning. And foam cushions for use in the tub can be pulled apart and swallowed by babies.

Baby washcloths and hooded baby towels are optional purchases. Any soft washcloth will do, as will any soft towel, so long as it is large enough to wrap your baby in. Special baby soaps can be expensive; whatever soap you choose, make sure that it is relatively free of perfumes, deodorants, antibacterial agents, and other additives, to prevent skin reactions. Soap can be used to wash baby's hair as well. But if you plan to use shampoo, choose a baby shampoo (without formaldehyde), because it will probably contain fewer additives than a regular shampoo.

Child Safety: Selecting the Proper Auto Seat Restraint

Overview of the Problem

Infants and children require special attention. Smaller size, lack of coordination, high center of gravity because of their proportionately large head size, and the greater activity level make them vulnerable to many risks in crashes. Unrestrained children are more prone to injury than adults in noncrash circumstances such as sudden braking or during sharp turns. The proper choice and use of child restraints is essential. Government statistics show a more than two-thirds reduction in risk of injury or death for properly restrained infants and children.

A child held on the lap of an adult or buckled into a seat belt with another person is in the worst situation in a crash. In a head-on crash, a child held by a belted adult in the front seat would collide with the instrument panel, because the adult would not be able to hold on to the child. In a similar circumstance a child held by an unrestrained adult would be crushed as both are thrown forward into the instrument panel. If the safety belt is buckled over both the child and the adult, the child would be crushed against the safety belt with tremendous force by the weight of the adult behind him.

All states now require that infants and children be buckled into an approved child safety restraint. The age limits covered by such laws vary from state to state. Safety belts are designed primarily for adults; they do not provide optimal protection for children. Child restraint systems have been designed for small bodies, and they afford the best protection when they fit the child, the vehicle, and the needs of the parent properly.

If a child restraint system is temporarily unavailable, using a safety belt, especially a lap/shoulder belt, is better than no restraint at all. However, a safety belt can be used only for children who are old enough to sit unsupported. (There is no safe way to transport an infant except in an infant restraint.) Proper fit of the safety belt is very important. The lap belt should be positioned as low as possible below the child's hips, never around the waist. If the shoulder belt crosses the child's face or throat, try moving the child closer to the center of the vehicle. If repositioning the child does not remedy this situation, as a last resort place the child in a lap-belt-only position with the lap belt positioned as low as possible below the child's hips. Avoid putting the shoulder belt behind the child's back. Pillows or other makeshift means to raise the child's height should not be used.

Selecting the Restraint: General Precautions

Parents should consider only child restraints that meet federal safety standards. The label on the restraint should state that it "conforms to all applicable federal motor vehicle safety standards." The label should also note the name and location of the manufacturer and the date the product was made. Restraints, particularly older ones, should be checked for hairline cracks, loose rivets, or broken parts. Parents are cautioned not to use child restraints manufactured before January 1, 1981; prior to that date, restraints had to meet less stringent governmental safety standards. A child restraint that has been in a crash should never be reused.

fitting the Restraint Properly to the Child

The age, size, and weight of a child are the major considerations in choosing an appropriate safety restraint system and in using it properly. In general, it is necessary to differentiate between three periods of childhood. The first period is from birth to when the child is about one year old and weighs at least 20 pounds. The second period is when the child is between one and about four years of age and weighs up to 40 pounds. The third period lasts until a lap/shoulder belt fits the child.

Restraint Systems from Birth to One Year

Caution: Never substitute ordinary baby carriers for a certified child restraint system. Ordinary carriers are not designed to withstand crash forces.

Rear-facing restraints. The most common type of restraint system for children from birth to one year of age and weighing up to 20 pounds is the rear-facing restraint, which provides support for the child's head and neck during a crash. There are two types: a small one for infants only and a larger, convertible restraint that can eventually be used forward-facing as well. If the child's head is higher than the top of the infant-only restraint, the child should be switched to a larger convertible seat and should continue to ride in the rear-facing position until one year of age. A rear-facing restraint provides effective protection when it is correctly installed in the car and the infant is securely restrained by the harness. Unfortunately, it is estimated that about one-third of parents who purchase safety seats fail to use them properly.

Here are some tips for using rear-facing restraints correctly:

1. Use a rear-facing restraint in a semireclined position. If the position is too upright, newborns may have trouble breathing. As the child gets older, a more upright but semireclined position may be preferable.

2. Always face the restraint backward toward the padded seatback. A rear-seat location is preferable to a front-seat location, especially if an adult can ride in back with the child. The center of the rear seat is best, if possible. If you are driving alone with a young baby, the American Academy of Pediatrics recommends that the

child be in the front seat so that it can be monitored, unless the passenger position is equipped with an air bag.

3. Follow carefully the instructions found in the child restraint and vehicle owner's manuals when securing a rear-facing restraint.

4. In the front, never rely on a two-point automatic seat belt. A snug-fitting lap belt is essential to secure the restraint properly. When the automatic belt is not adequate to secure the child restraint, you can install a separate lap belt using the existing anchor points in the vehicle.

5. Secure the infant snugly with the harness before any blankets are placed on him or her.

6. If the restraint has more than one pair of slots for the shoulder straps, use the slots *below* the child's shoulders.

Car Beds

If it is necessary for medical reasons to transport a child lying flat, there are two crash-tested car beds that can be safely used. Always position a car bed so that the child's head is toward the center seating position, not next to the door. Check for the label verifying that the car bed meets federal motor vehicle safety standards.

Restraint Systems for Toddlers (One- to Four-Year-Olds)

Forward-facing child restraints. These systems are designed for children who weigh over 20 pounds and who are over one year of age. They should be used in the fully upright position most of the time, but may be used occasionally in a semireclined position for a sleeping child, as recommended by the manufacturer. A convertible restraint used in the forward-facing position can accommodate most children until they weigh about 40 pounds and are four years old. Some children outgrow forward-facing restraints before they are four years old. When they no longer fit into the harness straps, a booster seat may be needed to help adapt the vehicle safety belt to the child's body.

Restraint vests. The restraint vest is a new type of restraint for children who weigh over 25 pounds. It is a lightweight child safety belt system with padded shoulder, lap, and crotch straps attached to a padded aluminum back or stress plate. Like other child restraints, it is held in place by the vehicle's safety belts, but it has the advantage of being small and compact enough to be placed in a suitcase.

Here are a few tips for using forward-facing restraint systems correctly:

1. Use forward-facing restraints in the upright position, which provides optimal protection.
2. A rear-seat location is preferable to a front-seat location; rear center is best, if possible.
3. Carefully follow the child restraint and vehicle manufacturer's instructions for installing the restraint, whether in the back or the front.
4. In the front-seat position, never rely on a two-point automatic shoulder belt to secure the restraint. A snug-fitting lap belt is essential to secure the seat properly. When the automatic belt is not adequate to attach the child restraint, you can install a separate lap belt using the existing anchor points in the vehicle.
5. If the child restraint has a tether strap, as do some older U.S. models and Canadian-made restraints, be sure to anchor the strap properly. If not, the restraint requiring a tether will offer less protection than a properly installed restraint that does not come with a tether strap.
6. Secure the child with the harness according to the manufacturer's instructions and always thread the shoulder straps through the *uppermost* slots.

Restraint Systems for Children Who Have Outgrown Forward-Facing Restraints

Booster seats. Booster seats are designed for children who have outgrown the forward-facing restraints but for whom safety belts do not yet fit properly. Most current booster models have a shield in front of the child's abdomen, and these are used with a lap belt alone. Some raise the height of the child and provide belt guides to position a lap/shoulder belt for proper fit. A few convert from one type to the other. When using a booster seat, make sure there is support behind the child's head and neck. Do not raise the child so that his or her ears are above the level of the seatback, unless the booster provides a built-in head and neck support (one booster seat manufactured by Volvo has this feature). Whichever model you choose, always check the label to be sure that it conforms to federal motor vehicle safety standards, and be sure to follow the manufacturer's instructions regarding the type of safety belt system (lap or lap/shoulder) to use with it.

Fitting the Child Restraint to the Car

The only way to be sure that the child restraint is compatible with your car is to try it out. Some belts cannot be pulled tight with some child restraints. The roof of your car may be too low to raise some over-the-head shields fully. Some safety belt systems call for the use of a special locking clip to secure a child restraint; others require installation of an auxiliary lap belt. Check your vehicle's owner's manual for the proper installation of a child restraint. In any case, after installation, give the restraint a sharp tug to be sure that it is secure and cannot be dislodged.

One final caution: If your car is equipped with a passenger-side air bag, check the vehicle's owner's manual regarding child-restraint installation in the front seat. It will probably tell you *not* to use a *rear-facing restraint* in this position, and for other types (including car beds), to move the vehicle seatback as far away from the instrument panel as possible.

Fitting the Needs of the Parent

If cost is an issue, infant and toddler safety seats can be rented or obtained through loaner programs. Hospitals and other service organizations often sponsor such programs. A list of these organizations can be obtained from your local pediatrician, family physician, or health department.

There have been numerous recalls of safety seats for various defects. Some of these flaws are more critical than others. Usually, recalled restraints can be fixed by replacing or adding a small part that is obtained directly from the manufacturer at no cost. You can check whether the model you are considering has been the subject of a recall by calling the National Highway Traffic Safety Administration (NHTSA) hotline or by contacting SafetyBeltSafe U.S.A. at 213-673-2666, P.O. Box 553, Altadena, CA 91003.

Choosing Clothing and Footwear Wisely

When it comes to baby clothes, it's easy to waste money by overbuying or by purchasing nondurable or inappropriate items. Here are some sensible guidelines.

In buying for a baby prior to birth, remember that your baby will need fewer sleeping gowns and other pieces of clothing during warm months. Your baby can get along with just a few shirts, gowns, and sleepers in the beginning. You can always shop for more when you have a clearer picture of what is needed and what will fit best.

Baby-shower clothes sometimes aren't practical for everyday use. For example, fancy sweater-bootie-hat sets may have weaves wide enough to trap a baby's tiny fingers. Exchange duplicate or impractical gifts for useful items, such as white cotton T-shirts with snap fronts or tie sides, waterproof pants (if you're using cloth diapers), or sleeping gowns.

Footed stretch suits are popular daytime and nighttime wear for babies. Avoid poor-quality suits, which tend to shrink in the dryer and quickly become too tight.

Selecting Baby Clothes

Baby sizes can be hard to decipher. To be sure a garment is correctly sized take it out of the packaging and judge the size yourself. Many parents buy shirts and other clothing one or two sizes larger than needed, since babies grow so rapidly.

Examine the weave of the fabric in T-shirts and gowns. Choose thick, well-finished shirts rather than thin, semitransparent garments or those that show signs of poor finishing, such as unclipped strings. Front-opening shirts are less likely to rouse wails of protest when being put on. If you purchase pullover T-shirts, look for overlapped shoulders and extra-wide neck openings.

Look for clothes that are easy to put on and take off. Until your toddler is toilet trained, you will want to have pants that offer quick and easy access for diapering. Snap-open legs are indispensable. Velcro closures do not launder well and eventually lose their holding power. Tiny buttons, bows, and other decorative fasteners only make dressing baby more time-consuming and difficult. Better alternatives are sweaters that zip up the back (to keep the zipper teeth from scratching small fingers or catching belly skin) and garments with large buttons, which make dressing the baby much easier.

Babies are most comfortable in simple, comfortable clothes. Dresses, for example, can get caught under a crawling baby's knees, frustrating her urge for forward movement.

All baby clothes should be able to withstand repeated machine washing and drying. According to law, a label has to state apparel's fiber content. Most baby clothing is made of cotton blended with polyester fibers.

Poly/cotton blends are less expensive than pure cotton clothing, are more wrinkle resistant, and are less likely to shrink—worthwhile qualities. Pure cotton garments, on the other hand, are more absorbent.

The most economical thing to do is to buy used clothing from other parents or from yard sales or recycling shops. For the price of one or two new shirts, you can supply your baby with a dozen bright outfits. And having a wide variety of clothing can cut down on how often you have to do the laundry. No one gives fashion ratings for this age group, so it's all right to be casual about how shirts and pants go together, and your tot couldn't care less.

Toddler Clothing

Clothing for this age needs to be durable and stain-repellent. Durability means sturdy fabrics, well-sewn seams with overcast stitching to prevent unraveling, and reinforcement, such as additional backstitching at the top and bottom of zippers or around buttonholes. Some manufacturers make children's pants with additional knee reinforcement.

Many parents today opt for a unisex dress code for their tots from crawling age through the early childhood years. The most practical shirts are colorful T-shirts with snap openings on one shoulder or down the front.

Crawling babies fare well in overalls or dungarees with shoulder straps and snap-open crotches for diaper changes. Pants with elastic waistbands are often too restricting and can ride down as the baby crawls. Overalls are also handy for hiding the shirt gaps that cause a tot's belly to stick out when rapid growth outdistances wardrobe. The best fabrics for overalls are soft knits or cotton/polyester blends for relatively wrinkle-free appearance without ironing.

When your baby begins to near the two-year mark, you will want to shift to elastic-waisted pants for potty training. Your child will need to be able to pull the pants up and down alone. Upon purchase, examine the waistband. It should not be overly tight, nor should it have scratchy seams that could cause discomfort on bare skin.

Underwear

Although manufacturers make thick, absorbent underwear called *training pants,* some parents find that regular underpants may give babies brought up on cloth diapers a better signal to use the toilet than bulky undergarments that feel much like what they've been wearing. Most training pants shrink considerably during washing, and they tend to bunch and lose stretch quickly.

Underwear should absorb moisture in order to prevent crotch irritations. Nylon knits, therefore, are not the best choice. The most comfortable underwear is made of 100 percent cotton or cotton/polyester blends with an absorbent cotton panel sewn into the crotch.

Winter Wear

Coats that specify "dry-clean only," such as those constructed of thick wool with insulated linings, are not practical for babies and young children. A garment that can't be washed is going to spend most of its time on expensive trips to the cleaners.

For the young baby, a thick blanket with a knitted tie-on hat is sufficient for most winter weather. A zip-up bunting or sack that encloses baby's body below the arms and has sleeves and a hood at the top is an excellent purchase until the baby can crawl. These cold-weather products are useful for keeping baby warm outdoors in stroller, car restraints, or backpacks. They should not be used indoors without supervision, nor should babies sleep in them.

Ideally, snowsuits or other winter outerwear for a child should be water-resistant. Purchase a winter garment with a built-in hood, and use it in conjunction with a knitted hat for maximum warmth.

Mittens offer more efficient cold protection than fingered gloves. They are also much easier to put on and take off. Ideally, mittens should have a nonslip surface sewn onto the palm and thumb area.

Most toddlers enjoy wearing low-cut rubber or plastic boots on slushy winter days. It's wise to purchase boots a size larger than your tot's shoes to make them easy to slip on and off.

Choosing Shoes

The main reason for putting shoes on a newly walking baby is to protect the feet from splinters, cuts, and other foot injuries and to keep them warm. So-called orthopedic shoes with artificial arches are of no benefit to a normal baby's feet, and they may even impede the development of balancing skills.

Choose shoes with soft sides and soles so that your child can sense the surface of the floor or ground under its feet. Sneakers are perfectly suitable, although crepe soles may catch on carpeting, causing falls. To fit your baby's shoes, choose a pair that has about ½ inch of room beyond the big toe to allow for growth. You should be able to get a pinch of the leather or fabric across the widest part of the feet.

As your baby grows, the main qualities to look for in shoes will be soles with a good grip, flexibility, and fasteners that make it easy to put them on and take them off, such as a single buckle or a Velcro strap.

Baby Nutrition

Breast Milk Versus Formula

In a baby's early months, you needn't spend money for infant formula and bottles. A mother could feed the baby her own milk. It's sterile and warm and requires no preparation. For their first six months of life, most babies get all the nutrients they need from breast milk or formula. In fact, their digestive system isn't mature enough to handle other foods; babies may even push food out of their mouths with their tongue, a reflex that protects them from substances they can't properly swallow or digest. Some studies suggest that introducing solids to infants younger than six months just adds needless calories, since the baby will continue to drink the same amount of milk.

The cost of formula. If you do opt for formula, you can spare yourself the bother of price shopping. All brands of infant formula are essentially the same; the government stipulates the basic ingredients. When it comes to price, the brands are also strikingly similar.

Three manufacturers command 90 percent of the infant-formula market. They do little or no competitive advertising and price their products almost identically. Since 1980, the retail price of formula has gone up more than 100 percent—three times faster than groceries, six times faster than milk.

When CU checked formula prices at supermarkets in the New York City metropolitan area, we found the major brands within 10 percent of each other. Supermarket managers we interviewed said formula rarely, if ever, is put on sale because the manufacturers seldom offer specials.

Raw milk for baby? Don't waste your money. Despite the well-documented dangers of drinking raw milk, at least one large raw-milk dairy used to advertise its product as the "safest, purest, most wholesome milk you can buy." The dairy called raw (unpasteurized) milk "the ideal formula for babies" and "a basic food for invalids."

But the fact is that raw certified milk products may contain dangerous bacteria. Those facing the highest risk of disease or death include babies and young children, along with pregnant women, the elderly, those with cancer or reduced immunity, and those taking cortisone, antibiotics, or antacids.

We believe there's some simple advice that should be applied to the drinking of raw milk: Don't. And that goes double for feeding the stuff to infants.

Introducing Solid foods

Somewhere around four to six months of age, babies develop the neuromuscular mechanisms they need to swallow solids. They also begin to grow too hungry to be satisfied by milk alone. But every baby is different, so the decision to start an infant on solids should be determined by a baby's readiness, not merely by weight or age.

feeding baby. Pediatricians usually recommend starting with infant cereals, which are fortified with vitamins and minerals, particularly iron, that complement the baby's diet of breast milk or formula. It's best to introduce other solid foods one at a time, at intervals of a week or so. It is then much easier to identify any food intolerances, which might show up as loose bowel movements, rashes, or other allergic reactions.

Each new food presents a new taste and texture experience for the child. So offer the food in small amounts, and don't worry if you're getting more on the baby than into his or her mouth. Some other feeding tips:

- Don't feed the baby straight from the original jar or storage container. Spoon what you need into a bowl, then cover the remainder and store it in the refrigerator for no more than a few days. If you use the food right from the container, bacteria from the baby's mouth can be transferred from the spoon to the jar, where they will grow.

- Rarely are there significant differences in nutrition or price among commercial infant and junior foods. You may want to avoid those few products that contain added sugars or salt or modified starches. Read the labels to find out which foods contain these additives.

A Sensible Way to Make Baby Food

If you stay away from mixed dinners, desserts, and some fruits, you *can* feed your baby nutritious, commercially prepared food. But homemade has its advantages.

Homemade baby food is usually cheaper, and it can be convenient. High temperatures involved in commercial processing can destroy trace nutrients that remain in carefully prepared home-cooked foods. Further, when you do your own mashing and chopping, you have control over variety and texture.

Making food for baby doesn't require a big production, but be sure to keep your tools and work spaces as clean as possible. Wash dishes, pots, silverware, and your hands with hot soapy water, and rinse with water as hot as possible. When you're cooking the food, don't put the tasting spoon back into the food.

All fruits and vegetables should be washed and peeled; seeds, if any, should be removed. Take the skin and excess fat off meat, and debone it before you cook it. Otherwise, especially with chicken, it's hard to find all the small bones. Taking the bones out before cooking also assures you that any bacteria from your hands will be destroyed by the heat of cooking.

Meats and vegetables should be baked, broiled, or steamed. Steaming retains the most nutrients. If you do boil fruits or vegetables, use little water. If you're feeding baby what you feed your family, separate out the baby's portion before you add sugar or seasonings. And if you buy canned or frozen fruit and vegetables, use those with no added salt or sugar.

A blender or food processor is helpful for mashing and chopping, but you don't need special equipment. Many cooked foods can be mashed fine by hand. Add formula, juice, or even the cooking water to thin the food. If you do use a processor or blender, note that vegetables purée best in large quantities and meats in small ones. Use the purée setting when the baby is little; as he or she grows, you can switch to "chop" or "grind" for a coarser consistency.

For about $5, you can buy a special food mill in the infant section of a department store to grind fruits, vegetables, and soft-cooked meats. The mill strains as it grinds, so it's useful for separating the hulls from foods such as corn or peas.

There are a few home-cooked foods to avoid in the early months. Certain vegetables—spinach, celery, lettuce, radishes, carrots, beets, turnips, and collard greens—shouldn't be fed to babies less than three or four months old. (That's too young to feed babies solid food anyway.) Those vegetables, bought fresh, may contain excessive nitrate, which can be converted to nitrite in the stomach of very young infants. Nitrite inhibits the blood's ability to carry oxygen.

Honey is perfectly safe for children more than a year old, but don't give it to infants. Honey sometimes contains spores of the bacteria that cause botulism, a deadly form of food poisoning. Adults and children pass these spores on without harm. But the bacteria can multiply in a baby's intestines, with potentially fatal results.

Don't feed a baby under a year old anything that he or she might choke on: raw peas and string beans, nuts, grapes, whole corn kernels, popcorn, whole or unseeded berries, hard candies, chunks of hot dogs, raw celery or carrots, or potato chips.

Save Money on Baby Bibs

Toddler eating time can be quite a mess. That's why bibs were invented. Bibs can be bought in disposable foam or paper versions and in more permanent washable, vinyl-backed terry or wipe-clean molded plastic. The disposable foam versions are lightweight, absorbent, and easy to store in a purse or diaper bag for use in restaurants or while traveling. Of the more permanent versions, the flexible, molded-plastic styles with a wide trough at the bottom are the most convenient. They don't have to be laundered, they can be easily wiped clean, they can be used over and over, and they catch liquids before they can reach the clothes. Rather than purchase a number of terry bibs or multiple packages of disposables, buy one flexible, molded-plastic bib, and wipe it clean after every meal.

Diapers: Options and Costs

All told, your baby will undergo 6,000 diaper changes in the first two and a half years. There are three basic diapering options today: buying and laundering cloth diapers, paying for a diaper service, or using disposable diapers.

Some parents use only disposables or only fabric diapers. But many get along with a combination of alternatives. For example, you may want to use a diaper service in the early months after your baby is born, since it saves the labor of laundering or toting home cases of disposables.

Later, you may want to launder cloth diapers for home use while using disposables for travel, outings, and stints at the baby-sitter's.

Cloth Diapers

Since they can be reused after every laundering, cloth diapers are more economical. (They can also be recycled as dustcloths when no longer needed as diapers.) They come in gauze and bird's-eye fabrics, in flat and prefolded styles. Prefolded models can be bought in larger (toddler) sizes; some brands come with an additional center fold to absorb wetness. Gauze is more comfortable than bird's-eye fabric, and its porousness lets air circulate, which helps prevent diaper rash. New cloth diapering systems are cut and styled to resemble disposable diapers. They come in several sizes and styles and close without diaper pins. The latest cloth diaper system models are fast drying and absorbent.

You will need about four dozen diapers (sold in boxes of 12) to begin with. You will also need at least three pair of diaper pins, preferably with locking heads, and at least four pair of waterproof pants (the snap-on styles are easier to use than pull-on varieties and allow some air circulation).

Terry cloth diapers, widely used in England, are now available from Dundee Mills, Inc. Supposedly, terry is more absorbent than gauze or bird's-eye fabrics. Newer versions of wool soaker pants—some with Velcro-type closures—are now being made by small companies such as Biobottoms.

Proper laundering is critical, since soap residue can remain if the diapers aren't rinsed well, causing ammonia buildup and possible diaper rash. Using hot water, a low-sudsing detergent, a water softener (not a *fabric* softener), and a vinegar rinse can help prevent ammonia buildup.

Commercial Diaper Services

About 25 percent of new parents still use commercial services that pick up soiled diapers and deliver freshly laundered ones each week. Diaper services offer a convenient, economical alternative to disposables; they provide the softness and comfort of fabric diapers without laundering hassles and eliminate the need to lug home cases of disposable diapers.

Many services now offer a variety of diaper designs, from fitted diapers to special diaper–diaper cover combinations that require no pins and have a variety of sizes to fit your baby's needs. Some offer twice-a-week delivery and the option of using new, rather than previously used, diapers. Most services are listed in the Yellow Pages.

The Cost of Diapering

Disposable diapers are definitely more convenient than laundering your own cloth diapers. But disposables are more expensive to use than either laundering your own diapers or using a diaper service. Their typical cost is about 25 cents apiece, which means an investment of more than $1,500 for the two years or more that your baby is in diapers. In comparison, diaper services charge 9 to 18 cents a diaper, which comes to $540 to $1,080 for that same amount of time. The cost of the home laundering of fabric diapers is not as easy to calculate, because water heating, washer and dryer energy costs, and the prices of detergents or other cleaning and softening agents used vary locally; nonetheless, from the standpoint of economy, doing it yourself is substantially cheaper. The initial investment is approximately $35 to $70 for four dozen diapers.

(For more information on baby care and products, you can consult Consumer Reports Books' *Guide to Baby Products,* third revised edition, by Sandy Jones and Werner Freitag and the Editors of Consumer Reports Books, 1991, $12.95. To order, call 1-800-272-0722 or 1-513-860-1178.)

FIVE

Staying Healthy

Saving on health costs needn't mean cutting corners. Drugs and remedies can be bought thriftily—by mail, in generic versions, or both. A few questions to your doctor may cut out some expensive and unnecessary tests. And avoiding health frauds spares you money wasted on quackery. Here's what you need to know.

Save on Medicine

Drugs by Mail: Economy and Convenience

Mail-order drug sales already account for about 5 percent of the $26 billion prescription market. That share may double by the mid-1990s. It's certainly convenient to buy medications by mail: Just fill out a form and mail it along with your prescription. You or your physician can often phone in the prescription.

But the main advantage is economy (see table, page 114). Prescription drug prices have risen nearly 90 percent since 1980, and they're still climbing steadily. From February 1989 to February 1990, for example, drug prices increased 10.4 percent—more than double the Consumer Price Index.

Ordering by mail makes the most sense for people on long-term med-

PHARMACY COST COMPARISONS: MAIL-ORDER VERSUS RETAIL

(As published in "Consumer Reports Health Letter," May 1990)

Drug[1]	Quantity	Dose (mg)	Retail price[2]	Mail-order costs: percent lower (−) or higher (+) than retail				
				AARP	Action Mail Order	American Preferred Plan	America's Pharmacy	PHARMAIL
Cardizem (diltiazem)	60	30	$21.65	−21%	−24%	−24%	−12%	−11%
Lanoxin (digoxin)	100	0.125	6.24	+ 5	− 4	+24	+ 2	+12
Premarin (conjugated estrogens)	21	1.25	10.00	−21	−16	−27	−27	−27
Seldane (terfenadine)	60	60	46.07	−22	−15	−25	−12	−17
Xanax (alprazolam)[3]	30	0.5	18.90	−18	−29	−32	−14	−25
Zantac (ranitidine)	30	150	40.20	−14	−19	−12	− 2	− 9

[1] Selected brand-name medications (with generic names).
[2] Average retail price based on March 1990 sampling of discount chain drugstores in the suburban New York area.
[3] Some states restrict interstate sales of controlled substances such as tranquilizers, including **Xanax** (alprazolam).

ication—for diabetes, heart conditions, or high blood pressure, for instance. They can save hundreds of dollars a year.

Retail pharmacists, who have the most to lose from the competition of mail-order sales, claim that high-volume dispensing leads to inadequate record-keeping and dispensing errors. But similar claims can be made against the retail industry. The process of dispensing prescription medications—whether by corner drugstores or large mail-order firms—is subject to human error. Either way, you must assume responsibility for managing the medications you take. For example, you should carefully check the label of any medication you receive to make sure that it matches the medication prescribed.

Retail pharmacists argue that they provide services well worth their higher charges for prescription drugs: They know their customers, counsel them on medications, monitor their progress, and provide information. But today, many pharmacists don't step out from behind their glass wall except to answer questions, and most consumers don't ask any questions.

Mail-order companies try to compensate for the lack of face-to-face contact by providing written information and other services. They typically provide a toll-free hotline staffed by pharmacists to answer customer questions. (In some states, this service is required by law.)

Of course, it can take up to two weeks from when you mail your order to when you receive your prescription. You may be able to save a few days by having your physician phone in the prescription directly or by calling in a refill yourself. With some mail-order companies, you can cut the time further by paying for overnight delivery.

The two largest mail-order drug services in the United States serve specific groups. The Department of Veterans Affairs (formerly the Veterans Administration) mails out more than half of the 58 million prescriptions it dispenses for veterans every year. And the American Association of Retired Persons (AARP) Pharmacy Service dispenses prescription drugs for about 10 percent of the association's 32 million members.

Most for-profit mail-order drug companies concentrate on the lucrative business of selling to large groups—companies, unions, and government employees. But some mail-order pharmacies sell directly to the public.

To find a mail-order program, check any large organization to which you belong. Often the mail-order option is not well publicized. If you're 50 or over, you can join the AARP for a $5 annual fee. Or contact one of the mail-order pharmacies that sell directly to individuals. Below, we list some companies that sell drugs to the public nationwide:

AARP (American Association of Retired Persons)
601 E Street, N.W.
Washington, DC 20049
202-434-2277
Annual membership fee of $5 (must be 50 or older). Prepayment for each order not required. Will bill insurance company directly.

Action Mail Order
P.O. Box 787
Waterville, ME 04903-0787
800-452-1976
Handling fee of 75 cents per order. Initial $100 credit line for 30 days.

American Preferred Plan
P.O. Box 9019
Farmingdale, NY 11735
800-227-1195
Does not sell over-the-counter drugs. Will bill insurance company directly. Delivery at no charge.

America's Pharmacy
P.O. Box 10490
Des Moines, IA 50306
515-287-6872
Handling fee of $1.40 per order.

PHARMAIL
P.O. Box 1466
Champlain, NY 12919
800-237-8927

Inclusion in our list does not imply endorsement by Consumers Union.

Generic Drugs: Often Cheaper by Half

Prescription drugs marketed under their generic names often are half the price of the same drug sold under a brand name—the name given it by the company that held the original patent.

Most generic drugs are manufactured not by fly-by-night factories but by the very same companies that develop brand-name drugs. In fact, the approximately 60 brand-name drug companies manufacture about 80 percent of all generic drugs as well. Some 300 smaller pharmaceutical companies produce the drugs for the rest of the generic market.

To realize the savings offered by generic drugs, you need the cooperation of both your doctor and your pharmacist. Doctors, for instance, frequently write the brand name when they prescribe drugs. It's shorter and easier to remember than the generic name. And since the brand name had no generic competition during the long life of its patent, the doctor is probably accustomed to writing it.

This medical habit doesn't prevent you from buying generically. The laws in every state allow pharmacists to substitute a less expensive generic version when the doctor prescribes by brand. Indeed, the doctor must make a conscious effort in order to limit you to the brand-name drug. In some states, this means he or she must write out "dispense as written," "medical necessity," or some other phrase on the prescription. In other states, the doctor chooses which of two lines on the prescription form to sign. Signing on one line means the patient must receive the brand specified; signing on the other means the pharmacist may substitute a less costly generic version.

If you switch from a brand name to a generic, the medication's color and shape may be different from the brand-name product you've been taking. The pill's appearance won't affect how the drug works. However, some patients can become confused about medications whose color and/or shape change, particularly if they are in the habit of transferring a day's worth of pills from the prescription vial to a pocket or purse container. An unfamiliar appearance can lead to taking the wrong pill at the wrong time and/or in the wrong amount. In such instances, prudence suggests sticking to the brand-name drug, even though it is more expensive.

The Medicine Chest

Countless over-the-counter remedies crowd the shelves. But Consumers Union's medical consultants suggest that you stock just seven basic single-ingredient drugs. We list some common brand names, but you'll save money if you buy store brands or generics whenever possible.

Analgesic. For most people, aspirin (**Bayer**, **Empirin**) is fine for occasional headaches or muscle aches and pains. Some people must avoid aspirin, most commonly because it can irritate the stomach but also because it interferes with blood clotting. And some people are allergic to aspirin. People who can't use aspirin can use acetaminophen (**Anacin-3**, **Tylenol**) instead, unless they are heavy drinkers or have liver damage.

Ibuprofen (**Advil**, **Nuprin**) is slightly more effective than aspirin or acetaminophen, but it's typically more expensive. It's probably best reserved for menstrual cramps, postsurgical dental pain, and muscle and joint injuries. Ibuprofen presents the same risks as aspirin, as well as potential impairment of kidney function from long-term use. People who are allergic to aspirin should not use ibuprofen.

Antacid. Use an aluminum/magnesium combination (Maalox, WinGel) for heartburn if you have normal bowel function. If you're easily constipated, try a magnesium-based remedy (Phillip's Milk of Magnesia, Uro-Mag). If you tend to have loose bowel movements, use an aluminum-based product (Rolaids, Amphojel).

Antidiarrheal. If you need medication to get through a minor bout of diarrhea, use a product containing attapulgite (in new formulations of Kaopectate) or loperamide (Imodium A-D). Also, temporarily cut down on fiber in your diet and drink plenty of fluids.

Antiseptic. All you usually need to do for a minor cut or abrasion is allow it to bleed a little, then wash it gently with soap and water. For a dirtier wound, flush it with water and gently swab rubbing alcohol (70 percent isopropyl alcohol) on the healthy skin around the wound to keep surrounding dirt and germs out. (Applying alcohol directly to the wound will irritate it.) Use tweezers, cleansed with rubbing alcohol, to remove splinters and other debris. Cover the wound with a sterile dressing.

Decongestant. Keep an unused container of nose drops or spray on hand for a stuffed nose. A product containing oxymetazoline (Afrin, Neo-Synephrine 12 Hour) or xylometazoline (Neo-Synephrine II, Otrivin) has the longest-lasting effect. To keep from infecting others or reinfecting yourself, toss out the bottle when you're finished with it. If you prefer to take a decongestant by mouth, use pseudoephedrine (Cenafed, Sudafed).

Emetic. Syrup of ipecac may be needed to induce vomiting of poisonous substances. But call your local poison-control center before you use the drug: Vomiting can be harmful—for example, when the swallowed poison is corrosive or the victim has esophageal or gastrointestinal problems. Never induce vomiting in an unconscious or semiconscious person.

Laxative. First try eating more high-fiber foods. For occasional relief when such dietary measures don't work, use a mild bulk-producing laxative, such as psyllium (Fiberall, Metamucil). Milk of magnesia works faster, but it may be a more powerful remedy than you need.

Storing Medicine

Don't store medications where they'll get too warm. And don't keep pills or capsules in the bathroom or other humid places.

Every few months, take stock of your supply. Throw out drugs that have passed their expiration date or that show any of these signs of age or spoilage:

- aspirin that gives off a strong smell of vinegar
- tablets that crumble or start to change color
- capsules that are melting or sticking together
- ointments that are hardening or separating
- liquids that are changing color, becoming cloudy, or separating

Medical Supplies

You'll also save by buying medical supplies in generic or house-brand versions. For common emergencies and ailments, stock these items:

Adhesive strips: Use ordinary strips with plastic-coated gauze (**Band-Aids**) that won't stick to the wound. Avoid medicated strips (**Band-Aid Medicated Bandages**). The medication they contain may cause allergic reactions.

Roll bandage: Cotton gauze, 2 inches wide

Sterile gauze pads: Four-inch-square pads, separately wrapped

Adhesive tape: One small roll, 1 inch wide

Scissors: Blunt-tipped

Tweezers: To remove ticks or splinters

Elastic bandage: About 3 inches wide, to wrap sprained joints or strained muscles

Ice pack: To minimize bleeding and relieve pain and swelling immediately after injuring a joint or muscle. Reusable cold packs (**ACE, 3M**) are available.

Thermometers: One rectal, one oral—with easy-to-read numerals

Humidifier: For relief of dry cough and sore throat. Cool-mist models must be cleaned frequently to prevent contamination by mold and bacteria. Ultrasonic humidifiers are less easily contaminated but must still be cleaned regularly, and they're much more expensive. (Electrolytic, or steam, vaporizers pose a risk of accidental shock or burn.)

First-aid manual: A good general guide is the American Red Cross's *Standard First Aid,* available from your local chapter.

Telephone-number list: Include your physician, pharmacist, poison-control center, police and fire departments, and rescue squad.

Your Money's Worth in Sore-Throat Remedies

You can prepare one of the best sore-throat remedies at home without spending an extra dime. Just add ½ teaspoon table salt to an 8-ounce glass of warm water and gargle until the glass is empty. The salt solution reduces the painful swelling, and the mechanical act of gargling often brings added relief.

If your throat is especially dry, suck on a hard candy—extra saliva helps soothe irritated mucous membranes. And since dry indoor air can aggravate a sore throat, consider using a humidifier.

However, over-the-counter remedies have one advantage over a salt-water gargle and hard candy: They're all topical anesthetics that, to varying degrees, deaden pain. The U.S. Food and Drug Administration (FDA) considers a number of ingredients safe and effective in sore-throat remedies, including:

Dyclonine hydrochloride. This is the safest, most effective, and longest-lasting of the group. **Sucrets Maximum Strength** lozenges and gargle contain the maximum effective dose of dyclonine. If allowed to dissolve slowly, a single lozenge may relieve sore-throat pain for a few hours. Sprays and gargles provide relief for up to an hour or so.

Benzocaine. This is the most widely used topical anesthetic in over-the-counter sore-throat lozenges. It's similar to dyclonine in safety but provides relief for less than an hour. None of the benzocaine products currently on the market contains the FDA's maximum recommended amount of the drug. **Spec-T** and **Tyrobenz** contain more than the others. Benzocaine is not currently available in sprays and gargles.

Menthol. This is the active ingredient in **N'ICE** lozenges and spray, as well as other brands. None contains the maximum effective dose. Menthol's anesthetic effect is relatively mild and brief, and it may irritate the mucous membrane in some people.

Phenol. Safe when used in the recommended dose, it can cause toxic reactions in high doses. As with menthol, the anesthetic effect of phenol is relatively mild and brief. Phenol is the active ingredient in **Chlorasep-**

tic lozenges and spray, as well as other brands. None contains the maximum effective dose. One product, **Dobell's** gargle, contains only 0.3 percent phenol, less than the minimum effective dose.

Hexylresorcinol. Hexylresorcinol has nothing special to recommend it. Lozenges **(Listerine, Sucrets Sore Throat)** provide some relief only as long as they last in the mouth. Hexylresorcinol is not currently used in sprays or gargles.

The amounts of the various ingredients in the many products on the shelves vary widely. In general, choose a product with a dose at the upper end of the range shown in the table below.

Antiseptics are also sold for sore throats. Those are chemicals that kill or inhibit the growth of microorganisms. Since the infection that causes

OVER-THE-COUNTER SORE-THROAT REMEDIES
(As published in "Consumer Reports Health Letter," January 1990)

Drug[1]	*Brand names*[2]	*Interval (hours)*[3]	*Dose*[4]
Benzocaine	Lozenge: **Spec-T** (10 mg) **Tyrobenz** (10 mg) **Oracin** (6.25 mg) **Children's Chloraseptic** (5 mg) **T-Caine** (5 mg)	2	2–15 mg
	Spray/gargle[5]	6	5–20% solution
Benzyl alcohol	Lozenge[6]	2	100–500 mg
	Spray/gargle[6]	6	.05–10% solution
Dyclonine hydrochloride	Lozenge: **Sucrets Maximum Strength** (3 mg)	2	1–3 mg
	Spray/gargle: **Sucrets Maximum Strength** (0.1%)[7]	6	.05–0.1% solution
Hexylresorcinol	Lozenge: **Listerine Maximum Strength** (4 mg) **Listerine Antiseptic** (2.4 mg) **Sucrets Sore Throat** (2.4 mg)	2	2–4 mg
	Spray/gargle[5]	6	.05–0.1% solution

(Continued)

OVER-THE-COUNTER SORE-THROAT REMEDIES (*Continued*)

Drug[1]	Brand names[2]	Interval (hours)[3]	Dose[4]
Menthol	Lozenge: **Vicks Throat**[8]	2	2–20 mg
	Ice Blue (6–7.5 mg)		
	Cherry or Lemon (2.5– 3.13 mg)		
	N'ICE (5.0 mg)		
	Oracin (2.5 mg)		
	Cēpastat[8]		
	Cherry (2.4 mg)		
	Spray/gargle: **N'ICE** (0.13%)[7]	6	.04–2% solution
Phenol[9]	Lozenge: **Chloraseptic** (32.5 mg)	2	10–50 mg
	Cēpastat[8]		
	Cherry (14.5 mg)		
	Spray/gargle: **Chloraseptic** (1.4%)	2	.05–1.5% phenol
Salicyl alcohol	Lozenge[6]	2	50–100 mg
	Spray/gargle[6]	6	1–6% solution

[1] Proposed by FDA for approval as safe and effective sore-throat remedies.
[2] Some brands with the drug as an active ingredient in the effective dosage range. Currently unavailable in generic versions, but may be available as store brands.
[3] Interval represents FDA's recommendations on how often to take drug—*not* how long effect lasts.
[4] Dosage range recommended by FDA as safe and effective for adults and children age 2 and over.
[5] Currently unavailable in spray or gargle form.
[6] Currently unavailable as an active ingredient in sore-throat products in effective dosage range.
[7] Contains alcohol. CU's medical consultants recommend that children and recovering alcoholics avoid over-the-counter products containing alcohol.
[8] **Cēpastat** regular, **Vicks Throat Menthol,** and **Vicks Throat** regular flavors contain ingredients not proposed for sore-throat remedies.
[9] For lozenges: Children ages 6 to 12 should not exceed 300 mg phenol in 24 hours. For sprays and gargles: Children under 6 should use only under direction of a physician.

a sore throat is within the throat tissues, a topical antiseptic makes no sense for treating sore-throat pain. Nevertheless, one antiseptic, cetyl-pyridinium chloride, is found in many sore-throat lozenges that also contain benzocaine, including **Cepacol Anesthetic**, **Colrex**, and **Oradex-C.**

There are also *topical analgesics,* drugs that relieve pain at the spot where they are applied, as opposed to internal analgesics, which are taken by mouth and absorbed into the bloodstream. Aspirin is an effective internal analgesic. But despite the claims of some manufacturers, aspirin has no topical effect. (What's more, aspirin can actually irritate mucous membranes.) Nonetheless, the aspirin-containing chewing gum **Aspergum** has long been advertised "for minor sore throat pain." In fact, **Aspergum** is not even especially useful for headache pain: One piece contains only 70 percent of the aspirin found in the usual 325-milligram tablet.

Cost-Effective Cold Remedies

Most cold products are "shotgun" remedies loaded with up to seven different drugs. Users often waste money on unnecessary drugs that can cause unwanted side effects. In addition, one of the main drugs in these shotgun cold remedies—the antihistamine—is a dud.

Antihistamines are useful for hay fever and similar allergies. Histamine plays no demonstrable role in colds, however. So any action of antihistamine on colds arises from the drug's side effects. In addition to inducing drowsiness, antihistamines cause some drying of nasal secretions. But that effect is so slight as to be almost undetectable.

Shotgun remedies usually boast two basic drugs: an antihistamine and a decongestant. Brands with just these two include **Contac, Drixoral** syrup, **Dimetapp,** and **Triaminic.** Other popular brands include a pain reliever as a third barrel—**Alka-Seltzer Plus**, **Benadryl Plus, Dimetapp Plus,** and **Dristan.**

The more drugs, the more symptoms a shotgun product can claim to bag. Consider **Dristan.** It's a three-barrel remedy that claims success against 12 different cold symptoms: sinus pain, body aches, chills, fever, headache, sneezing, runny nose, watery eyes, post-nasal drip, sinus congestion, nasal congestion, and sore throat. Proponents claim such remedies are economical and convenient: Just one purchase blows away all your symptoms. Most cold experts, however, consider the products to be irrational.

People differ greatly in their cold symptoms. Some suffer the whole gamut, while others escape with a mild runny nose and sneezes. As a result, users of shotgun remedies often pay for unnecessary drugs that increase the risk of side effects. Even when the drugs match the symptoms, the fixed doses in shotgun remedies may be inappropriate—inadequate for severe symptoms or too potent for mild ones. A more rational approach is to look for effective single-ingredient drugs. That way you can target just the symptoms you have, when you have them, and adjust the dose to fit their severity. The following table gives examples of the types of products to use for specific symptoms.

SELECTED COLD REMEDIES

(As published in *Consumer Reports*, January 1989)

All brands listed below contain a single active ingredient helpful against a specific cold symptom. Most of the ingredients are also available as generic products or store brands.

Symptom	Remedy	Ingredient	Products
Congestion	Topical decongestant[1]	Phenylephrine Oxymetazoline Xylometazoline	Dristan, Neo-Synephrine, Sinex Afrin, Duration, Dristan Long-Lasting Nasal Spray Neo-Synephrine II
	Oral decongestant[2]	Pseudoephedrine	Oramyl, Sudafed, Sudanyl
Sore throat	Medicated lozenges and sprays	Phenol compounds	Chloraseptic Sore Throat Spray
		Benzocaine Hexylresorcinol Menthol	Spec-T Sore Throat Anesthetic Lozenges Sucrets N'Ice Sugarless Cough Lozenges
Headache, muscle aches, and fever	Pain reliever	Aspirin[3]	Bayer, Bufferin, Norwich, St. Joseph Aspirin
		Acetaminophen Ibuprofen	Datril, Tylenol Advil, Nuprin
Coughs	Cough suppressant[4]	Dextromethorphan	Benylin DM, Delsym, Dr. Drake's, Pertussin 8-Hour Cough Formula, PediaCare 1 Liquid, St. Joseph Cough Syrup for Children, Hold 4-Hour Cough Suppressant
		Codeine	Cheracol, Histadyl EC, Naldecon CX, Novahistine DH
		Diphenhydramine	Benylin
	Medicated lozenges	Menthol	N'Ice Sugarless Cough Lozenges
	Expectorant	Guaifenesin	Colrex, 2/G, Hytuss, Nortussin, Robitussin

[1] More effective than oral decongestants, but overuse can lead to return of stuffiness; use sparingly, and only for a few days.
[2] May dry mouth or interfere with sleep. Can be taken daily for up to one week.
[3] Should not be taken by children with cold symptoms; use acetaminophen instead.
[4] People with lung diseases should use only under medical supervision.

Spend Less on Antifungal Preparations

Three of the most prevalent skin infections are all caused by the same family of fungi. *Athlete's foot,* the most common of the three, causes feet to itch, especially between the toes. *Jock itch* strikes in and around the groin—the pubic area, the inside of the upper thighs, and the buttocks. Athlete's foot and jock itch occur much more commonly in men than in women.

Common ringworm, the third condition, more often affects children than adults. In children, it typically affects the scalp, causing hair loss. In adults, it usually hits skin where there's less hair—especially the arms, back, chest, and legs.

The most effective and most widely used nonprescription topical medications for fungal infections belong to a class of drugs called imidazoles. These include clotrimazole (**Lotrimin AF**) and miconazole (**Micatin**). Tolnaftate (**Aftate, Tinactin,** and others) appears to be nearly as effective as the imidazoles.

Other nonprescription antifungal medications include clioquinol (**Torofor, Vioform**), povidone-iodine (**Betadine, Pharmadine, Povadyne),** and undecylenic acid (**Cruex, Desenex,** and others). They're less effective than the imidazoles or tolnaftate.

If you pay attention to the active ingredient listed on the label, rather than to the name of the product, you may save some money. **Micatin Antifungal for Athlete's Foot,** for example, often costs 10 percent more than **Micatin Antifungal for Jock Itch.** Both products contain exactly the same amount of the same active ingredients. You should also save with generic, rather than brand-name, products.

No matter which product you use, if a rash doesn't begin to clear up after two weeks on medication, consult your physician. While most people build up some resistance to repeated infection, as many as one in five develops chronic rashes. Severe rashes, especially athlete's foot, may lead to a bacterial infection requiring antibiotics. Rarely, an antifungal medication (most often clioquinol and povidone-iodine) may cause adverse reactions, including blistering, burning, itching, peeling, and redness.

Prevention. Whether you're trying to keep fungi away or to get rid of an infection, the idea is the same: Create a hostile environment for fungi. Since they favor warm, moist places, that means staying cool and dry:

• Towel off thoroughly after a bath, shower, or swim.

- Apply talcum powder each morning and evening to absorb moisture.
- Choose socks that keep your feet dry. Light cotton socks absorb sweat well. Some synthetics, such as orlon and polypropylene, draw sweat away from your skin. Others, such as nylon, trap sweat against your feet.
- Wear well-ventilated footwear, such as sandals or open-toed shoes. Leather shoes or athletic shoes made of synthetic mesh and leather also breathe well. Avoid plastic shoes or canvas sneakers. If your feet perspire heavily, wear different shoes on alternate days so shoes can dry out.

Regularity for a Whole Lot Less

Relieving Constipation—If You Really Have It

Bombarded by ads linking empty bowels to a full life, Americans spend about $300 million a year on the more than 700 brands of over-the-counter laxatives. Much of that money is spent needlessly because of tenacious misconceptions about constipation.

More than 60 percent of Americans believe that a daily bowel movement is necessary for good health. Actually the frequency of bowel movements among healthy people varies greatly—from three a day to three a week. If you aren't bloated and you move your bowels without discomfort, you're not constipated, no matter how infrequently you defecate.

Constipation is more likely to strike older than younger people, women more often than men. In some cases, it reflects an underlying medical problem: hormonal disorders (such as an underactive thyroid gland), elevated blood levels of calcium, neurological injuries or disorders, or mechanical blockages of the bowel (such as hemorrhoids or tumors).

Usually, however, constipation is caused by life-style and habits. The most common problem is having too little fiber in the diet. Fiber absorbs water and swells in the bowel, creating bulkier stools, which stimulate the bowel contractions that push the stool along.

People who are constipated should consume about 20 to 30 grams of fiber a day. (If you're eating more fiber, you should probably drink more fluids, too.) Good sources of fiber include wheat bran, beans, whole grains, whole-grain breads, and certain fruits and vegetables. Prunes are not only high in fiber but also contain an irritant that rouses the bowel muscles. Eat them sparingly; otherwise, they can cause renewed constipation when you give them up.

Inactivity can also contribute to constipation. Exercises such as jogging, aerobics, and brisk walking are good ways to stimulate the bowel, but any increase in activity helps.

Bowel movements are not just something your body does; you must heed the urge to defecate. Don't rush to catch the train right after breakfast, when the urge to defecate is often strongest. Set aside enough time to let nature take its course.

A host of common medications can be constipating. They range from iron or calcium supplements and aluminum antacids to prescription drugs, including antidepressants, antihistamines, antispasmodics, narcotics, tranquilizers, and heart drugs such as calcium-channel blockers, diuretics, and antiarrhythmic agents. If you became constipated after you started taking medication, ask your doctor whether drugs could be the cause.

There's no "safe and gentle" laxative. Used regularly, all methods of purging the bowel, enemas as well as laxatives, tend to weaken bowel function and cause dependence. Research suggests that about half the people who use laxatives regularly could regain normal bowel function by discontinuing those drugs. And all laxatives can have significant side effects. Laxatives should be avoided if possible or used only occasionally.

Temporary constipation may crop up when travel or illness disrupts your normal habits, when there's a change in your diet, or when you're taking a short course of medications. The problem often resolves itself in a few days. If not, an enema or laxative can help. In any case, your accustomed bowel movements generally return when you resume your normal routine.

If you've been constipated for more than two or three weeks without apparent cause, consult your physician. After ruling out serious disorders, your doctor will help you design a program of dietary and other life-style changes. If that doesn't work, an enema or laxative may be required.

Help for Hemorrhoids

Hemorrhoids are essentially swollen blood vessels in the anal canal and lower rectum, loosened by repeated episodes of increased pressure in the rectum. There are two types: internal hemorrhoids, which may bleed but are seldom painful, and external hemorrhoids, which can indeed cause pain.

Causes and Prevention

Most experts agree that chronic constipation is the main cause of hemorrhoids, although the frequent bowel movements associated with diarrhea, the pressure of pregnancy, and strenuous work or play can also encourage their formation.

Rectal bleeding is the most common symptom, with or without itching or pain, and hemorrhoids are the most common cause of rectal bleeding. However, since bleeding can also be symptomatic of colon cancer, persistent or recurrent bleeding demands medical attention. If you can rule out more serious conditions, you can attend to the various treatments that can alleviate hemorrhoid symptoms.

Increased fiber in the diet is both a preventive and a treatment. Fiber, which passes through the digestive tract virtually unchanged, retains water, adds bulk, and softens feces, helping to speed their passage through the colon. Fiber-rich foods include fruits, vegetables, breads, and cereals. For a fiber supplement, try miller's bran, which is cheap and convenient to use.

A *sitz bath*—sitting in plain warm water for 10 to 15 minutes—is a time-honored treatment for anal discomfort. A bathtub works fine, or you can buy a portable plastic sitz bath from a pharmacy or medical supply store.

Premoistened wipes, such as **Tucks Pads** or **Preparation H Cleansing Pads,** can help keep the area around the anus soothed and clean. After cleaning, patting gently with a cloth or soft tissue will dry the area without irritation.

Do Drugstore Remedies Work?

The short answer is "Partly." While they may reduce itching and irritation (with some potential side effects), none reduces swelling. The largest seller, **Preparation H,** claims to reduce swelling as well as reducing pain and itching. One of its active ingredients, shark liver oil, may be effective for soothing mild irritation, but there is no evidence that this medication reduces the swelling of hemorrhoids.

The other remedies contain ingredients that can cause allergic reactions. These include Peruvian balsam, found in **Anusol, Wyanoids,** and others, and the "caine" anesthetics (benzocaine, lidocaine, and others) found in **Lanacain, Nupercainal, Pontocaine,** and **Wyanoids** ointments.

Suppositories may lubricate the rectum but have minimal effect on hemorrhoids themselves.

Creams and lotions can help soothe irritation and are preferable to *ointments,* which retain water and promote the itching and irritation they're supposed to relieve.

Common Problems, Inexpensive Solutions

When You Can't Sleep

One in every three American adults has trouble sleeping. In search of slumber, many insomniacs—especially older ones—turn to pills. That's usually not a good idea.

Studies have shown that a prescription sleeping pill used occasionally helps people fall asleep only about 20 minutes sooner than they otherwise would have and stay asleep half an hour longer. Even this modest effect tends to fade with regular use. Worse, sleeping pills can actually cause sleep disturbances. And sleeping pills make some users, particularly older people, dangerously drowsy during the day.

There are problems with nonprescription sleep aids, too. The FDA now limits over-the-counter remedies to one of two active ingredients, both antihistamines: diphenhydramine (**Compoz, Nytol, Sominex,** and others) and doxylamine (**Doxysom, Unisom**).

The FDA considers these drugs to be safe and effective "for the relief of occasional sleeplessness." But some of their possible side effects— confusion, dizziness, urine retention, and visual effects—can make these drugs hazardous, particularly for older people. And the sedative effect of an antihistamine is weaker than that of a prescription sleeping pill.

Like the prescription drugs, over-the-counter remedies can cut into the quality of your sleep and make you drowsy the next day. Used regularly, they can lead to tolerance, which encourages higher doses and further disrupts sleep.

The most widely used self-prescribed medication for sleep is alcohol. But alcohol is metabolized quickly. As a result, one is likely to awaken early from an alcohol-induced sleep. In some people, that can lead to more alcohol and possibly also to other sedatives—a life-threatening combination in heavy users.

An expert panel for the National Institutes of Health recently concluded that sleeping pills—both prescription and over-the-counter—are overused and addictive. It advised older people not to self-prescribe over-the-counter sleep aids at all.

Consumers Union's medical consultants believe that prescription sleeping pills may be helpful only for brief episodes of insomnia, such as those caused by a temporary, stressful situation. But they see no use for over-the-counter sleep aids, which are far more likely to cause distressing side effects than to produce a good night's sleep. If you really need medication, ask your doctor to prescribe an effective drug in the smallest possible dosage for not more than a couple of weeks.

How to Help Yourself. Before you turn to your physician, however, there are several steps you can take yourself:

- Establish a consistent sleep schedule—go to bed and, more important, get up at the same time every day, including weekends. Most peoples' biological clock tends toward a 25-hour day. As a result, your body may want to stay up later. Don't let it.
- Don't use the bedroom for working, reading, or watching television. That way, you'll associate the bedroom more with sleep.
- If you don't fall asleep within 30 minutes, don't lie there and fret. Get out of bed. Read, listen to quiet music, perhaps have a light snack, until you start getting drowsy.
- Some people sleep better after a hot bath.
- Try to exercise regularly, particularly in the late afternoon or early evening. A walk before bedtime may be helpful.
- Avoid alcohol, caffeine, and nasal decongestants before bedtime.
- Try not to drink fluids close to bedtime, to avoid being awakened by the need to urinate. If you suspect a bladder, urinary tract, or prostate problem, see your physician.
- If you suffer from heartburn during the night, eat dinner earlier.
- If you're bothered by light in the bedroom, use darker window shades or wear an eye cover.
- If noise is a problem, try ear plugs. Wax, foam rubber, and silicone varieties are now available. (However, if you live alone, be sure the plugs don't also block the sound of a smoke alarm.) Some people prefer a "white noise" device, which emits a lulling sound to cover up disturbing noise.

- Sleep specialists generally recommend against a daytime nap if you have trouble sleeping at night. But some older people find such a nap helps them sleep at night. And a midday catnap may benefit those who can't stay awake in the evening until a desirable bedtime.

Flu Shots for Everyone: Why Risk Influenza?

Public health officials consider flu shots mandatory only for the people most vulnerable to pneumonia and other serious complications of influenza. Yet flu shots (trivalent influenza vaccine) make good preventive health sense for almost everyone. Although influenza rarely causes any lasting damage to otherwise healthy people, the miseries of the flu—sore throat, coughing, high fever—are largely preventable. So why not prevent them?

The cost of influenza is high. Even for those who slog through the flu without complications, there are the costs of medical care, medications, and lost work days. For the less fortunate, of course, the costs can include hospitalization and even death.

Flu is easily spread through contact with an infected person. The disease is caused by two main strains of the influenza virus—influenza A and influenza B.

Because outbreaks of flu rarely occur in the United States before December, there's a predictable "flu season" lasting through winter and into spring. (Travelers, however, may risk exposure at any time of year.) A flu shot, which costs about $15, takes about two weeks to provide protection, which then lasts about six months. November is the best time for vaccination, but September or October are acceptable.

You can't catch flu from a flu vaccine. And there's only a very slim risk of side effects—low-grade fever and muscle aches for a day or so.

Flu vaccine does not provide full immunity in all cases, however. It's about 90 percent effective in young and healthy people and 75 percent effective in elderly, high-risk people. (That's when the vaccine matches the current strain of influenza. If an unexpected strain pops up during the flu season, the vaccine may not work as well.)

As with any vaccine, of course, there are certain precautions. People allergic to eggs should not be vaccinated, and people with infections should wait until they recover. Although flu vaccine poses no known danger during pregnancy, delaying vaccination until after the first trimester is a reasonable precaution against theoretical risk to the fetus. (Pregnant women at high risk from influenza should not delay vaccination.)

High-risk groups. While public health guidelines permit vaccination for anyone who wants it, certain high-risk groups are targeted for flu shots:

- Anyone age 65 or older
- Adults and children with chronic lung or heart disorders, including children with asthma
- Adults and children who needed regular medical follow-up or hospitalization during the preceding year because of chronic diseases such as diabetes, kidney disorders, sickle-cell disease, or suppressed immune systems (including AIDS)
- Children and teenagers (ages 6 months to 18 years) who receive long-term aspirin therapy
- Those who come in contact with high-risk people: health-care personnel, providers of home care, and household members

Keeping Medical Expenses Down

About Costly Testing

"Were all those tests really necessary?" you may have wondered after leaving your physician's office. The answer, in many cases, seems to be no.

Many physicians overtest in an effort to rule out every conceivable cause of a patient's complaint. Such zeal may simply reflect extreme diligence. It may also reflect fear of being sued for malpractice for missing a diagnosis or an interest in using equipment already purchased.

And it's not just physicians who insist on unnecessary tests. Many patients demand tests to reassure them that nothing is wrong.

Some warning signs. Virtually every test has some potential value, however remote. And the doctor who recommends the test can probably describe that value persuasively. Still, you may be able to avoid some needless tests.

Watch for these two signs of possibly unnecessary testing:

- Your doctor keeps repeating tests. It's rarely necessary to order blood tests every week or two, for example, unless the patient is very sick or is taking a drug that requires frequent monitoring.

- The tests your doctor orders seem to have nothing to do with your complaint.

If you spot one of those patterns, you can either express your concerns to your doctor or get a second opinion.

What to ask. To avoid risky, painful, or expensive tests, start by asking your doctor about the purpose of the test. Then ask about the procedure itself. Will you feel discomfort? Will you be exposed to radiation? Can the test cause harm? If so, what are the chances of such harm?

Next, ask about the cost. "It's expensive, but your insurance will cover it" is not an acceptable answer.

If the test involves risk or significant discomfort or expense, here are some questions to ask:

What are the chances that the test will find something wrong? Those chances increase with the number of risk factors for, or symptoms of, a particular disease. Take sigmoidoscopy—insertion of a lighted, flexible tube into the large intestine to look for colon cancer. If you have no complaints, the test is not likely to find anything. But if your bowel habits have changed and you have rectal bleeding and a family history of colon cancer, the likelihood of finding disease is much greater.

What would happen if I waited? Suppose an ultrasound test has revealed a small ovarian cyst in a premenopausal woman. There's a very small chance that the cyst is cancerous. Her doctor wants to examine the cyst directly, through a surgical incision in her abdomen. The patient asks about delaying that procedure. The doctor says she could wait a few months and repeat the ultrasound to see whether the cyst is growing. If it's not, the cyst probably isn't cancerous. But if it is growing, it could be cancerous; there may be a much smaller chance of successful removal at that point. The patient must then decide whether the prospect of the surgical examination frightens her more than the minute risk of cancer.

Will the test affect treatment? A positive test result should have some practical application: Treatment will be started, stopped, or changed. Satisfying the doctor's or patient's curiosity is rarely a good enough reason to test. If your skin (but not your eyes) has turned yellowish, for example, your doctor may suspect carotenemia—excess carotene, a food pigment, in the blood. But there's little point in testing to confirm that suspicion. No other condition could produce such yellowing in an otherwise healthy person. And carotenemia, caused by a diet high in green and yellow vegetables, is harmless.

Any positive findings that might affect treatment should be confirmed. If a doctor recommends a change in life-style or medication based on a single result, ask to be retested—unless the test is risky or costly.

How reliable is the test? Mammography (breast X rays to detect cancer) is very sensitive in picking up possible abnormalities in women over 35. But it's not as useful in younger women. Moreover, the risk of breast cancer is very small in women under 35. Those are two reasons not to test a young woman with no symptoms. However, if you are in a high-risk group for breast cancer, mammography can be an important diagnostic tool.

A side benefit. When physicians are reminded how much a laboratory test costs, they're less likely to order one, according to a recent study conducted by researchers at Indiana University. Physicians who saw the costs displayed on a computer screen ordered 14 percent fewer tests than those who didn't. That saved about $7 per visit. Other studies have also shown that when physicians are forced to think about the usefulness of a laboratory test, they're less likely to order one.

Since calling attention to costs and usefulness did seem to help in the short run, you might be able to avoid an unnecessary test by asking your physician about those practical matters.

Getting answers. Most physicians dislike having their knowledge or authority challenged. A defensive or angry doctor may try to pressure you into undergoing a test or may not provide much useful information about it. So confrontation may not gain you much. But if your doctor doesn't answer your reasonable questions in a reasonable manner, you may want to look for another doctor.

Communicating with your doctor is much easier if you both have similar attitudes toward testing. If you can tolerate some uncertainty—and hate being poked and pricked—find a reliable physician who leans toward clinical judgment. If you like certainty, regardless of what you have to endure to get it, you'll do best with a physician who tests aggressively.

How Often Do You Need a Checkup?

An annual physical exam is not mandatory for every adult. According to our medical consultants, it's a waste of money for some people. Exams are more important in middle age, when chronic diseases such as heart disease and cancer become significant problems.

Here is the basic schedule we recommend for adults who have no health-related problems and no family history of inherited disorders.

Men should consider:

- Starting at age 30, an exam every five years up to age 45
- From age 45 to 60, an exam every two or three years
- After 60, an exam every year

Women should consider:

- Starting at age 20, an exam every three years to age 40
- From age 40 to 50, an exam every two years
- After 50, an exam every year

Tests a Checkup Should Include

No two doctors are likely to agree on which tests you should be given as part of a regular checkup. Out of the many available, our medical consultants recommend seven that they believe offer the greatest benefit. Each can detect serious disease before symptoms arise. And early treatment of the disease is likely to produce a better outcome than if treatment were delayed until after symptoms appeared.

1. *Urinalysis.* Perhaps the most widely used test in any complete examination, urinalysis can detect a variety of conditions. The presence of sugar in the urine may indicate diabetes. Large numbers of white blood cells (pus cells) may indicate an infection of the urethra, bladder, kidney, or (in men) the prostate. Microscopic blood in the urine requires additional testing for the presence of bladder and kidney tumors.

- Our medical consultants recommend that you have a urinalysis each time you have a physical. It's simple and inexpensive; your physician can usually do it in the office.

2. *Complete blood count.* A laboratory analysis of a drop of blood taken from the finger can detect the presence of anemia (a possible sign of internal bleeding) and of blood diseases such as leukemia.

- Our medical consultants recommend a complete blood count each time you have a physical. As with the urinalysis, it can usually be done in the doctor's office and is relatively inexpensive.

3. *Automated blood analysis.* This is a more sophisticated blood study. It can detect abnormal functioning of the body's organs. Most family physicians have the test done at a commercial laboratory, where special automated machines can determine the levels of up to 30 or more blood chemistries on a single blood specimen.

Some of the chemistries are more useful than others. Our consultants consider seven to be worthwhile: *blood sugar,* to detect diabetes (usually done on an empty stomach); *calcium,* to detect hyperparathyroidism; *cholesterol,* to judge the risk of heart disease; *creatinine,* to detect kidney disease; *serological test,* to detect syphilis; *transaminase,* to detect abnormal liver function; and *uric acid,* to detect gout.

The full battery of blood-chemistry tests usually provides the doctor with more information than is necessary or desired, and some of the information can be misleading. In this case, falsely abnormal results can lead to further diagnostic procedures that can be expensive and may involve some degree of risk.

• Our medical consultants recommend a blood-chemistry analysis, which is relatively inexpensive, each time you have a physical.

4. *Tests for colorectal cancer.* One out of every 25 people will develop colorectal cancer. It occurs equally in men and women. There are three tests that can effectively detect this cancer before symptoms appear.

The first is the *digital rectal examination,* done as part of a checkup by your physician, using a gloved finger. Of tests for occult (hidden) blood, the most commonly used one is the *hemoccult slide test.* Stool samples are prepared at home, using paper slides and a wood applicator, and returned to the doctor for analysis. The test is very inexpensive. The third test is *sigmoidoscopy,* which involves inserting a flexible illuminated tube, called a proctosigmoidoscope, into the rectum and up into the sigmoid colon.

• Our medical consultants recommend that the digital rectal examination should be a routine part of every checkup for those over 40. After age 50, you should have a hemoccult test once a year and a sigmoidoscopy every three years following two initial negative tests one year apart.

5. *Tests for breast cancer.* An American woman has about a 1 in 11 chance of developing breast cancer sometime in her life. Clinical studies suggest that early detection through use of mammography and physical examination may decrease mortality from breast cancer, particularly among women 50 and older.

Mammography—an X ray of the breasts—is the only test that can detect a breast cancer before it becomes large enough to be felt on physical examination.

If you have mammography, insist on a dose of less than one rad per breast. Because it uses ionizing radiation, mammography may itself increase the risk of breast cancer. But that minuscule risk is well worth the benefit.

Physical examination by the doctor involves careful palpation of the breasts for lumps. Every woman should also palpate her own breasts once a month after age 20. (The best time is one week following the onset of a menstrual period, when the breasts are less swollen and tender. After menopause, choose an easy-to-remember date for breast palpation, such as the first of the month.) Most breast cancers—at least 80 percent—are first detected by the woman herself.

- Our medical consultants recommend that an annual mammogram be performed beginning at age 50—sooner if there is a personal or family history of breast cancer or if your doctor recommends it. While routine mammography has been shown to be of definite benefit only for women 50 or older, the American Cancer Society recommends an initial baseline mammogram at age 35 and one every other year from age 40 to 50. Women between ages 20 and 50 who have annual gynecological examinations should use that occasion to have a breast exam. Otherwise, they should have breast palpation by a health professional at least every two or three years up to age 40 and then once a year.

6. *Pap test for cervical cancer.* Evidence suggests that cervical cancer develops slowly. Invasive cancer is usually preceded by a long stage (eight years or more) of localized cervical cancer that is detectable by a Pap test and almost always curable.

- Our medical consultants recommend that women should begin Pap tests soon after they become sexually active. Women can get good protection with a Pap test every three years, after two negative Pap tests a year apart (the American Cancer Society's recommendation). But the traditional schedule—a Pap test annually—gives women slightly better protection, especially if they have multiple sex partners. Many studies have shown that women who begin having sexual intercourse at an early age or who have multiple sex partners are at higher risk of developing cervical cancer. Women who have had a hysterectomy do not need a Pap test, but they should have a pelvic examination periodically to check for vaginal or ovarian (provided ovaries are still present) cancer.

7. *Skin test for tuberculosis.* This can show if you've been infected by tuberculosis bacteria since your last test, if that one was negative. If the test is positive, have a chest X ray to look for signs of active disease.

- Our medical consultants recommend a skin test (it's simple and inexpensive) each time you have a physical, unless a previous test was positive. (Once it is positive, it will remain so.)

Is the Deluxe Version Any Better?

Does Your Toothbrush Need a Tanning Booth?

Can you fend off disease by replacing your toothbrush? How about sanitizing it? According to The Sharper Image mail-order catalog, "**Purebrush** is a revolutionary new dental device that sanitizes your toothbrush after every brushing. Bacteria, sugars, molds, yeasts, and viruses are obliterated by an intense ultraviolet light." Its makers claim **Purebrush** is "the next best thing to a new toothbrush every day."

But there's no reason to sterilize your toothbrush. There's little evidence to support Murdock Laboratories' health claims for its $100 ultraviolet contraption—which president James Murdock has described as "basically a light bulb in a box."

The **Purebrush** brochure claims that toothbrushes are "a major source of bacteria, yeasts, molds, and viruses." Toothbrushes do indeed carry germs. But the number of germs on a toothbrush is minuscule compared with the billions of germs found in a healthy mouth.

The American Dental Association reviewed the skimpy evidence put forward for **Purebrush** and concluded that there's no proof that the relatively few germs on a person's toothbrush pose any threat when the brush is put back in the same person's mouth.

There's now a similar product competing for the privilege of zapping any harmless bugs on your toothbrush bristles. At about $50, the **Dentec 4000** is roughly half the price of **Purebrush.** But that's still $50 more than you need to spend to clean your toothbrush.

Consumers Union's dental and medical consultants see no danger from using a toothbrush carrying germs from your own mouth. They suggest that you simply replace your toothbrush every four to six weeks—when worn bristles make it less efficient at removing plaque.

What about germs from someone else's toothbrush? The Sharper Image pitch for **Purebrush** claims that your family will "unwittingly pass sore throats and infections back and forth—via your toothbrushes." But that remote and largely theoretical possibility is easily prevented: Simply store brushes so the bristles don't touch.

Fight Plaque for Less Money

Listerine—for years the only nonprescription mouthwash that could rightly claim to control dental plaque—now has some low-priced competition.

The American Dental Association has granted its seal of acceptance to the mouthwashes made by two big producers of private-label health and beauty products. Together, the two companies supply dozens of retailers—including K mart, Kroger, Target, Topco, Walgreens, and Wal-mart—who sell the mouthwash under their own store name. The products just granted the ADA's seal look and taste like **Listerine** and have a comparable formula. They are, however, different from **Listerine** in one key respect—price. In our area, a 32-ounce bottle of **Listerine** sells for about $4.75. The private-label products sell for one-third or one-half of that.

Sunglasses: Protection Without Spending a Bundle

Glamour has long been the stock in trade of companies that market sunglasses. But the stress now is on "performance": a promise of superior protection against potentially damaging sunlight.

Some companies claim their sunglasses offer protection from invisible ultraviolet light. Others claim they block out the blue segment of visible light, invisible infrared rays, or any combination of the three.

Consumers Union tested more than 180 pairs of sunglasses, sold under 21 brand names or no name at all, at prices ranging from $2 to nearly $200. Surprisingly, price had little relation to performance. Virtually all the models we tested, from the cheapest to the most expensive, did a commendable job of reducing potentially harmful ultraviolet rays of the sun—both UVB, which includes the shortest wavelengths of light reaching the earth's surface, and longer wavelengths of UV, called UVA. Most protected well against blue light, too—the shorter wavelengths of visible light that some scientists suspect may age the retina after many years of exposure.

When shopping for sunglasses, be aware of a voluntary labeling program adopted by the FDA in conjunction with the Sunglass Association of America, an industry trade group, which assigns a model to one of three categories—cosmetic, general purpose, and special purpose. Cosmetic models offer the least protection, special purpose the most. Sunglasses carrying the new labeling must meet that standard's requirements concerning blockage of UV and visible light. The basic label gives the category and the minimum requirements for that category; an optional label also indicates that particular model's actual UV blockage. For example:

> Meets ANSI Z80.3 General Purpose UV Requirements
> Blocks at least 95% UVB and 60% UVA
> These lenses block _____% UVB and _____% UVA

This system is a welcome improvement over the chaotic labeling we found in our most recent tests.

Among lens choices, polarizing lenses, which reduce reflected glare, are particularly useful for driving. A neutral, uniform-shaded lens is a good all-around performer. Medium-to-dark lenses with a gray tint, or ones with a slightly brownish or greenish tint, generally filter out much of the blue light with little distortion in color perception. You can find all of those qualities in many inexpensive pairs of sunglasses.

How to Duck Modern Health Hustlers

How can you tell the difference between reliable advice and a quack promotion? Here are six warning signs:

1. *Do they push vitamins?* Reputable health professionals don't recommend vitamins for a wide variety of problems. But many practitioners, including bogus nutritionists and some chiropractors, do. Sometimes they also sell vitamins, in megadoses at inflated prices.

Steer clear of physicians who give vitamin B-12 shots for fatigue and other vague complaints. Periodic injections of B-12 are appropriate only for people with documented B-12 deficiency and other disorders that result in inadequate intestinal absorption of the vitamin.

In high enough doses, certain vitamins (including A, B-6, C, D, and E) can cause disturbing or harmful side effects. Only individuals at risk of developing vitamin deficiencies—usually children under two and people with certain illnesses—stand to benefit from vitamin supplements, and then only as directed by a physician who doesn't sell them.

2. *Do they give phony nutrition tests?* There are any number of gimmicks, including amino acid analysis, cytotoxic testing, hair analysis, herbal crystallization analysis, and live-cell analysis. As screening tests for nutritional problems, they're all worthless.

Some entrepreneurs have devised questionnaires that ask about symptoms that could be due to a vitamin deficiency. But those symptoms often occur in many other conditions as well. Even if a vitamin deficiency does exist, such questionnaires don't permit accurate diagnosis or responsible treatment. That requires a physical examination and specific laboratory tests.

Your physician, a registered dietitian, or a reputable nutritionist with at least a master's degree in nutrition from an accredited institution can help analyze your typical diet and recommend dietary changes.

3. *Do they display fishy diplomas and certificates?* In recent years, many

unaccredited correspondence schools issued "degrees" in health-related areas, especially nutrition. You can check a school's status by contacting your state education department, the U.S. Department of Education, or the Council on Postsecondary Accreditation.

4. *Do they sell health by mail?* Most mail-order health schemes are "hit-and-run" operations set up to make a quick profit before the U.S. Postal Service intervenes. Common scams include antiaging products, baldness remedies, blemish removers, breast developers, and miracle weight-loss plans. Ads for these products typically offer a money-back guarantee that's no more legitimate than the product itself.

5. *Do they claim to have endorsements?* Companies marketing vitamins and other nutritional supplements sometimes claim that physicians or medical scientists have endorsed their products. Some of these companies establish so-called scientific advisory boards. Such companies often make false and illegal claims for their products.

In 1986, for example, a company called United Sciences of America began marketing food supplements supposed to help prevent cancer and coronary heart disease. These products, the company claimed, had been designed and endorsed by a scientific advisory board of 16 professionals. Of the 7 most prominent "board members," 6—including 2 Nobel prize winners—had neither developed nor endorsed the company's products.

6. *Do they promise to boost the immune system?* In recent years, AIDS—acquired immune deficiency syndrome—has focused widespread public attention on the immune system and generated all sorts of immuno-quackery. Some promoters, including many who had previously claimed to cure cancer, now promise to cure AIDS. Other hucksters appeal to the public by offering to boost immunity to disease in general. Since severe nutritional deficiencies can lower immunity, the quacks claim that various vitamin concoctions provide extra nutrients that will strengthen the immune system. But getting more than enough vitamins and other nutrients is no better than getting just enough of them. And most people get enough.

Shortcuts to Weight Loss: Usually Dead Ends

In 1989 alone, Americans forked over more than $32 billion for products related to weight control. Along with everything from low-calorie foods to hospital-based diet programs, this outlay also included a potpourri of generally worthless and even dangerous fat-melting pills and potions.

Although weight-loss drugs are regulated by the FDA, not much has been done to stop the sale of fraudulent products.

Some Dubious Aids

Here are a few concoctions in the bloated weight-loss marketplace:

Cyamopsis tetragonolobus. Commonly known as guar gum, this soluble fiber is used to thicken foods. It has some marginal value as a bulk laxative and as a cholesterol-lowering aid. It helps control blood sugar in some diabetics. But weight control is another matter.

Although some subjects have lost weight in studies of guar gum's effect on cholesterol and blood sugar, that has not been a consistent finding. And no controlled study has specifically tested guar gum's effect on weight. Guar gum does form a gel in the stomach that can impart a feeling of fullness. But that's a far cry from "automatic" weight loss.

Growth-hormone releasers. Purported to cause overnight weight loss, these products may contain the amino acids arginine, ornithine, or tryptophan. Promoters claim that ingesting so-called growth-hormone releasers on an empty stomach prompts the pituitary gland to secrete the hormone, which they say burns fat and causes weight loss. That concept is fake and the claim patently misleading. Although the intravenous injection of arginine can temporarily raise blood levels of growth hormone (this is one medical test used for growth hormone deficiency), the commercially marketed pills have no such effect.

Starch blockers. These contain an enzyme, extracted from certain plant foods such as kidney beans, that purportedly blocks the digestion of starches (complex carbohydrates). The enzyme works in the test tube, but the body produces more starch-digesting enzymes than these products could possibly block. The FDA has advised manufacturers to stop marketing these products and obtained injunctions against several who refused to do so voluntarily.

Sugar blockers. Containing an extract from *Gymnema sylvestre,* a plant grown in India, sugar blockers supposedly prevent the body from absorbing sugar. According to Purdue University's Varro E. Tyler, Ph.D., a leading authority on plant medicine, chewing the plant's leaves

HOW MUCH SHOULD YOU WEIGH?[1]

(As published in "Consumer Reports Health Letter," February 1990.)

Height	Recommended weight (Metropolitan Life)		Obesity[2] (NIH panel)		Age-adjusted recommended weight[3] (Gerontology Research Center)				
	Men	Women	Men	Women	20–29 yr.	30–39 yr.	40–49 yr.	50–59 yr.	60–69 yr.
4'10"	—	100–131	—	137	84–111	92–119	99–127	107–135	115–142
4'11"	—	101–134	—	139	87–115	95–123	103–131	111–139	119–147
5'0"	—	103–137	—	143	90–119	98–127	106–135	114–143	123–152
5'1"	123–145	105–140	157	146	93–123	101–131	110–140	118–148	127–157
5'2"	125–148	108–144	160	150	96–127	105–136	113–144	122–153	131–163
5'3"	127–151	111–148	162	154	99–131	108–140	117–149	126–158	135–168
5'4"	129–155	114–152	164	157	102–135	112–145	121–154	130–163	140–173
5'5"	131–159	117–156	167	161	106–140	115–149	125–159	134–168	144–179
5'6"	133–163	120–160	172	164	109–144	119–154	129–164	138–174	148–184
5'7"	135–167	123–164	175	168	112–148	122–159	133–169	143–179	153–190
5'8"	137–171	126–167	179	172	116–153	126–163	137–174	147–184	158–196
5'9"	139–175	129–170	182	175	119–157	130–168	141–179	151–190	162–201
5'10"	141–179	132–173	186	179	122–162	134–173	145–184	156–195	167–207
5'11"	144–183	135–176	190	182	126–167	137–178	149–190	160–201	172–213
6'0"	147–187	—	194	—	129–171	141–183	153–195	165–207	177–219
6'1"	150–192	—	199	—	133–176	145–188	157–200	169–213	182–225
6'2"	153–197	—	203	—	137–181	149–194	162–206	174–219	187–232
6'3"	157–202	—	211	—	141–186	153–199	166–212	179–225	192–238
6'4"	—	—	—	—	144–191	157–205	171–218	184–231	197–244

[1] Values in this table are for height without shoes and weight without clothes.
[2] Based on 20 percent more than midpoint of Metropolitan Life recommended weight range.
[3] Recommended weight ranges apply to both men and women.

can inhibit the sensation of sweetness. But there's no evidence that the chemicals they contain can block sugar absorption in the body or produce weight loss.

How to Lose Weight (Maybe) . . .

Most dieters who manage to lose weight inevitably gain it back. Going from diet to diet is demoralizing—and potentially harmful. Anything but a lifelong commitment to consuming fewer calories and burning more is doomed to failure. You can spare yourself time, money, and anguish by avoiding fads and gimmicks.

Of limited or no use are phenylpropanolamine (PPA) and benzocaine, the two over-the-counter drugs widely sold as slimming aids. PPA, marketed as **Acutrim, Dexatrim,** and other brands, can produce abrupt and even life-threatening rises in blood pressure in hypertensive people at only three times its maximum recommended dose. Benzocaine, a topical anesthetic marketed as **Diet Ayds,** is claimed to decrease appetite by diminishing the sense of taste. There's no convincing evidence that either drug is effective in long-term weight reduction.

Certain liquid formula diets, such as **Medifast** and **Optifast,** can produce marked weight loss and appear to be safe under close medical supervision. But most patients eventually regain most or all of their lost weight.

Body wraps, belts, sweat suits, and their accompanying gels and creams promise to burn fat. They only sweat away body fluids, which are regained as soon as you eat or drink.

At least one enterprising company offers to massage away "cellulite" in 10 sessions with a device similar to a vacuum cleaner. But cellulite doesn't exist. It's just a quack term used to exploit the idea that lumpy fat deposits respond to special treatment. They don't.

"Transdermal appetite reduction kits"—or diet patches—have been described as snake oil on a Band-Aid. A few drops of herbal or mineral liquid are placed on an adhesive bandage, which is then affixed to some strategic spot on the body. Diet patches are claimed to suppress the brain's appetite-control center. They have no such effect.

Beware of those who claim that certain foods or "dietary supplements" can burn off fat. Nothing you eat can do that. Sybervision's "Neuropsychology of Weight Control" program, for example, features the "**MetaboLean** nutrient system" that "goes directly to your cells." Read the promotional material closely, though, and you'll find that the success of the program still depends on eating less and exercising more.

. . . And Keep It Off (Definitely)

The only way to make weight loss last is to change your behavior permanently. To start with, you'll need to expend more calories than you consume. A combination of two strategies—diet and exercise—is most effective. Once you've reached your desired weight, you may be able to increase your caloric intake a bit. But don't expect to return to your old ways.

Diet. Trim your caloric intake by 500 calories a day and you'll lose about one pound a week. (That assumes your weight is now stable—that is, you're not gaining weight.) Keep a food diary for a few days to document your current intake. Once you've established how many calories you're taking in, you can set realistic goals for weight reduction.

Reducing dietary fat is a particularly good way to cut total calories. Each gram of fat contains 9 calories, while carbohydrates and protein have only 4 calories per gram. It doesn't take major dietary changes to cut fat from your diet; you can do it with such simple measures as trimming visible fat from meat, removing skin from poultry, using low-fat dairy products, and avoiding processed foods made with vegetable oils.

Exercise. Any physical activity burns calories. You'll burn them faster when you exercise harder, but you don't need strenuous workouts if that's not your style. Walking, for example, can help if you do it regularly.

Here are some examples of the average calories burned per 30 minutes of exercise by a person who weighs 150 pounds. Decrease these numbers by one-third for a body weight of 100 pounds; increase by one-third for a weight of 200 pounds.

Swimming (20 yd/min)	145 calories
Walking (4 mph)	175 calories
Aerobics (low-impact)	205 calories
Calisthenic circuit training	270 calories
Jogging (5 mph)	270 calories
Aerobics (high-impact)	280 calories
Bicycling (13 mph)	320 calories
Swimming (55 yd/min)	395 calories
Vigorous rowing	435 calories

Cross-country skiing (8 mph)	470 calories
Running (8 mph)	470 calories

Those numbers quickly add up. Just as you can lose 1 pound per week by reducing your daily caloric intake by 500 calories, you can also lose a pound per week by any combination of reduced food intake and increased exercise that totals 500 calories a day.

Exercise also raises your metabolic rate, causing calories to be burned at a faster clip for several hours after each workout. That tends to offset some of the metabolism-lowering effects of trimming calories from your diet. Exercise plus diet, then, work best in tandem.

A Nontreatment for a Nondisease

Candida albicans is a normally harmless yeast found in the mouth, intestinal tract, and vagina. While it may cause infections, these are rarely serious in otherwise healthy people.

During the past few years, however, various practitioners, including some physicians, have warned that 30 percent of Americans suffer from "candidiasis hypersensitivity," or "yeast allergy." They say the yeast can weaken the immune system and trigger a frightening array of symptoms, including abdominal bloating, anxiety, confusion, constipation, depression, diarrhea, dizziness, fatigue, irritability, mood swings, muscle and joint pain, and unexpected weight gain, as well as cravings for sugar or alcohol.

According to the American Academy of Allergy and Immunology, the nation's largest professional organization of allergists, the concept of yeast allergy is "speculative and unproven"—a polite way of saying it's rubbish. But proponents of the notion routinely diagnose "yeast problems" in their patients, and the health-food industry has encouraged people to diagnose and treat themselves for this nonexistent allergy.

Perhaps the most vigorous promoter of the yeast-allergy idea is William G. Crook, M.D., of Jackson, Tennessee, author of *The Yeast Conection: A Medical Breakthrough.* Crook's book contains a lengthy questionnaire to aid self-diagnosis of yeast problems. Shorter versions have appeared in magazine articles and in ads for products sold through health-food stores.

Spurred on by Crook's promotion, public interest in "candidiasis hypersensitivity" has grown rapidly. Other books have been published, and manufacturers now offer such products as **Candi-Care, Candida-**

Guard, Candida Cleanse, Candistat, Yeast Fighters, Yeast Guard, Yeastop, and **Yeast·Trol.**

Among the most publicized "anti-Candida" products is **Cantrol**—an assortment of vitamins, minerals, and herbs—from Nature's Way, of Utah. The company has promoted **Cantrol** with an ad that contained a 14-question self-test.

In 1989, the FDA seized a supply of **Cantrol** and issued a Health Fraud Bulletin instructing its field offices to initiate action against other illegally marketed "anti-Candida" products. And the Federal Trade Commission (FTC), which regulates the advertising of nonprescription products, charged that the self-test could not diagnose a yeast infection and that there was no reasonable basis for claiming that **Cantrol** is effective against yeast problems.

Early in 1990 the FTC announced that Nature's Way, while not admitting wrongdoing, had signed a consent agreement to stop making unsubstantiated claims for **Cantrol.** The company agreed to pay $30,000 to the National Institutes of Health to support research on yeast infections.

These actions should help deflate the market for bogus "anti-Candida" products. Meanwhile, be wary of doctors who diagnose "candidiasis hypersensitivity" in their patients or who recommend elaborate nutritional remedies for "yeast problems."

"Amazing Cures" for Arthritis Neither Amaze Nor Cure

"New help for arthritis sufferers" announces an advertisement for **CamoCare,** distributed by the American Association of Retired Persons Pharmacy Service. The "remarkable cream" is promoted as an "amazing new European discovery."

"'My pain is *gone,*' exclaims 'one satisfied user.'"

The only ingredients in **CamoCare** known to relieve pain when applied externally are camphor and menthol. (**CamoCare** also contains the herb chamomile and a few other ingredients, none of them pain relievers.) Camphor and menthol may be able to ease minor pains, but the results can hardly be called amazing. Camphor and menthol are the main ingredients in such venerable liniments as **Vicks VapoRub** and **Musterole.**

Arthritis is an ideal disease for hucksters to exploit. It's widespread, painful, chronic, and usually incurable. Symptoms flare up and subside spontaneously, so remissions can be attributed to "miracle cures." People with arthritis spend at least $1 billion a year on unproven remedies.

Innovative marketers have flooded the market with products ranging from daffy to dangerous. The **Vyrllium Tube,** which contained two cents worth of salt as its main ingredient, sold for $250. **Liefcort,** a potent combination of sex hormones and a steroid, was found to be dangerous even under medical supervision. These days, various "miracle diets," often promoted in books, are the most common kind of arthritis quackery.

Nine out of 10 people with arthritis try unproven remedies, and 10 percent of those people report harmful side effects. Compared with other products, **CamoCare** seems rather tame. However, any therapy arthritis patients try on their own can be harmful if it causes them to delay or quit conventional medical treatment. And, of course, they lose the money spent on worthless products.

Be especially wary of a product that:

- Claims to cure arthritis or work for all kinds of arthritis
- Offers case histories and testimonials from users as the only proof of effectiveness
- Offers only a single study as proof of effectiveness
- Claims to be a secret formula or available from only one source
- Doesn't list ingredients
- Has no instructions for use or warnings about potential side effects
- Claims to be harmless or stresses that it's "natural"

The Arthritis Foundation provides information about unproven remedies through its local chapters and its information line (1-800-283-7800).

Extra Vitamins? Most People Should Save Their Money

Are you concerned about getting enough vitamins in your diet? Worried that an undetected deficiency might be jeopardizing your health? Are you considering extra vitamins to help you cope with stress or to perk you up?

Marketers manipulate these hopes and fears to push vitamin supplements. Don't be misled. Only an extremely unbalanced diet could create a risk of a clinically significant vitamin deficiency. Emotional stress doesn't increase the body's need for vitamins. And vitamins provide no calories, so they provide no energy.

Vitamin supplements may be appropriate for pregnant women who drink alcohol or smoke, are vegetarians, or are carrying more than one fetus. And all pregnant women should consider a daily supplement containing 30 milligrams of iron, an essential nutrient that their diets are likely to lack. (Iron supplements should be taken with meals.)

Women generally don't get enough calcium; pregnant women should be especially sure they do. The National Academy of Sciences recommends 1,200 milligrams of calcium a day during pregnancy; those who don't get enough calcium from their diet should consider a supplement.

The theory that vitamin C (ascorbic acid) can prevent or cure colds is another hardy fallacy. In 1970, that "remedy" hit its peak of popularity with publication of Linus Pauling's "Vitamin C and the Common Cold." Pauling ultimately argued for large daily doses of from 1,000 to 2,000 milligrams in times of health and as much as 20,000 milligrams at the onset of a cold. (The adult Recommended Dietary Allowance, or RDA, is only 60 milligrams a day.)

The thesis has been tested and retested, and most researchers are now satisfied that vitamin C neither prevents nor cures colds. At best, the aerosol form of ascorbic acid may have a mild antihistaminelike effect—drying nasal secretions slightly. But there are many more potent antihistamines on the market than vitamin C, and they certainly do not cure or even treat the common cold.

A few studies have suggested that taking extra vitamin C regularly may diminish the severity, though not the duration, of colds. But the benefit was only slight.

Were it only a matter of risking $20 to $100 a year on heavy doses of vitamin C for even the possibility of warding off colds, some people would doubtless be willing to gamble. But megadoses of vitamin C are not harmless. Too much vitamin C can produce diarrhea and diminish the ability of white blood cells to kill harmful bacteria. Megadoses may encourage the formation of urinary-tract stones in some people, urine tests for glucose can be thrown off by the presence of ascorbic acid, and the effect of anticoagulant therapy may be decreased.

According to the AMA, the amount of any vitamin used as a therapeutic agent "should not exceed two to ten times" its RDA. Considering that the doses recommended by vitamin C proponents range from 16 to more than 300 times the RDA, the risks are real.

People who have been taking large doses should stop gradually. "Rebound scurvy"—caused by a rapid drop in blood levels of vitamin C—can occur in infants whose mothers took large doses during pregnancy.

Will Mercury Fillings Poison You?

Hundreds of dentists across the country are removing allegedly dangerous mercury-amalgam fillings and replacing them with new ones. Our advice: If a dentist wants to remove your fillings because they contain mercury, close your mouth and watch your wallet.

One hundred million Americans have "silver fillings"—actually alloys, or amalgams, of silver and several other metals. One of those metals is mercury, which makes up about half the filling. In 1979, University of Iowa researchers found that chewing can release minute amounts of mercury vapor from old fillings. That finding sparked the present controversy over amalgam safety, which was fanned into flame by a December 1990 report on amalgam fillings that aired on the popular CBS-TV show "60 Minutes." The report featured, among other elements, a 1990 study at the University of Calgary in Alberta, Canada, in which sheep fitted with amalgam fillings, eating a normal diet, lost 60 percent of kidney function in two months as a result of mercury poisoning, while a control group eating the same diet and not having their teeth filled with amalgam lost none. After the show ran, thousands of worried amalgam wearers lit up switchboards at state dental societies, dental schools, and the American Dental Association.

However, experts in toxicology, biochemistry, and veterinary science have been critical of the Alberta study, pointing out that sheep are inappropriate models for amalgam problems in people. Not only did the amalgam used in the study contain a higher level of mercury than amalgam fillings placed in humans, but sheep wear their teeth down far more quickly than people—chewing, swallowing and rechewing their abrasive diet of grass and grains for 15 hours a day. The animals in the study were literally swallowing their fillings daily, in bits and pieces. An additional blow to this study is the opinion of renal specialists on the ADA panel that reviewed it. According to them, there is little evidence of damage to the kidney function in the sheep.

A Mercury Threat?

Mercury is a potent poison when swallowed, inhaled, or absorbed through the skin. Prolonged exposure to high levels can damage the brain and nervous system. The classic example occurred in the nineteenth century, when makers of felt hats dipped material into mercuric-nitrate solution to make the felt easier to shape. In so doing, the workers absorbed mercury through their skin and inhaled mercury vapor. Tremors, incoherent speech, difficulty in walking, and feeblemindedness resulted. Smaller amounts of mercury vapor can cause less drastic symptoms, including anxiety, insomnia, and minor tremors.

Can mercury in fillings cause those or other health problems? "Anti-amalgam" dentists contend that mercury fumes from amalgams can cause problems ranging from depression and multiple sclerosis to fatigue and irritability. Their solution: Drill out the amalgams and replace them with fillings made from other materials. The American Dental Association (ADA), on the other hand, insists that amalgam fillings are safe. Only people allergic to mercury—less than 1 percent of the population—need avoid them, the ADA says.

Alternative Fillings

Dentists make up amalgam with mercury because it's strong and durable. An amalgam filling can withstand the tremendous forces of chewing for a long time before breaking down. A mercury-amalgam filling usually lasts 5 to 10 years and may last as long as 40 years.

The main alternatives to mercury-amalgam fillings are composite resin fillings, made mainly of plastics. When amalgam fillings are removed because of "mercury toxicity," composite fillings usually take their place. Composites can be mixed to match the color of the tooth and so are often used for front teeth.

But composites have several drawbacks, particularly in back teeth, where they are subjected to heavy biting pressure. Typically, they last no more than three years. They're also more expensive than amalgam, and teeth filled with composites are less resistant to recurrent decay.

Composites are being continually tested and improved. Research is under way on composites that can be chemically bonded to teeth. Such composites could rival amalgam fillings in durability. CU's dental consultants say that composites strong enough for use in back teeth may become available sometime in the 1990s. However, composites have been in only limited use for the last 20 years, and health-care professionals have not completely ruled out potential long-term health problems, according to Dr. J. Rodway Mackert, Jr., associate professor of dental materials at the Medical College of Georgia.

Gold inlays are also sometimes used instead of amalgams. They're durable but cost a lot, both for the gold and for the installation. They are not a practical alternative to amalgam fillings.

Assessing Exposure

Dentists who are looking for a reason to remove amalgam fillings typically use a mercury-vapor analyzer to evaluate the air in the patient's mouth. These devices are customarily used in factories, where they measure the mercury levels in workplace air. Is it appropriate for dentists to use them? CU's dental consultants say that use of the mercury analyzer is a scare tactic to get patients to part with their fillings. The device makes it easy for a dentist to contend that a mercury level exceeds occupational standards.

When using the analyzer, the dentist has the patient chew vigorously for 10 minutes, creating heat and friction that maximize the release of mercury vapor. The analyzer senses the mercury contained in about ½ cup of air and multiplies it by 8,000. That gives a readout corresponding to the mercury level in a cubic meter of air—about the amount inhaled in an hour. But for the patient, the exposure lasts only a few minutes during chewing—and only a fraction of the vapor may be inhaled. Most people don't inhale through their mouths while chewing. And even when they're not chewing, most people breathe through the nose, so that inhaled air bypasses any mercury vapor that may be in the mouth. One recent study showed that the analyzer technique tends to produce estimates that are some 16 times higher than the actual daily dose of mercury vapor.

In assessing mercury vapor's effect on health, the key issue is how much actually gets absorbed by the body's tissues. Thomas W. Clarkson, M.E., of the University of Rochester School of Medicine, is one of the world's leading authorities on mercury toxicity. He says that a mercury-vapor analyzer can't answer that question.

Clarkson told CU that a person's mercury exposure can best be assessed by measuring the mercury levels in blood and urine. If dental amalgams really were poisoning people, Clarkson pointed out, the mercury levels in the general population would be at dangerously high levels. That's far from the case. In one study of 1,107 people (mainly in the United States), 95 percent had urine levels of mercury lower than 20 micrograms. Adverse health effects appear when the level reaches about 150 micrograms or more, Clarkson said.

Another study examined the claim that dental amalgam interferes with immune function. But the researchers found that subjects with amalgam fillings had the same number of disease-fighting white blood cells as people who were amalgam free. And a Swedish researcher found no connection between amalgam and nonamalgam groups in measures used to assess immune system, liver, kidney, and skeletal-muscular health.

If anyone faced a health hazard from mercury fillings, it would be dentists and their assistants. A dentist typically handles between 2 and 3 pounds of mercury every year. Skin contact can result in absorption, and careless use and accidental spills can produce significant levels of mercury vapor in the air. In fact, surveys have shown that as many as 10 percent of dental offices have mercury-vapor levels that exceed 50 micrograms per cubic meter of air—the upper limit that the National Institute for Occupational Safety and Health considers safe for eight-hour exposures in the workplace.

Yet, despite their higher exposures, dental personnel aren't being poisoned. Since 1982, the ADA has sponsored a mercury-testing service that measures urine mercury levels in dentists and dental workers. While average levels are about four times higher than in the general population, they are still well within the acceptable range.

One major reason some dentists are jumping on the antiamalgam bandwagon can be summed up in one word: fluoride. Largely because of fluoridated drinking water and fluoride toothpastes, the incidence of tooth decay over the past two decades has been cut roughly in half. So some dentists are experiencing a falling-off of business. Removing and replacing amalgam fillings helps to fill that financial hole.

Reinvading a tooth—drilling out amalgam and installing a replacement—can also increase tooth sensitivity and weaken the tooth. And studies show that the very action of drilling out amalgam can produce brief but significant increases in mercury levels in the mouth.

SIX

Moneywise

The United States economy goes up and down. Taking measures to protect your money—controlling your cash flow, accumulating cash, and cutting your debts—makes sense in any economic climate.

Step 1: Control Cash Flow

To cope with a job loss or a large drop in income, you first need to know what your living expenses are and how much of your take-home pay is left over after paying them. You can find out easily if you keep a household budget. If not, go through your check registers, credit-card and charge-account statements, bank statements (for cash withdrawals), and paycheck stubs. If you have trouble accounting for your total cash outflow, keep a spending diary for the next 60 days.

Divide your expenses into two categories: those that you can't reduce and those you could probably lower in a pinch. The first group of expenses includes mortgage or rent payments, car payments, utilities, commuting costs, insurance premiums, and real-estate taxes. The second group includes grocery and restaurant expenses, long-distance phone calls, clothing, personal care, children's allowances, gifts and charitable donations, cable TV, hobbies, vacations, and other recreation.

Your investigation can pay off in the discovery of cash leaks that are easily plugged now and discretionary spending that can be cut back if necessary. You can even map out an austerity budget for the worst of times.

Step 2: Accumulate Cash

Every household needs an emergency fund—ideally, enough to cover six months of living expenses if you lose your job or become sick. Exclude income taxes and any business expenses (which will temporarily drop off) but not much else. In two-income families whose breadwinners both are secure in their jobs, three months' expenses should suffice for emergencies.

To qualify as "cash," funds should be kept available in safe, easily liquidated accounts. Those include money-market accounts at banks, money-market mutual funds, short-term certificates of deposit, and 13-week Treasury bills.

If your household is like many, it has nowhere near enough cash on hand. The bulk of many families' surplus income goes into retirement plans at work, where it's inaccessible. Employee contributions to 401(k) salary-withholding plans, for example, can be borrowed only while you remain on the payroll and only if your plan permits loans. If you are ever let go, you must pay off the balance due on any outstanding loans; otherwise, the loan will be treated as a distribution on which you will have to pay income taxes plus a 10 percent penalty if you're under the age of 59½.

Besides taking stock of cash flow, you may be able to raise cash in other ways:

- Stash any raises or bonuses in your emergency fund.
- Put the proceeds of maturing long-term certificates of deposit in three-month CDs or money-market accounts.

Step 3: Reduce Your Debts

The lower your debts, obviously, the more you save on interest. More important, by paying off debts you also reduce your fixed monthly expenses. As a general rule, monthly payments of debts other than a mortgage loan should never equal more than 20 percent of take-home pay; a maximum of 15 percent is safer, especially in uncertain times.

Where to Keep Your Cash

Liquid Assets

It's important to keep some of your money liquid, easily accessible as an emergency fund for life's unpleasant surprises. For an asset to qualify as liquid, it must meet two tests.

First, you should be able to get your hands on the money almost immediately—within a week at most. Bank accounts most obviously meet the test. But any asset that you can redeem or exchange for cash whenever you wish qualifies as well—certificates of deposit, mutual-fund shares, and stocks and bonds, if you can count on selling them anytime (that is, if they are highly marketable).

Second, you must be able to convert an asset into ready cash at a constant, or very nearly constant, value. Bank deposits again meet the test. So do money-market mutual funds, which are redeemable at a fixed price of $1 per share. Securities that you can sell readily, but only at the risk of getting less than you paid for them, do not qualify as liquid.

All the assets discussed in the following sections meet those two tests of liquidity. But some assets work a bit harder than others at earning interest.

Demand-Deposit Accounts

Most banks, savings and loans, and credit unions allow immediate access to cash put in "demand" deposits—checking accounts, share-draft accounts, savings accounts, and money-market accounts. You'll always get back the dollars you put in if the institution is backed by a federal deposit insurance fund; the safety of your principal as well as any interest earned is guaranteed by the government up to $100,000 per depositor.

Though very liquid, bank savings accounts pay relatively low interest rates. Checking accounts often pay no interest. Savings accounts typically pay 5 percent, as of this writing. Even bank money-market accounts, which usually require minimum deposits larger than that on savings or checking accounts, average only about a percentage point more than passbook savings accounts.

Bank Certificates of Deposit

Compared with bank money-market accounts, bank CDs give you a bit more interest and meet the first test for liquidity—they are payable on demand from their issuer. They're also covered by the same federal deposit insurance as demand-deposit accounts. But only the principal deposited in a CD meets the second test of liquidity—constant value. You risk losing part of the interest if you cash a CD before it matures. The penalty for early withdrawal ranges from as little as seven days' interest to as much as six months' interest. This means that you shouldn't break a CD except in emergencies. As a contingency measure, you might consider using the CD as collateral; banks will often let you borrow against a CD at 2 percent or so more than its rate.

Money-Market Mutual Funds

Money funds meet the constant-value test of liquidity and the test of immediate access—their shares are almost as readily redeemed for cash as bank deposits. In addition, money funds pay higher returns.

Money in a money fund is not quite as safe as in a federally insured bank account. No government insurer stands behind the deposits in money funds. In their brief (two-decade) history, though, no money fund has gone belly-up. The best assurance of a fund's safety is the high quality and short-term nature of its portfolio, usually a mix of commercial paper, bank CDs, and Treasury securities. These assets must mature in an average of 100 days or less. Banks, by contrast, invest heavily in longer-term, intrinsically riskier mortgages and bonds.

You can arrange for maximum liquidity by authorizing wire transfers from your money-market fund to your bank. Then, by dialing a toll-free number, you can have amounts of $1,000 or more sent to your bank account the same day or overnight. (Some funds charge $5 for wiring amounts under $5,000.) For less pressing withdrawals, you can write money-fund checks, usually limited to amounts of $500 or more. Those who wish to write smaller checks can do so through an arrangement commonly called an asset-management account, which is available at brokerage houses and a few mutual-fund companies. Account holders can write checks of any size and get a debit or credit card activated to withdraw cash at automated teller machines of banks affiliated with national or regional ATM networks.

Major brokerage houses charge from $30 to $100 a year for their

asset-management accounts and require five-figure initial deposits.
National discount brokerages are cheaper. So shop around.

Savings Accounts

Consider the following elements when you shop for a savings account:

- *APR.* The annual percentage rate is the basic yearly interest rate
  that the account pays.
- *Compounding.* The more frequent the compounding period, the
  better off you are. However, continuous compounding yields only
  a tiny bit more than daily compounding.
- *Yield.* The annual percentage yield takes into consideration both
  the APR and the frequency of compounding. It tells you by what
  percentage a deposit will grow if you leave it in the account for a
  full year.
- *Balance method.* How does the financial institution determine the
  amount on which interest is paid? The fairest method is called day-
  of-deposit-to-day-of-withdrawal (sometimes known as day-in-to-
  day-out, or DIDO). With it, you get interest each day on the actual
  balance in your account. Another common method is day-of-
  deposit-to-end-of-interest period. This means that withdrawals
  before the end of the interest period (usually the end of the
  month) don't earn interest for any of that period. The least equi-
  table is the low-balance method. This system pays you interest only
  on the lowest balance in your account during the interest period
  and ignores the rest.
- *Fees, charges, and penalties.* If your balance falls below a certain
  minimum, is there a service charge (or do you cease to earn interest)? Is there a charge for withdrawals after a certain number is
  reached? Is there a charge for so-called inactive accounts? What
  other special charges are there?
- *Delaying interest on deposits.* Does the financial institution start paying interest the day checks are deposited, or does it wait for the
  check to clear?
- *Deposit insurance.* Be sure to find out whether you would be covered by federal deposit insurance. Unless you have a basis to form
  an independent judgment on the adequacy of a state deposit-
  insurance fund, stick with a federally insured institution.

Getting the Most from Your Checking Account

Shop Around for Low Fees

Banks generally used to provide the same checking and saving services to all customers, no matter how large or small their balances. No more. But if you carefully shop around, you still can find some checking account bargains.

To shop for a better-than-average checking account, look over your checkbook for several months last year—say, January, May, August, and November. Figure out how many checks you usually write and what your balance typically is. Then you can realistically shop for an account in a way that will minimize bank fees.

Some of the best deals are available through smaller banks and savings institutions. The checking account worksheet on page 160 should help you make comparisons.

Who's at Risk for a Forged or Lost Check?

What should you do if your checkbook is lost or stolen? Your banker will probably advise you to stop payment on all outstanding checks and close down the account. But that would mean getting in touch with everyone you owe and sending out new checks. If you miss anyone, you'd have to suffer the ignominy of bouncing a check. And each stop-payment order might cost $12 or more.

Banks may well urge customers to order a stop payment whenever they think there's a risk. But what most customers don't realize is that they generally aren't at risk—their bank is.

If your checkbook is lost or stolen, you should report that to the bank immediately. But you don't have to stop payment on a batch of checks. All you need to do is spot a forged signature and notify the bank that you didn't sign the check. It's the bank's job to verify your signature against the one kept on file. Of course, banks don't check every piece of paper. But a forged check cashed at a bank becomes the bank's responsibility. That's true of any business or individual who accepts checks.

You also don't need to stop payment on a check you forget to sign. Say you realize you've mailed off the utility bill with an unsigned check. If you stop payment, the power company may slap you with a late charge because it hasn't received its money on time. But if you let the unsigned check go through, the bank may clear it.

Almost the only time a stop payment makes sense is when goods or

Checking Account Worksheet

1. Name of bank: _____

2. Covered by Federal Deposit Insurance?
   ☐ Yes   ☐ No

3. Type of checking account:
   ☐ Regular   ☐ NOW   ☐ Super-NOW

4. Interest rate paid on account balance:
   ☐ No interest
   ☐ 5¼ percent
   ☐ Other fixed percentage: _____ percent
   ☐ Split rate: _____ percent on first $_____ in account,
     _____ percent on amount above that

5. Do I have to pay fees on this account?
   ☐ No   ☐ Yes   ☐ Depends on balance kept in account

6. If fees depend on balance, how is balance calculated for this purpose?
   (Average daily balance is best.)
   ☐ Minimum balance
   ☐ Average daily balance
   ☐ Other: _____

7. When fees apply, what are they?
   ☐ Monthly maintenance charge: $_____ per month
   ☐ Fee for each check written: $_____ per check
   ☐ Other fees: _____

8. If interest is paid, on what balance is the interest calculated?
   ☐ Interest paid daily on that day's balance
   ☐ Average daily balance
   ☐ Other: _____

9. What is the charge for:
   Bouncing a check (insufficient funds): $_____
   A certified check: $_____
   Making a deposit (if any): $_____
   Using an automated teller machine: $_____
   Printing 200 checks with name and address: $_____

10. Convenience factors:
    How close is nearest branch to my home? _____

    How close is nearest branch to my office? _____

    Number of branches: _____
    Number of automated teller machines: _____
    Bank hours: _____

services turn out to be unsatisfactory. By stopping payment on the check, you gain some leverage in your effort to get a contractor to do the job right or a seller to replace the goods.

A stop-payment order may also make sense if a vendor sheepishly reports that your check was misplaced and you write a second one. It may be prudent to stop payment rather than trust the vendor to tear up the lost check if it's found.

You Can Get Cheaper Checks by Mail

If you have to reorder checks, don't assume that your bank is the only place to buy them. There's a better deal: checks by mail.

Buying checks through your bank may be convenient, but you'll pay dearly. Banks take a hefty profit on check printing—as high as 100 percent. If you like checks decorated with ducks in flight or sunsets, you'll pay even more. But checks printed by independent companies cost from 40 to 65 percent less than the ones supplied by a bank.

You can order checks from Current, Inc., a mail-order greeting-card company in Colorado Springs (800-426-0822). It has a special introductory offer for 200 checks; reorders only cost several dollars more. Mailing address: Current, Inc., Check Printing Department, Box 19000, Colorado Springs, CO 80935. Or, you can try Checks in the Mail, Irwindale, California (800-733-4443), a family-run business that's been printing checks for banks since 1922. It also charges a low fee for 200 checks and a slightly higher fee for subsequent orders. Its mailing address: Checks in the Mail, P.O. Box 7802, Irwindale, CA 91706. Both companies offer wallet-type checks and a selection of a dozen or more designs.

A Consumers Union staffer who ordered checks from Current was quite satisfied. The company required one of the check reorder forms from the reporter's supply of bank checks, a deposit slip, and payment by check. The company says all that helps get the account number at the bottom of the check correct and assures that it's a legitimate order. The checks arrived in about four weeks and were every bit the equal of higher-priced models from the bank.

Money and Your Home

Home-Equity Loans: Borrow with Care

Once called "second mortgages," home-equity loans became a booming industry in the 1980s. They owe their popularity to comparatively low

interest rates, tax-favored status, and easy availability. Though tradition-
ally used to finance home improvements, they have become all-purpose
loans. For many years, their drain on home equity was more than offset
by steeply climbing home prices. But homeowners can no longer count
on similar appreciation to help them finance their future needs, such as
retirement.

Even more ominous, households laden with both first- and second-
mortgage debt risk financial disaster if times get hard. Faced with both
falling real-estate values and prolonged unemployment, for example, a
family might be forced to sell its house for less than the debt on it or to
suffer a foreclosure.

Moral: Borrow cautiously. Here are some of the basics.

Sources for loans. Banks and savings institutions now compete with
credit unions, finance companies, brokerage houses, and insurance
companies. Home-equity loans come in two forms:

- *Closed-end loans.* You borrow a fixed amount all at once and repay
  it in monthly installments over a set period, such as 10 years.
- *Home-equity lines of credit.* You borrow money as you need it, drawing against a maximum amount established when you opened the
  account. You pay interest on the balance due, as with a credit
  card. There is often a choice of paying down the loan on a prear-
  ranged schedule or paying only interest for the first several years.
  The interest rate is usually adjustable.

  Open-end lenders frequently give you a book of special checks
  with which to tap into your line of credit, or they may let you borrow through your regular checking account. At some banks you
  can draw cash at a teller's window or from an ATM.

Interest rates. Most lenders base their adjustable interest rates on the
prime rate (what banks charge their best commercial borrowers). Your
rate may be one or two percentage points higher.

Other indexes lenders use include the 90-day Treasury bill rate and
the average 30-day jumbo ($100,000) CD rate. Both those indexes are
more responsive to interest trends than the prime rate and therefore are
more volatile.

In addition to interest, many lenders charge a yearly fee of $25 to $45.

Rate caps. Federal law requires lenders to set an upper limit, or cap,
on an adjustable interest rate over the lifetime of the loan. Lenders set

their own ceilings, which recently averaged 19 percent. By law, lenders can deny you further cash advances once the cap is reached. The loan contract may also set a floor of 8 to 9 percent on your rate, no matter how low the index sinks.

Closing costs. Up-front charges for such items as a property appraisal, attorney's fees, a credit investigation, and title insurance can mount up to $750 or more of closing costs on home-equity loans. In the heat of competition, however, some lenders waive all closing costs.

Loan amounts. Your equity in your house—its market value minus the unpaid balance owed on existing mortgage debt—becomes the basis for deciding how much you can borrow against the property. Few financial institutions will let you extract more than 80 percent of the value of your home, and on a house worth $500,000 or more the cut-off may be as low as 50 percent. This limit is called the loan-to-value ratio.

For example, say your house is appraised at $200,000 and has a $100,000 mortgage balance. If the lender applies a 75 percent loan-to-value ratio, the most you can borrow is $150,000 minus your $100,000 debt, or $50,000.

Tax advantages. If you itemize deductions, none of the interest you pay on car loans, credit cards, and other so-called consumer loans can be written off against taxable income for 1991 and the following tax years. But interest on home-equity loans up to $100,000 remains 100 percent deductible on federal Form 1040 and on many state income-tax returns as well.

Note, however, that closing costs are not generally deductible, except for points charged up front on a closed-end loan.

Guidelines. Taking out a home-equity loan can make sense under certain circumstances, so long as you impose a few restraints.

- Treat the loan as an investment, whether in improving your house, financing an education, or starting a business. Use it cautiously to consolidate debts whose interest is not tax deductible or to cover emergency expenses. But don't use it for vacations or luxuries.
- Use open-end loans to cover deferred costs such as college tuition and multiphased home improvements. Use closed-end loans for refinancings and other lump sums.
- Beware of teaser rates, the kind that ratchet up after a year or two.

- Whenever possible, reject the interest-only option. Schedule installments that will retire the debt in 10 years or less.

- Base the size of your loan on your ability to repay, rather than on the amount of equity available to you. A useful rule is that your mortgage and home-equity loan payments should not exceed 35 percent of your gross monthly income.

Reduce or End Your Escrow Account?

As a condition of giving you a mortgage, many lenders insist you set up an escrow account to accumulate money for taxes and insurance. You often don't, however, earn interest on that account. If you think you could handle payment of your tax and insurance bills yourself, consider contacting your lender to see if your escrow account can be ended. Some lenders will let you pay tax and insurance bills if you can convince them that you'll pay the bills on time. You may succeed in having your escrow payments eliminated simply by sending a written request to your bank.

Reducing an escrow account. If you can't end your escrow account, maybe you can cut it. A 1975 law called the Real Estate Settlement Procedures Act (RESPA) allows lenders to maintain a cushion of no more than two months of insurance and tax payments at any given time.

To check if your escrow account is too large, you'll need a month-by-month statement for the past year. Many lenders send those out annually; if yours doesn't, request one. It will show the monthly balance in your escrow account and the disbursements the lender has made. The lowest monthly balance during the year is the lender's cushion. If that amount is more than one-sixth of the yearly disbursements from the account (in other words, two months of escrow payments), it's excessive.

You may not even be required to keep a two-month cushion in your account. The terms of some mortgages allow the lender only a one-month cushion or no cushion at all. Check your mortgage documents.

Homeowners should also beware of any increases that lenders demand for their escrow accounts. Mortgages taken out at a hometown bank often are sold to faraway companies for servicing. Those companies predict tax increases based on regional or national averages, not on what's happening in your community.

If your escrow account appears to be bloated, first complain to your lender or the company that services the mortgage. If that doesn't produce results, contact your state's banking department or attorney general's office.

When escrow accounts are required. Virtually all borrowers in certain categories are required to pay their property taxes and insurance through an escrow account:

- When the mortgage is insured by the Federal Housing Administration or by the Department of Veterans Affairs.
- When the loan is for 90 percent or more of the value of the house.

When escrow accounts are acceptable:

- Despite the loss of interest, some homeowners prefer the "forced savings" that an escrow account requires. With an escrow account, they pay one-twelfth of their annual tax and insurance bills every month instead of having to come up with the entire amount when the taxes and insurance become due.
- Thirteen states require lenders to pay interest on escrow accounts. But the required interest rates in states with such laws ranges from 2 to 5 percent—typically even less than the rate on a passbook savings account.

Mortgage Payments

If you already have a mortgage or are in the market for a new one, you can probably save tens of thousands of dollars by "investing" in your mortgage. By simply making accelerated principal payments, you may net a higher return than you would by investing the money elsewhere.

To prepay, notify your lender that the extra amount should go directly for repayment of principal, not for interest. You may want to write a separate check to ensure that the lender services your loan properly. Keep track of how much extra principal you've paid, and compare your figures with the year-end statement issued by your mortgage holder.

Home Insurance and Other Protection

Should Your Next Home Carry a Warranty?

The next time you shop for a home, you may find the real-estate agent talking up the warranty on a house, not just its location, tax rates, and the like.

The trend stems partly from the high cost of real estate. Many buyers, stretched financially, can't afford to have anything go wrong after they move in. And sellers can't always use the "buyer beware" defense; courts more frequently hold sellers liable for hiding defects these days.

Builders offer warranties on new houses through companies such as Home Owners Warranty Corporation. It provides 10-year coverage with rates based on the selling price of the home.

Warranties on existing houses are typically sold by real-estate agents through an arrangement with insurance companies or service-contract firms. Purchasers include both buyers and sellers. One of the biggest home-warranty firms, Homeowners Group, Inc., sells through 18,000 real-estate offices and charges a flat fee in the range of $300 to $400 for a one-year warranty with a $100 deductible.

Most warranties cover all the essential systems in the house—heating, air-conditioning, plumbing and plumbing fixtures, water heater, fans, electrical wiring, and major appliances. The warranty on a new house typically covers roof or structural problems. A warranty on an existing house won't cover structural or roof problems or termite damage—all major exclusions.

A warranty can be a good deal on an older house or one that's not in the best of shape. But like many types of insurance, the overall risk of loss is much less than the cost to consumers.

Companies marketing these contracts claim that houses with warranties sell faster and at higher prices. That can be a plus for the seller. Buyers, however, might do better to forgo a warranty and keep some money aside as a repair fund. Buyers should also hire an impartial inspector to provide a complete report on the house. That should reveal any major defects before the sale is executed, while there's still time to renegotiate or back out of the deal.

Paying Too Much to Protect Your Home?

If you bought a home during the past few years, you may have had to buy excess insurance as a condition of getting a mortgage. A closer inspection of your insurance policy could save you a lot of money.

For years, mortgage companies in most states have forced some homeowners to insure their homes for the full amount of their mortgage—the loan for the house plus the land, not just the replacement cost of the building.

Years ago, the cost of a typical house represented about 80 percent of the selling price of a piece of property. Most buyers made a 20 percent down payment, so mortgage companies figured they could protect the rest of their investment by requiring insurance for the full amount of the mortgage. But in many areas, such as the East Coast, in California, and near metropolitan centers, the house often accounts for as little as 55 percent of the purchase price.

If you bought a $250,000 house in metropolitan New York, where land values are exceedingly high, you might have made a $50,000 down payment and financed the balance. The replacement cost of the house might be only $162,500, but under the old formula, you'd have needed $200,000 worth of insurance to get the mortgage. Paying for the extra $37,500 of coverage could cost close to $160 annually.

Recent homebuyers should check to see if their insurance covers only the full replacement cost of the house. More is waste; less means you're underinsured.

If you suspect you might be protecting the dirt that your house sits on, ask your mortgage lender to have your insurance requirements revised. You'll probably need to have your home appraised and to provide documentation to the lender. (An independent appraiser usually charges about $150 to $300.) In most cases, the mortgage lender will permit you to carry less insurance if the house is covered for its full replacement cost.

Reach for a Discount on Homeowners Insurance

Many property casualty insurers give 5 to 15 percent multipolicy discounts for the privilege of writing both your auto and homeowners policies. Make sure you're being credited for at least a 2 percent discount if your house has smoke detectors and burglar alarms. And while you're at it, consider raising your deductibles—the amount you have to pay in case of loss or damage before the insurance coverage kicks in. Compared with the usual $250 deductible, you can typically save 10 percent on a boost to $500, 25 percent on a $2,500 deductible, because a higher deductible means you are assuming a greater share of the coverage.

Avoiding Credit Brokers

Your Credit Rating in Tough Times

Your economic well-being can rise and fall on your credit rating. While there is no such thing as a universal credit rating, most lenders get information about credit applicants from the files of the nation's consumer credit bureaus.

Whenever you open a credit account, one or more credit bureaus will open a file on you that notes the relevant information from your application and details about the initial credit transaction. Once a month, the accumulated files go to one or more of the three big national credit bureaus—Equifax, TransUnion, and TRW Credit Data.

Information on the promptness of consumers' payments goes into those files, along with notices of any judgments against them for unpaid debts, liens against their property, or personal bankruptcies. (Federal law requires credit bureaus to erase most adverse information after 7 years, however. The major exception is personal bankruptcy, which can remain on file for 10 years.) Local and regional credit bureaus hook into the Big Three's computer networks, making everybody's files widely accessible.

How accurate are credit reports? In mid-1991 there were some 400 million credit files in the credit-bureau computers, and the bureaus claim that less than 1 percent of their consumer files contain errors that would affect someone's chance of getting credit. Not a bad record, but also apparently not true. We conducted an informal poll and found that some 48 percent of credit reports contained inaccuracies, with nearly 20 percent of them being major enough to affect a consumer's credit eligibility. One participant in our poll was denied credit during the course of our study due to errors in her report. Just as disturbing was the fact that one in three participants reported that third parties had gained access to their reports without their consent, and another one in three couldn't tell *who* had reviewed their reports because the information was impossible to decipher. About half of all respondents reported that some of their current credit accounts were missing from their report.

How you are judged. A mistake in your credit record can make you ineligible for an auto loan, a credit card, or a mortgage. These days, most lenders decide whether to grant you credit through a process called *credit scoring*. The traits that help to determine your acceptability are likely to include the following:

- How long you have lived in the same place, worked for the same employer, or practiced the same profession.
- How old you are. People in their forties and early fifties, the peak spending years, tend to lose points here.
- What you do for a living. Blue collars tend to score lower than white collars.
- How much you earn.
- How much you have in the bank.
- How much you owe, and to how many lenders.
- How promptly you pay your installment debts.

How to correct errors. Your score, of course, is based on data provided by credit bureaus. If the data are wrong, so is the score.

Fortunately, federal law provides some correctives. Among them:

- *The right to know why you have been rejected.* If a credit bureau's report supplied information that led the lending institution to make a thumbs-down decision on your application, you must be told the name and address of the bureau.

- *The right to know what's in your file.* If you are denied credit, you have 30 days to demand to see—free of charge—the information in your report. Consumers who haven't been denied credit can learn what's in their files for a fee, typically $10 to $20.

- *The right to correct errors.* Credit bureaus must reinvestigate any information you dispute, usually within 30 days of the time you've called it to their attention. You can then tell them to send corrections to creditors who looked at your file during the previous six months. In case of an unresolved dispute, you have the right to insert your version in your file in 100 words or less.

FINDING YOUR CREDIT REPORT

Most lenders and retailers send data about their customers to local credit bureaus that are linked by computer to one or more of three national credit-reporting companies. To find out how to request a copy of your report, contact the following:

EQUIFAX

Your best route is to check your local phone directory. (Equifax's headquarters address is P.O. Box 4081, Atlanta, GA 30302; 404-885-8000.)

TRANSUNION

East: P.O. Box 360, Philadelphia, PA 19105; 215-569-4582.
Midwest: Consumer Relations, 222 S. First St., Suite 201, Louisville, KY 40202; 502-584-0121.
West: P.O. Box 3110, Fullerton, CA 92634; 714-738-3800.

TRW CREDIT DATA

National Consumer Relations Center, 12606 Greenville Ave., P.O. Box 749029, Dallas, TX 75374-9029; 214-235-1200, ext. 251.

Precautions to take. Pay your bills on time, of course. If you ever paid a court judgment, make sure that courthouse and credit-bureau records list it as satisfied. If you ever signed a home-improvement contract, make sure that any mechanic's lien has been lifted.

At least once, ask all three national credit bureaus whether they have a file on you. Inspect your files and ask that any errors or omissions be corrected.

Credit Insurance—a Bad Buy

Credit insurance, also called credit life, sounds like a reasonable insurance deal: It pays off the balance of the loan if the borrower dies. But check carefully before you buy. Consumers are grossly overcharged for credit life, and few people need it in the first place.

A report from the Consumer Federation of America shows that in one year, borrowers paid some $2.1 billion in premiums on 70 million policies. But only $900 million in claims were paid out, an appallingly low average loss ratio of 43 percent. By contrast, auto insurance policies pay out 60 to 80 percent in claims.

One reason for the excessive cost has to do with the way credit life is sold. Lenders offer borrowers just one policy; consumers can't shop. To earn the highest possible commission on their credit-insurance sales, lenders tend to affiliate with the insurer whose rates are highest.

State insurance departments regulate credit insurance, and maximum allowable premiums vary by state. Maine, New Jersey, New York, and Vermont consumers pay the lowest rates. Consumers in Alabama, Georgia, Louisiana, Mississippi, North Carolina, Oklahoma, and South Carolina pay the highest.

Credit insurance makes sense only if all of the following apply: You live in a state with a low maximum rate. You're over 50 years of age or in poor health. You're concerned about your heirs being able to pay off your loan.

For everyone else, term life insurance is a much better deal. In most cases you buy two or three times as much term life for what credit insurance would cost you. And if you should die, the proceeds will go to your beneficiaries—not to your lender.

Credit Card Come-Ons

Choosing the right credit card is a bit complicated, but the right choice can save you a bundle. A good card has three attributes: a low interest rate, a 25- or 30-day grace period, and little or no annual fee.

Interest rates. Many banks have never reduced credit-card interest rates from the highs reached in 1981. Why? Because consumers don't usually shop for credit or switch cards for a more favorable rate. Many mistakenly think all credit cards are alike, with rates set by Visa, MasterCard, or other organization. (In fact, the terms of a card are set by the individual bank issuing the card.)

Those who do shop, however, can find rates well below the average. The worst banks may charge almost twice the interest of the best ones. With credit unions, the range of interest rates tends to be somewhat narrower, and the rates fall roughly in the middle of the range banks charge.

RAM Research of Frederick, Maryland, is a banking research firm that tracks some 500 credit cards, including variable-rate cards, in terms of interest rates charged. Interested consumers can obtain a copy of Card Trak, a 12-page newsletter that's updated each month by RAM. For a copy of the latest newsletter, send $5 to Card Trak, Box 1700, Frederick, MD 21702.

Grace period. If you always pay your credit-card bill in full, you don't need to worry much about the interest rate. Instead, keep your eye on the grace period—the period within which you may pay your credit-card bill without incurring interest charges. If there is no grace period, you'll be charged interest even if you pay the full bill on receipt.

The difference adds up fast. Let's say you make five $50 purchases during a monthly billing cycle and pay your bill in full. At a bank with a 30-day grace period, you'd owe no interest. If your card had no grace period and a moderate interest rate of 16.5 percent, you'd pay as much as $3.50 in interest, depending on when you charged the purchases. Avoid getting a card without a grace period.

Annual fee. The issuer may charge $15 or so for a standard card and $36 for a premium card. Some banks will give you the option of trading in the annual fee in return for a higher interest rate—for example, 19.8 percent interest and no annual fee, or 17.76 percent and a $20 annual fee.

Which is better? If you usually pay off bills within the grace period, incurring no interest charges, you needn't worry about the interest rate. So you'd choose the card that has no annual fee.

If you maintain a monthly balance due of $150, you would also come out ahead without the annual fee, since the two-point difference between 19.8 percent and 17.76 percent would result in additional interest charges of just $3 a year. Only those who normally leave more than $1,000 of credit charges unpaid would benefit from the lower interest rate, which would pay for the $20 annual fee.

Some banks make the deal even more complicated. For example, one bank offered a Visa Premium with a $35 annual fee and a variable-interest rate that floated 2 percentage points above the prime rate. (At one point, the card's rate was 12 percent.) It also offered a regular Visa with a fixed-interest rate of 17.9 percent but only an $18 annual fee. The lower-rate and higher-fee premium card looked attractive to those who carry an unpaid balance of $288 or more. However, its variable rate could rise. Most cardholders are better off choosing the lowest annual fee they can find, even at the cost of some interest points.

Another innovation is the tiered account in which you pay one interest rate for balances up to a certain point and a lower rate for balances above that amount. For example, First American Bank in Atlanta recently offered a credit card with a 17.4 percent interest rate on balances up to $2,500 and a 14.4 percent interest on balances above that amount. Even if you carry enough credit-card debt to qualify for the eye-catching lower rate, the reduced rate applies only to balances above the $2,500 mark. You'll still pay 17.4 percent on every dollar below that amount.

Fine print. A growing number of banks impose penalties for late payment of the bill and for exceeding the credit limit, as well as transaction charges and cash-advance fees. Some fees amount to a couple of dollars; others are exorbitant. One bank charges a whopping $20 each time a cardholder exceeds his or her credit limit, as well as a 5 percent penalty (up to a $5 maximum) for late payment. Another charges 5 percent of any cash advance, with a minimum fee of $5 and a maximum of $25 per advance.

Additional fees must be disclosed to consumers, but not before they receive their cards. All too often, consumers don't realize a card issuer imposes such fees until their monthly billing statement arrives in the mail.

Thrifty Cheer for the Holidays

When November rolls around, you're apt to get a cheery offer with one or more of your credit-card statements. "Need extra cash for the holidays?" it may ask. "Because of your excellent credit standing, you're eligible to skip your December payment."

Look on such an offer as a gift—for the company issuing the credit card, that is. Should you accept, interest charges will continue to accrue on any amount you owe. And even if you usually pay your bill in full each month, you'll be charged interest on all the new purchases you make as well. At the interest rates most department stores and banks charge for their cards, skipping payment is the same as taking out a loan at 19 to 21 percent interest.

Ho, ho, ho.

Is a Debit Card a Good Idea?

Debit cards differ from credit cards in two basic ways: They take money from your checking account automatically and, usually, instantaneously, and they impose a potentially heavier financial risk on you than credit cards do if thieves happen to get hold of your card.

Debit cards do have their points. They're far more welcome than personal checks in the commercial world. They make it easier for consumers to withdraw cash from their banks through automated teller machines that are often accessible 24 hours a day.

You can also get money from your checking account at banks throughout the United States and Canada, in Europe, and, soon, in Japan. There are a couple of other advantages: The cards make it less necessary to carry cash, and you can get a card with no credit investigation at most banks, if you qualify for a checking account.

The costs. Some banks exact a fee every time you withdraw cash from an ATM. Others charge only for withdrawals through regional or national ATM networks. About 14 percent of banks charge their depositors for using their own ATMs; as of this writing, the average fee is 20 cents per withdrawal. But 69 percent of banks charge for withdrawals via regional networks, and that fee tends to be higher—an average of 75 cents. Fees for using either of the two national networks (Cirrus and Plus) tend to be higher still: 77 percent of banks charge a fee averaging $1. Check with your local bank about its ATM policies as well as for information on the national networks that offer its services.

Some banks also charge fees if you use your debit card at a store. Other things being equal, a no-fee bank obviously beats a fee-charging one. Even the best debit cards have some drawbacks, however:

- *Lost interest.* If you use a debit card, your withdrawal from your account is instantaneous. With a well-chosen credit card, however, you can wait at least 25 days and, depending on the date of a purchase, as long as 55 or 60 days to pay the bill without incurring interest. During this "float" period, your money can continue to earn interest for you in a bank account or a money-market fund.

* *Liability on stolen cards.* A debit card can be a time bomb in dishonest hands. You could lose the entire balance in your checking account—plus the maximum amount of credit available if you have an overdraft privilege on the account.

There are some safeguards. A thief needs to know your personal identification number, or PIN, in order to use the card. Don't write your PIN on your card or on any slip of paper that you carry with it. And don't choose as a PIN an obvious number—your birth date, telephone number, or social security number—that a thief might easily learn.

More important, the penalty clock doesn't start ticking until a bank statement arrives revealing unauthorized charges. Your liability during the first two days after you receive your statement is limited to $50—another good reason to review your statement as soon as it arrives each month.

Store and brokerage cards. In areas where banks market debit cards for use in stores, the same card that works in your ATM will also work at checkout counters and cashiers' booths.

A few large gasoline and supermarket chains also issue debit cards for use only in their own outlets. These systems usually give customers two days' grace before deducting the money from their bank accounts. But watch out for membership fees. Mobil, for example, was recently charging $12 a year.

Ordinary Visa or MasterCards that come with some multiservice brokerage accounts, such as Merrill Lynch's Cash Management Account, can also function as debit cards. When you charge something, the money either comes right out of your money-market account or activates a loan against your securities.

You don't need a PIN to use a broker's card in stores because your withdrawals are not instantaneous. They travel through the banking-industry clearinghouse like any credit-card transactions or personal check. So you get a day or two of interest on your money before it departs.

Save on Life Insurance: Figure Out Your Needs

There are huge differences among life insurance policies. Here's how to sort out what you need:

Estimating Insurance Needs

Don't depend on an agent to figure out how much insurance you need. Do that yourself, using the worksheet on page 176. You need to consider your family's future expenses, including child care and college costs, and your family's current assets. Don't be surprised if the calculation reveals that you may need $100,000 to $200,000 or more in life insurance coverage.

Affordable Insurance

The three basic types of life insurance are term, whole life, and universal life. For most families, term insurance provides the greatest coverage for the lowest cost. At the time of purchase and for many years afterward, term premiums are the least expensive. Whole life premiums are generally the most expensive. Premiums for universal life policies are often lower than whole life premiums but higher than term premiums.

Term premiums do rise as you get older and the cost of providing insurance protection increases, but they usually don't reach the level of whole life premiums for many years. By that time you may need relatively little insurance coverage—or perhaps none at all.

Some insurance agents know that whole life or universal life is too expensive for most people, so they often suggest a combination of term and either whole life or universal. It's best to avoid these combination plans. They're a way for the company to hook you to the "permanent" type of coverage it really wants to sell.

Term insurance is perfectly respectable. It is not "poor man's coverage," as some agents would lead you to believe.

Insurance as Savings

A life insurance policy is not a very liquid investment. You can get locked into either a universal life or a whole life policy for several years because the start-up costs of these types of policies are high.

But universal life policies appear to have better rates of return in the

Worksheet: How Much Life Insurance Do You Need?

What you need

Immediate expenses
  Federal estate taxes $_____
  State inheritance taxes   _____
  Probate costs   _____
  Funeral costs   _____
  Uninsured medical costs   _____
    Total final expenses $_____
Future expenses
  Family expense fund   _____
  Emergency fund   _____
  Child-care expenses   _____
  Education fund   _____
  Repayment of debts   _____
    Total future expenses $_____
      Total needs $_____

What you have now

Cash and savings   _____
Equity in real estate   _____
Securities   _____
IRA and Keogh plans   _____
Employer savings plans (e.g., 401[k])   _____
Lump-sum employer pension benefits   _____
Current life insurance   _____
Other assets   _____
  Total assets $_____

Extra insurance needed

(Total needs minus total assets)
Total needs $_____
Total assets $_____
  Additional insurance needed $_____

early years than whole life policies. Furthermore, a universal life policy has more flexibility. But the flexibility of its elements requires that you pay attention to all notices and statements from the insurance company so you'll know if the policy is in danger of lapsing.

Dividend-Paying Insurance

A policy that pays dividends is called *participating*. Insurance policy dividends are a partial return of the premiums you've paid. Premiums for a participating policy are generally higher than for a nonparticipating one.

If you buy term insurance, dividends are likely to be small, so it hardly matters whether the policy is participating or nonparticipating, and, practically speaking, a universal life policy is priced to pay no dividends. Therefore, the dividend issue is important mainly if you buy whole life. A participating whole life policy is likely to be a better buy than the nonparticipating variety.

Which Company?

Insurance companies do sometimes go bankrupt, but state insurance regulators usually get another company to take over the failed company's policies. Nevertheless, such a bankruptcy could cause you red tape and delay at best, reduced dividends or cash value at worst.

Unless you have independent knowledge of a company's financial condition, buy from a company rated A+ or A for financial stability by *Best's Insurance Reports*, a reference book available in many libraries.

Comparison Shopping

Ask three or four agents to present one or more policies of the type you want. Compare *interest-adjusted net cost indexes* (if it's a term or a whole life policy). The lower the index, the less costly the policy. If an agent refuses to give you the index, go to another agent.

Keep in mind that bigger doesn't necessarily mean better. Some of the best life insurance buys are from small or medium-size companies.

The Agent

If you find an agent who is attentive to your needs, explains policy details clearly, and puts your family's interests ahead of his or her commission income, you may be willing to pay a little more for a policy to keep his or her services. Service may be especially important with universal life. A good agent will contact you periodically to see whether the policy still meets your needs and whether you should consider any adjustments in premiums or in the amount of coverage.

Avoiding Unnecessary Warranties and Products

Who Needs an Extended Warranty?

Extended warranties on home appliances and electronic goods are not worth buying. Extended warranties are really insurance policies. The purpose of insurance is to protect you from financial disaster. It makes little economic sense to insure against small risks that you can, if need be, cover out of your own pocket.

According to retailers themselves, only 12 to 20 percent of people who buy a warranty ever use it. And many warranty holders who do call for service don't need repair work but simply didn't understand the instructions.

Many extended warranties also go unused because their owners move out of a retailer's area, customers' families split up, or customers simply forget they have the warranty.

Some consumers who buy a warranty find it useless if they ever do need service. Crazy Eddie, a chain that once dominated the home-electronics business in the New York metropolitan area, aggressively sold extended warranties—right up to the day it went bankrupt in June 1989. In California recently, University Stereo, FedMart Stores, and Pacific Stereo all closed their doors, leaving consumers with worthless contracts.

At least 19 independent companies supply warranties to stores around the country. In most cases, neither they nor the stores that issue their own warranties are subject to state insurance regulations. They don't have to put money aside to cover their warranty obligations should they go out of business.

Buying products with a proven record of reliability is the best way to avoid breakdowns. Every year, *Consumer Reports* surveys hundreds of thousands of readers about the repair records of goods they own and prints the results as Frequency-of-Repair records. CU believes you have the best chance of buying reliable goods if you stick to brands whose repair record has been good.

Selling It to the Elderly

Elderly people who live alone dread a fall or a sudden attack that renders them helpless, far from the phone. A spate of TV commercials and door-to-door selling preys on those fears to sell expensive emergency-response systems that are supposed to summon help quickly. By one count, some 350,000 such emergency-response devices are now in use, supplied by perhaps a dozen companies.

Some companies are using high-pressure tactics to unload merchandise. In one case, recounted by an investigator in the San Francisco district attorney's office, the salesperson reportedly used grisly details about a fictitious crime to sell some systems. In Baltimore, some 200 elderly people bought expensive but useless equipment—the seller hadn't paid the answering service responsible for monitoring calls.

According to an official at the American Association of Retired Persons (AARP), some people have paid thousands for systems embellished with smoke detectors and burglar alarms.

If you or an elderly relative wants an electronic help line, you may need no hardware at all. In some areas, the police or local social-service agencies run programs to telephone elderly individuals or people with disabilities daily. If no one answers, someone goes to the house to check on the person.

If an emergency-response system seems the best option, you may be able to rent one from a local hospital. The typical charge: $40 a month, including monitoring, plus an installation fee. Private companies also rent the equipment.

The AARP has a booklet explaining how emergency-response systems work and comparing several companies' offerings. To request a copy, write to AARP Fulfillment, 1909 K Street, N.W., Washington, DC 20049. Request publication ADN D12905, "Meeting the Need for Security and Independence."

Job-Loss Strategies

Losing a job at any time can be a frightening and painful experience. But for those who are terminated, there are steps to take to help them through the financial uncertainty that usually follows.

Early Retirement Packages

These deals are generally the same for all employees in a company's division or branch. But unless you have been with the company for many years and are past 50, early retirement packages are rarely worth considering.

Typically, the main inducement is to enhance your future pension by crediting you with, say, five extra years of employment and five extra years of age. You can usually choose to take a reduced pension immediately or wait and receive a higher one when you are older.

However, that often hardly compensates for the larger pension you might have earned by working until normal retirement age. "The bulk of a pension, as much as two-thirds, is earned in your last 10 years of employment," one expert points out.

As a sweetener, the package might include severance pay equal to several months' or even a full year's salary. The company may also offer to continue your health-insurance coverage, at regular employee rates, until you become eligible to receive Medicare benefits at age 65.

Early retirement "windows" generally close after four weeks. Although most employers don't pressure anyone into early retirement, the decision involves a dilemma: If you stay on and times get worse, you risk losing not only your job but the early retirement benefits you would have received as well.

So who should accept? People who would have retired in a couple of years anyway, those who sense that they are likely to be fired later, and, finally, those who probably can find another satisfactory job and who might do well to accept the offer of an immediate pension and invest the money for future use.

Severance Benefits

In recessions, layoffs are more likely than early retirement deals. Employees not covered by collective-bargaining agreements most often get only one week's pay for each year of service. But some companies double that formula, and a few do even better.

Under a 1985 federal law called COBRA (Consolidated Omnibus Budget Reconciliation Act), laid-off employees can continue their group health coverage at their own expense for 18 months. The premium can be no higher than 102 percent of your group insurance premium. Even so, the bill for family coverage can run as high as $600 a month.

Fortunately, many employers continue to pay fired employees' health coverage for a limited period, as a severance benefit. More than 40 percent of larger companies (those employing at least a few hundred people) provide such payments for laid-off managers, supervisors, administrators, and technicians. Nearly as many companies keep up fired employees' life insurance for a few months. Another frequent benefit for midlevel employees is job counseling by an outplacement firm.

HOW MUCH SEVERANCE TO EXPECT

Nine out of 10 companies employing at least a few hundred people pay severance to middle- and upper-level employees laid off in staff cuts. Collective-bargaining contracts often control the benefits paid to others. The percentages shown here apply to companies with formal severance policies; firms with informal policies often pay less. And remember: Severance benefits are negotiable.

Frequently used formulas	Percentage of companies applying them to:		
	Managers %	Supervisors %	Administrators and technicians %
One week's pay per year of service	36	41	42
Two weeks' pay per year	16	16	16
Three weeks' pay per year	2	2	2
One month's pay per year	8	5	5

Source: Right Associates, Philadelphia, 1990 survey.

Negotiating Better Terms

You don't have to accept the early retirement package, severance pay, or benefits your employer tries to hand you. Instead, you can hire a lawyer to negotiate a better deal. So many fired employees do so that employers began requiring people to sign a release from further obligations before receiving benefits. This action led to the passage in 1990 of a law giving employees 40 or older 45 days (21 days if you're the only employee affected by the layoff) to decide whether to sign a release and 7 days after signing to revoke it. Attorneys specializing in employees' rights report that they often succeed, under threat of litigation, in improving their clients' severance benefits.

According to one expert, people over 40 may even persuade their employer to designate a lump-sum payment as compensation for the hardship of being fired, making it free of income tax.

Unemployment Insurance

This coverage pays weekly benefits theoretically designed to replace 50 percent of your salary, but only up to maximums that vary widely from state to state and are often meager.

As a rule, you can collect only if you lose your job through no fault of your own. If you qualify, you can collect checks for 26 weeks in most states. In states where joblessness is severe, benefits may be extended to 39 weeks.

S E V E N

Traveling Smart

In bad times or good, people persist in trekking, touring, jetting, junketing, and all-around peregrination when vacation time rolls around. We've asked our colleagues at the *Consumer Reports Travel Letter* to share the best nuggets of travelwise information they've collected over the past few years. Here are tips that can save you time and money.

Airfares

Why Pay List Price?

Would you like to fly overseas at a discount of up to 30 percent? Or pay less than half an airline's asking price for an unrestricted transcontinental Coach ticket? Get your ticket through a consolidator, a little-known kind of discount travel broker.

There's nothing shady about such tickets—they're for seats that the airlines want to unload rather than let go unsold. The tickets can often be bought directly from the consolidator; otherwise, you can get them through a travel agent.

Consolidator tickets to Asia, for instance, provide the best airfare discounts you're likely to find. Tickets from the United States to Bangkok, Hong Kong, Singapore, and other major Asian cities should remain an outstanding value. At this writing, for example, you can buy a round-trip ticket from the West Coast to Hong Kong for as little as $600.

Consolidator tickets are also available to Europe and South America. The discounts are usually a bit less than for tickets to Asia, but they can still be attractive; it's easy to save $200 or more per ticket. You'll find the best consolidator deals to Europe in the summer. In winter, airlines often cut their advertised Economy excursion fares to consolidator levels (although with stiffer restrictions).

For a while now, savvy travelers to points abroad have been saving with consolidator tickets. But there's a new wrinkle: Several consolidators now sell unrestricted Coach tickets on some domestic flights. Three that we know of are RMC Travel Centre (800-344-7439), British European Travel (800-747-1476), and Unitravel (800-325-2222).

You won't necessarily save on domestic tickets—they're priced somewhat above the airlines' cheapest excursion fares—but, like the international tickets, they don't carry the airlines' usual advance-purchase and length-of-stay restrictions. The savings come in when you need a domestic ticket in a hurry (you often have to buy an airline's cheapest regular tickets weeks in advance) or when your trip won't require a Saturday night stay at your destination.

Consolidator tickets do carry some special restrictions: If your plans change, you can't switch to another airline. And refunds—if given at all—must come from the consolidator, not the airline.

For an idea of available fares, start by checking ads in Sunday travel sections. Then phone the consolidators or travel agents who advertise to ask about restrictions. If you can't find an ad, try phoning a few consolidators directly to see what's available. We suggest you ask if they accept credit cards, an important safeguard should your tickets go astray.

Many consolidators also arrange discount lodgings, especially for their air-ticket customers. Rates are usually 20 to 40 percent off a hotel's regular rate.

Become a "Frequent Flier"

You say you don't fly enough to earn a free trip through airline frequent-flier programs? Sign up anyway. There's no cost to join the program of any U.S. airline. And if you don't, you may never hear about some of the biggest bargains in domestic airfares.

Within the past year or so, several lines have offered deep, short-term fare cuts to some or all of their frequent fliers—but not to the general public. Some of those fares were one-half to one-third of the airline's cheapest published Coach excursions for coast-to-coast trips. Further, some promotions included a discounted car rental.

True, these short-term promotions come with various restrictions. But you'll find similar restrictions on much pricier tickets.

Good Deals: Short-Term Promotional Airfares

For a few years now, U.S. airlines have been offering short-term airfare deals. Those promotions help build traffic in slack periods—early winter, for example, or days in the middle of holiday periods. Typical fares for a transcontinental round trip have run $300 or less.

Short-term promotions have become, in effect, a new low-end fare, at least 25 percent below the cheapest year-round Coach excursions. Typically, you're given three to four weeks to buy tickets and up to six months to complete your travel. But sometimes you have to move fast: Some low-end tickets may be on sale for less than a month.

To take advantage of those fares, you need flexibility—willingness to travel when the airlines want you, not necessarily at the time most convenient for you. You must know where you want to go and be able to schedule your trip—and buy tickets—on relatively short notice, as soon as an attractive promotion is announced.

Short-term airfare deals aren't limited to round trips. The bargain sometimes comes as a free or low-cost companion ticket or as a dollars-off certificate that can be applied to a trip or vacation package. There's often a tie-in with some other organization's promotion—say, a supermarket chain's, a charge card's, or a bank's. Some deals may be available only through mailings to some airlines' frequent fliers.

Airlines offer promotions unpredictably. As a rule, competitors quickly match a major line's openly advertised specials but not frequent-flier, merchandise, and charge-card promotions. To keep abreast of the offers, watch for ads in big-city newspapers, and check your frequent-flier mailings and the stuffers in charge-card billings.

Deals for Seniors

Travel and entertainment companies have paid increasing attention to the older traveler in recent years. Airlines, hotels, and even some car-rental companies have introduced many ways for older travelers to save money.

- Among associations offering benefits to seniors, the American Association of Retired Persons (AARP) is largest and best known, and welcomes members as young as 50 years of age. Many travel companies extend accounts to AARP members.

• Whether you make travel arrangements yourself or use the services of a travel agency, always ask about discounts available to seniors.

It pays to grow old these days, at least if you like to travel. Many travel benefits are available to travelers who cross that golden line. Discounts offered directly by airlines, car-rental companies, and hotels may not be as good as those you can get by purchasing travel through a consolidator or other discount travel source. But senior discounts can sometimes be applied to services that have already been priced below full rate. The harm is only in *not* asking.

Senior organizations. Membership in the American Association of Retired Persons is available to anyone 50 years or older. As of this writing, it costs only $5 per year and brings many benefits, including some discounts on travel.

Several hotel chains extend discounts to AARP members. American Airlines offers discounts that are lower than the cheapest available Coach excursion fares to AARP members and their spouses (of any age). Fares cover travel on American routes within the United States (except Alaska), the Caribbean, and Mexico.

Other senior organizations also offer travel benefits to their members, including discounted travel services. The smart policy is to list the organizations you belong to when making your airline, hotel, or car-rental reservation, and ask if you're eligible for any perks.

Airfare deals for seniors. If you or your spouse are 62, you are eligible for special discounts. You can always get at least a minor price break on your plane tickets.

In the past, most airlines required seniors to join an airline "club" to get access to discounted airfares. In 1987, eight of the major lines had clubs that offered a 10 percent discount and a few other benefits. Only United still has a seniors' club. (And even United has added a senior coupon program.)

Aside from United's club (see page 192), seniors have three main discount alternatives: passes, coupons, and standard discounts. The fare to choose depends in good part on your travel needs. All require that you provide proof of age when you buy your pass, book, or ticket, and often again when you board the plane.

Continental's airline pass. As of this writing, a senior who does a great deal of traveling will find the best bet by far is Continental's fly-every-week **Freedom Passport**. For a fixed price, this pass lets you take a one-way flight (including connecting flights with no stopover) every week during a 12-month period wherever Continental flies, within certain limits. The program offers a variety of options:

CONTINENTAL'S FREEDOM PASSPORT*

Area	*Coach/Economy*	*First Class*
Domestic basic⚀	$1,799	$2,499
Add-ons (per trip):		
Mexico	150	250
Caribbean	150	250
Central America	150	250
Hawaii	300	450
Europe	400	800
South Pacific	500	900
Global⚀	3,599	5,999

*All rates are subject to change. Rates quoted as of September 1991.
⚀ For first purchase; renewals $300 less.

- The basic domestic **Freedom Passport** lets you visit each city served by Continental or Continental Express in the lower 49 states, Canada, and the U.S. Virgin Islands up to three times (arrivals and departures at your home city and connections don't count against that limit).

- You can buy up to three add-ons each for Mexico and the Caribbean and one each for Hawaii, Central America, Europe, and the South Pacific (Australia, New Zealand, or Guam).

- The Global option gives you the domestic pass plus all the add-ons. It doesn't save you any money over buying the options separately if you're traveling Coach/Economy. But it will save you $600 if you're traveling First Class.

- Domestic and international **Freedom Passport** travel is blacked out on some days.

- Within the lower 48 states, and to Canada, Hawaii, Mexico, the Caribbean, and Central America, travel is permitted noon Monday to noon Thursday, plus all day Saturday; to Europe and the South Pacific, you can fly any time Monday to Thursday plus Saturday (with exemptions on a few routes where flights operate only on Friday or Sunday). Saturday travel to or from Europe is not allowed in June, July, or August.

- Seats can be reserved no more than 7 days in advance for domestic travel and 21 days for the Caribbean, Europe, Hawaii, Mexico, and the Pacific.

- Seats for **Freedom Passport** trips are limited, and travel does not earn frequent-flier mileage. Seniors can buy a nontransferable **Companion Passport** for a spouse, friend, or relative under 62, for use only when accompanying the qualifying senior.

As of this writing, no other airlines have similar programs. Note two major caveats with the **Freedom Passport:** (1) Continental's financial position has been shaky. The airline appears to be gaining some ground under its bankruptcy restructuring program, but any purchases made today for services to be rendered in the future involve some risk. (2) Seats are limited, especially in First Class.

Coupon books. Books of four or eight coupons are now sold by all the major U.S. airlines. Each coupon is good for a single one-way trip (even if it requires connecting flights) between cities served in the lower 48 states. On some lines, nearby cities in Canada, the Caribbean, and Mexico are included. United includes San Juan and Puerto Rico. All the coupon programs share certain features. The minimum age is 62. Coupons are valid for a year. Seats allocated to senior-coupon travel are limited. And travel is blacked out on some dates.

AirCanada offers a multistop travel program, meaning that you can set up a travel itinerary of 4, 8, or 12 flights over a 3-month period for a discounted price. You do not actually purchase a coupon book. This program is available to anyone 55 or older, and a companion of any age can travel the identical itinerary with the senior for the same reduced rate. The program is subject to many restrictions and is generally offered only for travel in the autumn months.

The table on page 189 shows prices and terms for coupon offerings of the major airlines:

- *Prices.* Coupon book prices range from approximately $379 to $473 for four coupons, and $720 to $792 for eight. These prices

SENIOR COUPON PROGRAMS*

Airline	Program Name	4-Coupon Book	8-Coupon Book	Travel Days	1-Coupon Buys [1]	2-Coupon Buys
Air Canada[2]	**Freedom Flyer Multistop Ticket**	$570[3]	$680[3]	7 days	one-way flight with connection within Air Canada system	any flight with stopover
Alaska Airlines	**Senior Discount Coupon Book**	$473[3] Peak $432[3] Off-Peak	$790[3] Peak $724[3] Off-Peak	7 days T, W, Th, Sa	one-way within lower 48 or from U.S. to British Columbia	Alaska to lower 48 or British Columbia
America West	**Senior Save Pack**	$430	$720	Noon M–noon Th and all day Sa	one-way within lower 48 except coast-to-coast	one-way to or from Hawaii
American Airlines	**Senior TrAAveler Coupon Book**	$473	$791	7 days, but only Tu, W, Th to Puerto Rico	one-way within lower 48, but not Alaska	one-way to Hawaii
Continental	**Freedom Trips**	$449	$749	7 days	one-way within lower 48	one-way to or from Alaska or Hawaii
Delta	**Young-at-Heart**	$472	$792	7 days	one-way within lower 48 and Puerto Rico	one-way to or from Alaska or Hawaii
Northwest	**Senior Ultrafare Coupon Book**	$472 Peak $432 Off-Peak	$792 Peak $725 Off-Peak	7 days M, Tu, Th, Sa	one-way within lower 48	one-way to or from Alaska or Hawaii

189

SENIOR COUPON PROGRAMS*

Airline	Program Name	4-Coupon Book	8-Coupon Book	Travel Days	1-Coupon Buys [1]	2-Coupon Buys
TWA	**Senior Travel Pak**[4]	$436	$758	T, W, Th, Sa	one-way within lower 48	one-way flight of 2,000 miles or more in peak months (5/15–9/15) one-way to or from Hawaii
United	**FlightPac**[5]	$473 Peak[6] $432 Off-Peak[7]	$790 Peak[6] $725 Off-Peak[7]	7 days Tu, W, Th, Sa	one-way within lower 48	one-way to or from Alaska or Hawaii
USAir	**Senior Citizen Coupon Booklet**	$473	$790	7 days	one-way within lower 48	

*Effective September 1991. Programs and prices are subject to change.

[1] Except where indicated, flights requiring a connection require only one coupon. Stopovers require two coupons.

[2] Multistop group of fares (not a coupon book). Travel September through mid-December; 55 years of age minimum. Twelve segments available for $790, tax included. Numerous restrictions apply.

[3] Tax included.

[4] TWA **Europe Bonus** certificate available for $449 off-peak (September through June) and $649 peak (June through September). Blackouts apply.

[5] Flights taken with coupon do not earn frequent-flier mileage.

[6] Peak fare (unrestricted travel anywhere in the continental United States, San Juan, and Puerto Rico).

[7] No travel from or to San Juan, Puerto Rico, or Hawaii.

are subject to change, however. Senior discount programs are becoming another area for frequent promotion wars among the airlines.

- *Days of travel.* Some lines let you travel any day of the week (though with seat limitations). Others permit travel only on selected days. United and Northwest have two different types of coupon: peak and off-peak. The off-peak books limit travel to four days a week.

- *Mileage caps.* TWA requires two coupons each way for a trip segment of over 2,000 miles during peak-travel months (May 15 to September 15). Airlines that fly to Alaska or Hawaii require two coupons each way. America West requires two coupons for domestic travel from the West Coast to the East, or vice versa. All other airlines permit coast-to-coast travel with one coupon, unless you make a stopover en route.

- *Frequent-flier mileage.* With the exception of United, all the airlines in our survey said that flight segments flown on the senior coupons do earn frequent-flier mileage if the traveler belongs to the airline's frequent-flier program.

- *European travel.* TWA offers the **European Bonus** certificate for an additional cost ($449 for off-peak September through June, and $649 for peak travel times, June through September). While those prices are attractive from many Midwestern and Western points, they may be higher than some excursion fares from East-Coast points. As of this writing, no other major domestic airline offers a European travel coupon for seniors.

Coupons are ideal for seniors who take at least two long-haul round trips each year but do not travel enough to warrant Continental's **Freedom Passport.** The net cost of travel with senior coupons can be much lower than with the cheapest published Coach excursions. Even on shorter trips, senior coupons can be less expensive than an individual ticket (even one that has been reduced by 10 percent with a senior discount). But be sure to check the current airline policy on mileage caps before you buy. If you plan a long trip with stopovers, the double-coupon requirement could reduce or eliminate any savings.

Standard senior discounts. All major U.S. airlines offer seniors a straight 10 percent discount on domestic travel. Typically, the discounts apply to any published adult fare, from First Class to the cheapest Coach excursions.

Ordinarily, you must be at least 62 to qualify for a senior discount.

Some airlines give the same or a similar discount to a companion of any age who accompanies an eligible senior traveler. Just show proof of age when you buy your ticket.

The table on page 193 summarizes the discount offerings of the major airlines (as of July 1991). United Airlines is the only line that requires you to join an airline-sponsored senior "club" to get a senior discount. However, membership in United's **Silver Wings Plus Club** is free, and it offers additional merchandise and travel benefits publicized in the club's newsletter.

Both of Canada's major airlines, Air Canada and Canadian International, now give 10 percent discounts to seniors as well. The discounts apply year-round on flights to Canada and to the United Kingdom via Canada, and seasonally to most Caribbean points. They apply to all published fares—Economy excursions through First Class. There are no restrictions other than those that apply to the prediscounted fare. Both lines also give a 10 percent discount to a senior's companion of any age who travels on an identical itinerary and uses the same fare class.

Most lines treat discounted senior tickets as ordinary tickets. They normally earn frequent-flier credit, and frequent-flier upgrades can be used. However, senior discounts often do not apply to short-term promotional fares offered through frequent-flier programs or to joint promotions with merchants. The discount is sometimes applicable to promotional fares offered directly by American, Continental (except on published senior fares), Northwest, Air Canada, America West (except 21-day advance purchase, nonrefundable fares), Delta, and USAir. Only United limits discounts exclusively to full-fare coach tickets.

Senior discounts are also available for travel to many overseas destinations, including much of Western Europe. The standard formula applies on most routes: 10 percent off for travelers 62 or over.

The typical 10 percent senior discount is much smaller than discounts available through coupons and, for many overseas trips, through a consolidator. But even 10 percent is better than no discount. You can also get an extra 5 to 8 percent off by buying your senior ticket through an agency that rebates a portion of the commission.

Discounts on rental cars. Some car-rental companies also extend discounts to seniors, although most go to those who are members of AARP.

- Alamo Rental Car is aggressively courting the mature market. The company offers *Golden Wheels* discounts to customers 62 or older

AIRFARE DISCOUNTS FOR SENIORS*

Airline	Minimum Age	Percent Airfare Discount	Companion Discount	Available All Fares?	System Pass Available?	Seniors Club
Air Canada ②	62	10	Yes	①②	No	No
Alaska Airlines	62	10	No	②	No	No
America West	62	10	Yes	③	No	No
American Airlines	62	10	Yes	Yes ④	No	Yes ⑤
Canadian Intl.	62	10	Yes	①②	No	No
Continental	62	10	Yes	⑥	Yes	No
Delta	62	10	Yes	④	No	No
Northwest	62	10	Yes	②⑦⑧	No	Yes ⑨
TWA	62	10	Yes	②	No	No
United	62	10	⑩	④	No	Yes ⑪
USAir	62	10	Yes	⑦	No	No

*Effective September 1991. Programs and prices are subject to change.
① Applies year-round on flights to Canada and to United Kingdom via Canada, seasonally to most Caribbean points.
② Applies to all published fares.
③ Some variation by market. In Southwestern states offer senior promotional rates. When discount applies, it applies to all except 21-day advance purchase.
④ Some promotional fares excluded.
⑤ However, new memberships are not being accepted.
⑥ Except published senior citizen fares.
⑦ Some special fares excluded. Check with airline for current restrictions.
⑧ Applies year-round to published fares to travel to U.S. destinations, including Alaska and Hawaii, and to Canada, Netherlands, United Kingdom and Germany.
⑨ **World Perk Seniors Club.**
⑩ Only on occasion, on special rates.
⑪ **Silver Wings Club.**

who book rentals through a travel agent or tour operator. Alamo also offers some varying discounts to customers 60 years of age or older who rent directly.

- Avis, Budget, Dollar, General, Hertz, and Thrifty offer discounts ranging from 5 to 10 percent to members of AARP. Dollar offers its own senior discounts, which vary depending on the rental contract.
- American International and Enterprise offered no discounts for seniors when we contacted them in July 1991.

Discounts on rail. Most rail systems offer discounted fares for seniors. In the United States, Amtrak extends discounts on some of its Coach fares to travelers 65 and over. In Canada, VIA Rail offers travelers 60 and over a 10 percent discount that can be compounded with off-peak travel discounts, for total savings of up to 50 percent. European railroads offer senior discounts ranging from 25 to 50 percent off standard point-to-point fares.

Over 50? Save money at hotels. Budget-conscious senior travelers hardly ever need to pay list price for a hotel room. In addition to half-price clubs, there are other options. Some national chains, as well as individual hotels, offer discount programs targeted to the older customer. So do senior organizations such as AARP. Older travelers can even get discounts for the asking at many hostelries. The trick is to find the best deal for the time you are traveling.

The table on page 195 summarizes the discount policies and programs of many of the big chains operating in the United States and Canada as of October 1991. (Discounts are usually the same in a chain's overseas locations, if any.)

Deals for any senior. The simplest hotel discounts are based on a senior's age. To qualify, you just present identification that shows you are over the minimum age (50 to 65, depending on the hotel). With many chains, the age-based discount is as good as any other you are apt to find. Often, a standard fixed discount is given at all hotels in a chain, but sometimes the availability and amount of discount vary from hotel to hotel or by season.

Over the last few years, more and more hotels have added senior discounts to their marketing mix. Today, several chains give seniors up to 50 percent off room rates. Discounts that deep are based on sophisticated yield-management pricing. They are usually on a "space-available" basis, so they may be tougher to find than more modest discounts. Furthermore, the big discounts may not apply to minimum-rate rooms.

Several chains require seniors to reserve in advance to get a discount. Howard Johnson and the seven chains in the Choice group offer a higher discount for advance reservations than for walk-in bookings.

SENIOR HOTEL DISCOUNTS*

Hotel/Resorts	Any Senior		AARP Percent Discount	Hotel Senior Club	
	Minimum Age	Percent Discount		Minimum Age	Percent Discount
Aston	—	—	—	55	20 [1][2][3][4]
Best Western	55	10	10	—	—
Budgetel Inns	[5]	4–10	4–10	—	—
Choice [6][7] Prime Time, Prime Time Senior Saver	60	10 / 30 [3][8]	10 / 30 [3][8]	—	—
Colony [7]	60	20	25	[9]	[9]
Courtyard by Marriott [7]	62	15	15 [3][8]	—	—
Days Inns [7]	—	—	10	50	15–40 [2]
Doubletree	60	15–50	15–50 [3]	—	—
Fairfield Inn [8]	62	10	15	—	—
Hampton Inn	—	—	—	50	[2][10]
Hilton (U.S.)	—	—	10–15	60	25–50 [3]
Holiday Inn	55	[5]	10	[11]	20
Howard Johnson	60	15 / 30 [3][8]	15 / 30 [3][8]	—	—
Hyatt [12]	62	25	25	—	—
Journey's End	55 [13]	10 [8][17]	10 [8][17]	—	—
La Quinta	55	10	10	60	20
Marriott	—	—	10 [3] / 50 [14]	—	—
Master Hosts [15]	[6]	10–15	10–15	—	—
Outrigger	50	20 [3][9][16]	20 [3][9][16]	—	—
Radisson	62	[5]	[5]	—	—
Ramada	60	25	25	—	—
Red Lion [17]	—	—	20 [3]	—	—
Red Roof Inns [6]	—	—	—	60	10 [2]
Residence Inns	62	15	15	—	—

(Continued)

SENIOR HOTEL DISCOUNTS* (*Continued*)

Hotel/Resorts	Any Senior		AARP Percent Discount	Hotel Senior Club	
	Minimum Age	Percent Discount		Minimum Age	Percent Discount
Sheraton	60	25 [3][18]	25 [3][18][19]	—	—
Shoney's Inn	—	—	10–15 [3]	50	15–20 [2][10]
Stouffer Hotels	60	10–50 [3]	[3][5]	—	—
Travelodge	50	15 [6]	15 [6]	50	15 [6]
Vagabond Inns	50	10 [5]	10 [5]	55	10 + [5]
Westin	[5]	10–50 [3]	[3][5]	—	—

*Effective October 1991; subject to change.
Note: Except as noted, senior discounts available only at participating locations. Unless otherwise indicated, discount available on minimum-rate rooms. Advance reservations required for discount only where shown. Where discount column shows a range of values, discount varies by location or season.
[1] But 15–32% at 2 Molokai hotels.
[2] On-the-spot enrollment available.
[3] Requires advance reservation.
[4] Free economy rental car at all properties except Molokai, Mexico, San Francisco.
[5] Varies by location.
[6] Discount available at all locations.
[7] Includes Clarion, Comfort, Econo Lodge, Friendship, Quality, Rodeway, Sleep Inns/hotels, suites/ resorts.
[8] Subject to availability.
[9] Club to be launched Spring 1992. Call Colony for details.
[10] Up to 4 persons can share room at the single rate.
[11] Varies by membership requirement in participating seniors' organizations.
[12] United States, Canada, Caribbean, and Guadalajara (Mexico) only.
[13] At Canadian locations 60 years of age (CAPR or other identification required).
[14] Applies to 21-day, nonrefundable advance purchases.
[15] Includes Red Carpet and Scottish Inn.
[16] Cannot be combined with any other discount; subject to change without notice.
[17] Sears Mature Outlook members also get 20% discount.
[18] Discounts not available on minimum-rate rooms.
[19] Also offered to NRTA and NARP members.

All listed chains have toll-free national reservations numbers. But you'll often have a better choice of discount options—promotional deals as well as senior offers—if you reserve directly with each hotel.

Senior organizations. Membership in AARP is probably the easiest and best way to qualify for hotel discounts. Several other senior organizations offer similar programs, but AARP membership is very inexpensive (currently $5 per year) and its program very broad.

- You can get AARP hotel discounts at age 50. That is 5 to 15 years younger than the typical minimum for age-based discounts.
- Several hotel chains offer senior discounts only to members of AARP (or other senior organizations).
- None of the discounts that hotels offer to seniors solely on the basis of age was any better than AARP rates. Only members of a few of the hotel-sponsored senior clubs earn better discounts than AARP members.

Hotel programs. Several chains run their own "clubs" for seniors. Some clubs are free; others charge a one-shot fee of $10 to $50 a year. Travelers who use the sponsoring hotels extensively may find their programs a bit more useful than AARP:

- Aston and Red Roof offer senior discounts only through their own programs.
- The senior-club programs at Days Inn, Hilton, La Quinta, and Shoney's are more generous than AARP or straight age-based discounts.
- Hotel-sponsored programs usually offer minor extras, such as small discounts at hotel restaurants and shops.

With most chains, you can join the program on the spot and get the senior discount the first time you check in at a participating hotel. But Hilton, La Quinta, and Travelodge give you the discount only after you receive your membership card. If you plan to use any of those programs, enroll at least six weeks before your trip.

Some Good Airline Values

Here are some outstanding values for tight-money times—some cheaper than competitors, others better:

- *Midwest Express.* This tiny airline is the only one that provides acceptable comfort for a traveler on any Coach ticket, including the cheapest excursion. It flies from a Milwaukee hub to major cities in the Midwest and on the East and West coasts. Its all-Coach DC9 fleet is outfitted with four-across seating, typical of First Class on other lines. You're never stuffed into a middle seat, and you have adequate seat space even in a full plane. The line also features premium meal service. However small its present market, this niche carrier is a welcome exception to the sameness of most U.S. Coach air travel. If you want a comfortable trip at an affordable price, look for the improbable *YX* airline identifier in the *Official Airline Guide* or a reservations computer.

- *Southwest.* This one small low-fare airline has forced the industry giants to hold the price line in much of the United States. When Southwest moves into a new route, fares drop; when it leaves, they go up again. True, Southwest's planes are crowded and there's no meal service. But cost-conscious travelers owe this line a debt of gratitude—best expressed at the ticket counter.

- *Martinair.* Last year, this big Dutch charter line introduced **Star Class** on most flights from the United States to Amsterdam—you get the equivalent of major-line Business Class for less than half the major-line Business Class fare. We've heard good reports on Martinair's Economy service in 767s as well.

- *For skyborne comfort.* You can usually increase your odds on a comfortable Coach/Economy trip by selecting an airplane with wider-than-average seats and a below-average number of middle seats. By both measures, the **Boeing 767** earns top rating—seats are 20 inches wide, and there's only one middle seat in each row of seven.

  Among the narrow-body planes, the 20-inch seats installed in most **MD80s** are noticeably roomier than the 19-inch seats in 727s, 737s, and 757s. The MD80s also have only one middle seat per row of five, rather than two in each row of six seats, as you find in the narrow-body Boeings. While the new **A320** shares the Boeing's undesirable six-across arrangement, its wider body permits the use of 20-inch seats. Of course, the legroom you get is still up to each airline.

Arranging Elbow Room

Seating in the Coach section of airplanes is getting tighter and tighter. You'll be a lot more comfortable if you're not jammed into a filled row.

If the discomfort tempts you to consider a pricey Business Class or First Class ticket and you're traveling as a couple, try this money-saving ploy instead: Book a window and an aisle seat in a three-seat row. When single travelers buy a ticket, airline computers assign a window or an aisle seat first. Since center seats are sold only when all others are taken, you and your companion are apt to have the row to yourself and a lot of extra room. If the plane fills up, you can always offer to swap a seat with the traveler in the middle seat.

Act as a Courier, Save on Airfare?

It's possible to travel cheaply by acting as a courier for an international delivery service. But be aware that courier flights aren't suitable for most travelers, and trips to the most popular destinations are often hard to get. Still, for a few travelers, a courier flight can cut several hundred dollars off the cost of a typical ticket. Be wary of scams: Some ads for courier flights bait and switch; some promoters collect a "listing" fee but never get you a flight. Legitimate courier services have plenty of candidates, all screened before assignment. If you're interested, here are two newsletters that regularly publish listings of available trips, fares, and information on how to sign on as a courier: *Travel Secrets,* Box 2325, New York, NY 10108 (monthly, approximately $30 per year); and *Travel Unlimited,* Box 1058, Allston, MA 02134 (monthly, approximately $20 per year).

Other Ways to Travel and Save

Ferries

Ferryboats generally offer a seductive combination of transportation and spectacular vistas. New York's Staten Island ferry is still the best 50-cent ride in the country. And, at 15 cents, the Hong Kong *Star Ferry* ride may be the world's best value in short scenic trips. Whenever you're in a coastal or river city, from Sydney Harbor to Venice to London, chances are there's an inexpensive ferry trip that will take you somewhere interesting—and provide great views along the way.

Transit Passes

Subways, streetcars, and buses may be more prosaic than ferries, but they cover a lot more territory. Transit systems in many of the world's

major cities offer one-to-three-day travel-all-you-want passes, usually a
good deal for visitors who want to make the most of a few days in town.
Whenever you arrive in a new city, ask about a transit pass—it almost
always saves money and is also a great convenience.

Metroliner

If you're traveling from New York to Washington (or anywhere in
between), ignore the strident claims of the jet shuttle, which is grossly
overpriced. Amtrak's high-speed **Metroliner** trains will convey you
almost as quickly door-to-door for about $79, a bit over half the price
(less than half if you use taxis to and from the New York airports). Moreover, the **Metroliner** offers a much more comfortable trip—and lets you
laugh at air-traffic delays.

Renting Cars

Do You Need Extra Car-Rental Insurance?

Ads blare a car's base rental price—so much per day, so much per week,
perhaps "unlimited" mileage. But zingers are tucked away in the fine
print as extra charges for insurance. Depending on what other coverage
you have, there's a good chance you can rent a car safely at the come-
on, base price.

There are two sorts of coverage, for collision and liability.

Collision. Covers damage to or theft of the car you've rented—plus,
possibly, rental charges for the period the car is out of service. Rental
companies are only too glad to sell you a waiver of their right to collect
collision damages from you, variously called "collision damage waiver"
(CDW) and "loss damage waiver" (LDW). But, at typical charges of $9
to $14 a day, CDW/LDW is an increasingly bad buy.

Most American drivers are at least partially protected against paying
for rental-car damage or theft under the *liability* coverage of their regular auto insurance. True, the coverage may be limited—most policies
apply only to rentals within the United States, and many have a dollar
ceiling. In addition, some limit coverage to cars rented while your own
car is being repaired.

However, many major charge cards provide no-extra-cost protection
against collision damage to a car rented with the card. Most American
Express cards and some basic versions of MasterCard and Visa cover you

for collision damage up to the full value of the car; Diners Club covers up to $25,000. All premium MasterCard and Visa cards provide collision protection.

Most charge-card coverage is *secondary*, paying only what's owed after you've collected from your own insurance. Diners Club and some premium MasterCards provide *primary* coverage; you needn't make a claim against your own insurance. Since typical auto insurance doesn't cover collision damage on rentals outside the United States, charge-card coverage on foreign rentals is, in effect, primary.

If you decide to rely on charge-card coverage, simply decline the CDW/LDW option. You don't have to ask a car-rental agent whether the company "accepts the CDW the charge card provides." The car-rental company has no say in the matter. But you may have to assume temporary responsibility for damage, pending reimbursement from your own insurance or the charge card. About the only valid reason to buy CDW/LDW is if you're unwilling or unable to carry a large short-term damage payment, assessed on your charge card, until your own insurance or the charge card reimburses you, or if you are traveling in New Zealand, where the government allows car-rental companies to require CDW/LDW on all rentals, regardless of whether the driver has other protection.

Be aware that some companies place a "hold" against your credit card if you don't buy collision protection, often for several thousand dollars, occasionally for the full value of the car. Such a hold could immobilize your credit card for other purposes.

Liability. Coverage is the other consideration with rental cars. It covers "third-party" damage to persons or property (including other cars) that a driver's car hits. But many people already have at least some protection from two sources. If you own a car, your own automobile liability insurance almost always covers you when you're driving a rented car—if you're not sure, ask your agent. And in most parts of the world, car-rental companies are required by law to carry liability insurance.

The amount of liability insurance required on a rental car varies widely among the U.S. states and country by country. The $10,000 minimum in several states is barely enough to cover damage to another car in a moderately severe accident, let alone the huge settlements that may be awarded in personal-injury cases.

At this time, the major car-rental companies provide only the minimum liability insurance required by state law. The companies' insurance is primary—damages are paid entirely out of that coverage, up to the policy's limits. But if a judgment is higher, the claimant (or the car-rental company, if it's defending the suit) can go after you (through your auto insurance policy) for the difference.

Some car-rental companies sell additional liability coverage at a daily rate. There's no reason to buy it. The liability insurance you need depends on your financial position, not the car you're driving. You'd hardly need more liability insurance for a rented car than for your own car.

About the only travelers who need special liability coverage are those who don't usually drive at home and therefore carry *no* auto insurance. If you don't have year-round insurance and plan to drive for a while, contact an insurance agency to buy protection for that period.

Scouting Out Cheap Car Rentals

These days, it's easy to find the cheapest base car-rental rates for anywhere you're heading. Airline-sponsored reservations computers make comparison shopping easy, with displays of three rate options for all major rental companies: a weekly "touring" rate, a "weekend" rate (often good for up to four days), and a daily rate (usually relatively high).

You're apt to be eligible for some sort of discount—through a charge-card program, a frequent-flier program, a travel club, or your employer. But the "big" discounts (up to 30 percent) those sources promote are almost always confined to the pricey daily rates—you're lucky to get 10 percent off on weekly and weekend rates.

It doesn't pay to spend too much time chasing rental-car discounts: Prices available to members of local American Automobile Association (AAA) affiliates are usually as good as—and often better than—those available through travel-club, frequent-flier, or corporate programs.

Mileage charges make the major pricing difference among car-rental companies. Currently, the industry is swinging toward "unlimited" mileage. But some companies still limit you to a set mileage, with per-mile charges added after that; the mileage caps may vary from 70 to 150 miles per day (usually depending on location).

Unlimited mileage isn't always your best deal. If you're using a rented car mainly for local errands in your destination area, a low daily or weekly rate with 100 or 150 "free" miles per day may be cheaper than a competitor's unlimited-mileage rate. You have to estimate how far you're going to drive on each rental and compare alternatives.

A mileage cap isn't the only variable to consider when comparing car-rental costs. You may have to call the car-rental company to ask about other charges, often hidden or unexpected:

- Some companies charge up to $5 a day for each additional driver; others charge nothing. If more than one person in your party plans to drive, include extra-driver charges in your cost comparison. Spouses are usually covered at no extra charge.
- Some of the lowest rates require you to return the car to the rental station or city at which it was rented. Others let you return a car anywhere within a state or urban area at no additional cost.
- Some rates require that you drive only within the state in which you rent the car, or within the state and a few adjacent ones. Be sure your rate is valid for *all* states in which you plan to drive.
- Most weekend rates and some weekly rates require you to return the car on or before the day specified.

There are teeth to most of these conditions: If you don't fulfill them completely, your entire rental can revert to a much higher daily rate plus mileage. Thus, if you rent a car on a weekend rate and want to keep it an extra day, you may have to turn the car in at the end of the weekend and *rerent* it for the additional day at the daily rate. Some weekly rates, on the other hand, let you extend a rental at a prorated cost without rerenting, a point to check if you aren't sure how long you'll need a car.

Don't gamble that a car-rental company won't detect violations of extra-driver or territorial restrictions. Should you need mechanical service or be involved in an accident when driving in violation of the contract, you could face huge towing and servicing charges.

Best Car-Rental Deal: U.S. Weekend Rates

It isn't easy to find an appealing car-rental deal. Prices—especially for weekly "touring" rates—are fairly consistent among the major companies. But the car-rental industry is strongly geared to business travel in most areas, so the rental companies usually have lots of cars idle over weekends. They'll rent you one with unlimited mileage, starting at about $20 a day (plus taxes and such extras as additional-driver charges and insurance, if you're careless enough to buy it) during those slow days. Depending on location, a "weekend" may start as early as Thursday and last into Monday.

Caution: With a weekend rental, you have to get the car back before weekend rates expire or the entire rental will revert to a much higher weekday rate. If you want to keep a car an extra day, turn it in and rerent it. And, of course, don't look for weekend deals in those few places where weekend demand exceeds weekday demand—in New York City and a few vacation areas, for instance.

Rooms and Lodging

Coupons for Half-Price Hotel Rooms

There are several coupon books you can buy that can save you a bundle on lodgings when you travel. For example, the 1991 edition of *Travel America at Half Price* ($32.95) contains coupons good for 50-percent discounts at more than 1,000 U.S. hotels. The 1992 edition of *Half Price European Directory* has similar coupons for 500 hotels, most in Western Europe but a few in Turkey, Cyprus, Egypt, and Malta. Both books also contain coupons for discounts on meals, attractions, and the like. For a trip of more than a few days, both should repay your investment well.

In general, to get a half-price room in the United States, you phone a listed hotel directly—not its toll-free reservation number. For lodgings abroad, you can reserve half-price rooms in two chains through a U.S. reservations office (Sheraton: 800-325-3535; Occidental, for certain hotels in Spain and Portugal: 800-332-4872; 212-838-3322 in New York City). With the other overseas hotels, you reserve through a European reservations office or directly with each hotel. When you reserve, identify yourself as a user of the coupon book.

Note that all rooms are on a "space available" basis—the discounts will be given only when a hotel doesn't expect to be full. The discounts may not be given on a hotel's cheapest rooms, and they may be blacked out in a hotel's busiest periods. Don't buy one of these books if you want a deal at one or two specific hotels for one or two specific dates. But if you can be flexible in your vacation plans, both programs can provide good bargains.

Half Price European Directory and *Travel America at Half Price* (national directory version) are available from Entertainment Publications, 2125 Butterfield Rd., Troy, MI 48084 (800-521-9640; 313-637-8400 in Michigan).

The American Budget Motel

That's your best all-around list-price lodging deal. Travelers along the main U.S. highways can enjoy a spacious, modern room—typically with two queen beds or a king and a well-equipped bath—and free on-site parking. You get far more for your money than in any other class of accommodation we know of, anywhere in the world.

In addition to a serviceable room, almost all budgets now offer the usual basics: phone, color TV, and pool. Many add such inducements as free local phone calls, cable TV, in-room refrigerators, in-room VCRs, and free morning coffee or continental breakfast. You don't get large, opulent lobbies, meeting rooms, room service, an on-site restaurant, or help with your baggage—but who needs them?

Inexpensive Lodgings

The college dorm. If you're looking for a cheap room, you can often take advantage of summer "off-season" rates at college dorms. Here are two excellent references:

- Peterson's *Directory of College Accommodations* by Jay Norman, Peterson's Guides, Princeton, NJ, 1989; $9.95 in bookstores. Lists 175 colleges in the United States and Canada that accept paying guests in summer. Brief description of colleges and surroundings, plus booking and price information.
- *U.S. and Worldwide Travel Accommodations Guide,* Campus Travel Service, P.O. Box 8355, Newport Beach, CA 92660, $13 including postage. Lists 650 colleges and universities in 25 countries (about 350 in the United States), with tables of prices, dates of availability, booking and price information, brief summary of activities.

Some colleges offer more than dorm rooms. Bentley College (outside Boston) promotes "Summer Suites" early June to mid-August—3-bedroom (5 twin beds) apartments with air-conditioned living room, dining area, kitchen, and bath, $72 daily (two-night minimum) for two people (minimum); children 17 and under stay free; each additional adult pays $15 per night. Advance reservations required (MasterCard, Visa). (You can arrange with the telephone company for a phone hookup.) Bentley College Summer Suites, Conferencing and Special Events, 175 Forest Street, Waltham, MA 02154-4705; 800-292-8782 (617-891-2292 in Massachusetts).

Campus Holidays USA has a voucher program for campus accommodations as well as budget hotels in North America and the United Kingdom. Campus lodgings (dorm rooms, shared baths) are available only during school holidays, hotels year round. You buy a book of 7

($91) or 21 vouchers ($252) and receive a directory; you reserve your room directly and pay with 1 voucher per person per night. Most accommodations require a cash supplement (examples: $23 for two at San Francisco State University, $36.40 for two at Howard Johnson's in Miami, $14 for a single dorm room at a Kings College residence hall in southeast London). At present, there are 32 locations in the United States, 10 in Canada, and 10 in the United Kingdom. Campus Holidays USA, 242 Bellevue Avenue, Upper Montclair, NJ 07043; 201-744-8724, FAX 201-744-0531 (American Express, MasterCard, Visa, Discover).

Price-Wise Holiday Ideas

Here's a selection of pleasant vacation ideas for value-conscious travelers:

- *U.S. big-city weekend.* In major U.S. cities, hotels that cater mainly to business travelers actively court leisure travelers to fill rooms on Friday and Saturday nights. Many offer a combination of reduced rates and tickets to some local event. Several big chains offer standardized, nationwide package deals; individual hotels often put their own programs together. Decide on a city and start calling for deals.

- *U.S. festivals.* You needn't travel to Europe to enjoy a great music or drama festival; the home-grown product can give you far more for your money. The Ashland (Oregon) Shakespeare festival and Santa Fe Opera festival, for example, provide wonderful entertainment experiences in charming settings. So do Marlboro, Saratoga, Tanglewood, and dozens of other summer programs across the United States. Cut room costs by staying at a budget motel (see page 205).

- *Major universities.* At just about any major U.S. university you'll find multiple athletic, cultural, and entertainment events every day during the school year—often of surprisingly high quality. University towns usually offer a reasonable range of budget accommodations and an eclectic selection of inexpensive restaurants, too.

- *U.S. national parks.* The U.S. national parks present—and preserve—some of the world's true scenic wonders. If you're willing to accept accommodations that are a bit dated and a bit basic, you can't beat the immediacy of staying in an in-park concession, but those rooms are limited and sell out early. You'll find a wealth of other lodging options, including half-price and budget choices, in the gateway communities that abut most major parks. Perhaps the best value of all is the $25 **Golden Eagle Pass,** which allows a full car of visitors into all parks for a year; buy it at the gate of the first park you enter in the year.

- *Ski area off-season.* Whether it's Aspen or the Alps, you can usually find very attractive off-season hotel and condo prices in ski areas. Some ski areas actively promote summer programs (such as the Aspen Music Festival) to beef up summer occupancy. Others just let the mountain scenery do the job.

- *No dice at the casino.* Hotel and restaurant prices in Atlantic City, Las Vegas, Laughlin (Nevada), Reno, and Tahoe are designed to lure you to the gaming tables. If you can resist that lure—or gamble only enough to qualify for a tour package—you can take advantage of some attractive rates, while enjoying plenty of entertainment options and opportunities to observe a major indoor spectacle in a glitzy atmosphere. The cheapest packages are usually bus tours that originate in nearby major cities—Los Angeles, New York, or San Francisco (local newspapers give details). But you can also find good rates for individually booked hotel accommodations, especially during midweek.

- *Three value cities.* Vancouver is our Canadian choice, for its hospitality, cosmopolitan ambiance, scenic setting, mild year-round climate, and reasonable hotel and restaurant prices. For good value in Asia, it's hard to beat Hong Kong. It offers a unique combination of a warm welcome, Asian bustle, and good-value hotels. In Europe, Budapest remains our first value choice, especially for its affordable dining and cultural events.

Money Matters

Foreign-Currency Traveler's Checks

Problem: You arrive abroad with dollar-denominated traveler's checks when banks are closed. You need cash. Bad solutions: You change checks at a nonbank exchange office, where you lose up to 10 percent to steep fees and adverse exchange rates. Or you cash checks at a hotel, restaurant, or store, where your loss can run twice as high.

There's a better answer. Buy some traveler's checks in foreign currency and you'll lose nothing: Just about any hotel, restaurant, railroad ticket office, gas station, or even corner grocery will take the checks at face value. (But don't overbuy—you'll lose a bit when you exchange left-over checks back into dollars when you return home.)

Banks with foreign-exchange offices sell the checks. But now so do travel agents, through two airline-sponsored reservation systems such as PARS and System One. The agent takes your money and a fee.

To compare costs, "Consumer Reports Travel Letter" bought checks in 1990, in a number of currencies, in amounts worth exactly $500. The checks were bought through American Express, an airport Bank of America office, and the two airline systems.

In general, holders of **American Express** cards would have done best. Platinum-card holders would have paid about $512 to $516 for checks in Canadian, British, French, German, or Japanese currency; green-card holders, who pay a 1 percent service charge, would have paid about $5 more. Those costs are almost exactly what it would have cost to convert cash or U.S. traveler's checks to foreign currency at a bank after arriving abroad.

For virtually every currency, PARS was the most expensive (by as much as about $28, in the case of checks in Japanese yen). System One was cheaper than the airport bank for some currencies, more expensive for others.

Using Plastic

Overall, however, you may well do best by putting as many foreign purchases as possible on a charge card. You get the best rate and pay little or no fee. Foreign-currency checks are a good idea mainly when:

- You know you'll arrive in a foreign country at a time when exchange offices are closed.
- You don't want to carry a lot of foreign cash, you don't want the bother of exchanging U.S. traveler's checks at a bank every day or so, *and* you don't want to charge purchases.
- You want to lock in the exchange rate at the time you buy checks.

Use Your Bank Card Overseas

When you convert dollars to foreign currency, steep fees and bad exchange rates can cost you more than 10 percent of your transaction.

But in many countries, you can now sidestep such expenses. If your automatic teller machine (ATM) card works in the **Cirrus** or **Plus** network at home, you can use it abroad to withdraw cash from foreign-bank ATMs that belong to the same network. Your withdrawal will be converted at the *interbank exchange rate*—the "wholesale" rate that banks use for large-scale financial transactions.

That's quite an advantage. If you exchange currency or traveler's checks at a bank exchange counter, you'll get a *retail* rate that is often 3 to 5 percent less favorable. At many banks, an additional fee—per transaction, per check, or a percentage of the transaction—can add another 2 to 5 percent to your cost. The expense can be even worse if you exchange at hotels and nonbank exchange counters when banks are closed.

Overseas, **Cirrus** and **Plus** work exactly as ATMs work at home. At a foreign ATM, punch up your personal identification number (PIN) and the amount of a withdrawal (in local currency). The machine issues the currency, and your home account is debited automatically. Both systems always give you the interbank rate; the foreign bank imposes no fees. The only possible extra is a per-use fee your bank may impose for using an ATM elsewhere on the network.

As do ATMs at home, most foreign ATMs operate 24 hours a day. You need never wait until the banks open to get an acceptable exchange rate. And, as at home, a maximum daily withdrawal limit protects you if your card is stolen.

Both **Cirrus** and **Plus** ATMs abroad are being programmed to provide instructions in English as well as one or more local languages. Despite some early technical snags, both systems are now building foreign networks quickly. **Cirrus** and **Plus** already have thousands of locations in Canada, Mexico, Europe, and Asia. By now, **Plus** may have opened planned locations in South America, too.

Both networks provide worldwide directories. You can get a worldwide **Plus** directory from your bank (call the **Plus** home office, 303-573-7587, if your bank can't get you one). **Plus** hopes to handle requests for directories through its toll-free line soon (800-843-7587). **Cirrus** overseas directories are also available from U.S. member banks.

On August 20, 1990, **Cirrus** and **Plus** announced that holders of an ATM card in either system would be able to use both systems' machines. The only foreign country in which cards are currently interchangeable is Mexico (at Banco Nacional ATMs), but Hong Kong, the Philippines, Singapore, Spain, Thailand, and Venezuela will be added as soon as banks in these countries activate the **Cirrus** system. You may have to have your PIN changed before you can use your card overseas—check with your bank before you leave on a trip.

If your present bank or credit union isn't affiliated with the network offering ATM locations in the countries you visit most frequently, consider opening a new account with one that is. If you plan to use the system extensively, it pays to shop around for the local bank with the lowest per-use ATM charge.

Using your ATM card to buy pounds, say, might save you 7 to 8 percent over currency. You'll save less in countries such as Japan, where the government limits bank fees and charges on foreign exchange. Even so, you're almost always better off with the ATM system than at a bank counter.

Of course, you can still get foreign currency abroad through ATM networks with a charge card. Such a transaction is treated as a cash advance. Individual card-issuing institutions vary in their treatment of such advances:

- Many charge interest from the date of a cash advance until you pay your bill. (Of course, charge-card advances treated as loans don't debit your checking account until you pay the bill, either, but they're counted against your card's credit limit.)
- Some charge either a percentage of the advance (up to 3 percent) or a per-transaction fee on foreign cash advances.

Either treatment adds to your cost: A foreign-currency withdrawal almost always costs more with a charge card than with an ATM card.

It's still too early to rely on ATMs for all your foreign-exchange needs. Even in countries where **Cirrus** and **Plus** have substantial local networks, you may not always be able to find a participating ATM, and your card may not work at all locations. A few traveler's checks are still a good idea for most trips.

Also, the ATM's cost advantage is limited to hard-currency countries (including Western Europe and many Asian/Pacific countries). In countries with official (or tolerated) two-tier exchange rates you're often better off exchanging U.S. currency or traveler's checks at a tourist rate than having a bank make the exchange at an official rate.

Overall, then, in hard-currency countries, you'll usually minimize your foreign-exchange costs if you follow these guidelines:

- Use a charge card for major expenditures—tickets, hotels, rental cars, and the like. You get a decent exchange rate, the protection

of the card's chargeback provisions, and (often) an extra guarantee on your purchases.

- Wherever possible, use an ATM card for incidental cash.
- As a backup, carry a small amount of money in traveler's checks—
preferably foreign-currency checks.

Cheap Calls Home

Why pay top dollar for calls to the United States from abroad? AT&T
offers **USA Direct,** a service available in many countries in Europe, the
Pacific, and Latin America. In most cases, a local or toll-free call from
any phone in the foreign country connects you directly with an AT&T
operator in the United States. You then place your call and bill it to your
calling card or your home phone. Rates can be up to 40 percent higher
than local carriers, but they are not marked up with surcharges—up to
200 percent—that foreign hotels often add to international calls billed
to your room. Unfortunately, some foreign hotels are blocking access
from room phones to **USA Direct.** If you run into that problem, call
from the nearest public pay phone.

Call **USA Direct** at 800-874-4000 (before you leave) for more information and a plastic card listing the toll-free access numbers abroad.
MCI offers a similar service from many of the same areas (call 800-444-
4444).

Cutting the Cost of Shopping Abroad

Buying a big-ticket item overseas? You can typically save 6 to 25 percent
if you trim the tax-collector's take. Here's how.

Many of the world's advanced nations raise revenue with VAT, the
value-added tax. It's something like a sales tax, but it's concealed in the
price of goods and services. It can range from just a few percent to as
high as 28 percent (the equivalent of 39 percent of the retail purchase
price). Many countries allow foreigners to avoid paying some or all of
the VAT.

The VAT reduction is not the same as "tax-free" shopping at airports
and on ships where part of the *import duty* or *excise tax* is waived on
liquor, tobacco, jewelry, and a few other luxury (and heavily taxed)
items. (You can't get VAT refunds on tax-free purchases.) As the table
on page 213 shows, VAT recovery applies mainly to merchandise; only

a few countries offer refunds on services (lodgings, meals, car rentals). Some countries refund the entire VAT amount, others only a portion. The table's *Price Reduction* column shows what you'd actually get back, calculated as a percentage of the posted price (including tax) of your purchase, not the percentage VAT rate. Unless noted, our calculations are based on a mail refund. In many countries, refunds are subject to small "handling" fees that may amount to as much as 3 percent of the purchase price.

Where VAT percentages vary, lower rates (sometimes no tax at all) usually apply to basic necessities (food, clothing, books); higher figures apply to various categories of luxury goods (cameras, electronics equipment, jewelry). Most countries provide brochures describing VAT rates (and refunds) for foreign visitors; ask at a visitor center or official information booth. If you're not sure about a specific purchase, ask the merchant where you're shopping about the amount of VAT refund on each item.

Many countries require a minimum per-store purchase amount (shown in the table) for a tax refund to eliminate paperwork for small refunds; some countries allow merchants to impose their own minimum. The minimum normally applies to all purchases made at one store during a single shopping session, not the price of any single item, so long as all the purchases are listed on the same form.

In some countries, giving VAT refunds is optional for the store. If you see no tax-free sign or sticker (it will usually be in English), be sure to ask before you buy anything.

Getting a rebate can be cumbersome. The refunds or reductions may be handled in any of several ways, as described in the following sections.

Mail Refund

When you buy merchandise, you pay the amount on the price tag, including VAT. You also show your passport, and the merchant produces the required tax-refund forms, on which the details of the transaction are entered. (In a few countries, you have to get your own forms from customs officials or tourist offices.)

The merchant then gives you a copy of the form and a self-addressed envelope. In major cities, large department stores—Harrod's in London and Galeries Lafayette in Paris, for example—have special offices that facilitate VAT refund paperwork.

When you leave a country, you show your purchases to a customs official, who validates your form(s). You mail the validated form back to the

VAT REFUND AMOUNTS AND PROCEDURES

Country	Price Reduction (%)	Applies to[1]	Minimum Purchase[2]	Mail Refund	Border Refund	Direct Export	Tax-Free Purchase
Austria	17–24	M,A[3]	$ 89	✔	✔	✔	—
Belgium	7–25	M	153	✔	—	—	—
Denmark	15	M	99	✔[4]	✔[5]	✔	—
Finland	11–13	M	53	—	✔	✔	—
France	13–23	M	226	✔	—	—	—
Germany	12	M	—	✔	✔	—	—
Ireland	8–16	M	[6]	✔	✔	✔	—
Israel	13	M,A,S	50	✔	✔[5]	—	✔[7]
Italy	15–28	M	452[8]	✔	—	—	—
Luxembourg	6–10	M	103	✔	—	✔	—
Netherlands	15	M-	167	✔[4]	✔	—	—
Norway	10–14	M	49	—	✔	—	—
Portugal	14	M	71	✔	✔[5]	—	—
Spain	6–11	M,A[3]	102	✔	—	—	—
Sweden	12–13[9]	M	34	—	✔	✔	—
Switzerland	6	M	384[8]	✔	—	✔	—
UK	13	M	[8]	✔	—	✔	—

[1] Key: A = automobile rentals, M = merchandise, S = services.
[2] Official government limit, per store, except as noted (can include more than one item purchased from the same store at the same time); dollar values calculated at August 1990 rates; stores may set their own limits in some countries.
[3] Tax refunded on auto rentals for any driving outside country.
[4] Refund checks available in any currency you specify, a major advantage.
[5] At major international airport(s) only.
[6] Each merchant sets own minimum; averages about U.S.$50–100.
[7] No tax on rooms, hotel meals, rental cars, and other services if paid in U.S. dollars (see text).
[8] Per item.
[9] Reduction is 12–13% if you use border-refund system, 17% for direct-export system.

store. If you paid for your purchases by cash or check, your refund will usually be a check in the currency of the store's country (which may take a little hassle—and extra commission—to cash). If you paid by charge card, your refund may be a credit to your account or, again, a local-currency check.

Border Refund

In this system, you fill out forms essentially as before. But when you leave the country, you can submit the paperwork to a customs office in the departure area and receive a check on the spot, usually issued in local currency. Several countries provide border refunds only at one or two major international airports, plus, possibly, a few major seaports.

Direct Export

Some countries let you deduct the VAT from the purchase price if the merchant mails your purchases directly to you at a foreign address. But you may have to pay extra for the shipping. You also have to cope with customs and pay U.S. import duty when the merchandise arrives in the United States. (At this writing, the United States requires you to pay duty on all purchases shipped home, even if you remain under your total duty-free allowance for the trip.) This system is useful mainly for purchases that are so cumbersome that you'd have them shipped home in any case; otherwise, your potential VAT saving can easily be wiped out by U.S. duty and clearance expenses.

Procedural Tips

If you're making relatively small purchases, forget VAT refunds—for most travelers, a refund of a few dollars is more hassle than it's worth. But it's well worth avoiding the VAT on a big purchase. Here's how to proceed in countries with refund programs:

- Before you buy an expensive item, make sure a store participates in the local VAT-reduction program.
- Where possible, concentrate purchases in large stores where employees are used to VAT-reduction paperwork.
- Buy in as few stores as possible. Try to do all your buying in a single shopping visit. The fewer separate checks you receive, the less you'll lose in currency conversions.
- Buy with your charge card in countries that permit merchants to credit your account rather than to issue a local-currency refund

check. You'll get a better exchange rate on both the initial purchase and the refund.

- Allow plenty of time for the paperwork the tax refund requires—both when you shop and when you leave the country.

- Intra-European trains often don't allow time for tax-refund paperwork at border crossings. If you leave by train, you may have to get off at the border stop, handle the paperwork, and wait for the next train. All systems except direct export require you to show the merchandise as you leave the country. That procedure can be a hassle.

- If you leave by plane, your purchases—however large and cumbersome—must be in your carry-on baggage. Allow enough time for tax-form questions to be dealt with at the airport. There may be long lines.

- If you leave a country by car, you have to cross the border when stations are open. If a border station is closed or unmanned, you'll miss your refund.

Cashing small refund checks in foreign currency can also be a problem. Some banks won't handle them at all; others give you a very poor exchange rate. However, three U.S. organizations can help:

- Chequepoint USA Currency Exchange Bureau converts British VAT refund checks (no other countries) for a 5 percent fee. Go to the office at 551 Madison Avenue, New York, NY 10022 (212-980-6443), or endorse your check to Chequepoint and mail it with a self-addressed stamped envelope.

- The foreign-currency department of Deak International cashes VAT refund checks in any currency at current exchange rates, less 1 percent, with a minimum fee of $3.50 per check. Checks that are less than the equivalent of $150 are cashed immediately; larger checks must clear a European bank first. Visit Deak's office at 630 Fifth Avenue, New York, NY 10111 (800-448-6516, 212-757-6915 in New York).

- Ruesch International converts VAT refund checks at what the company describes as "competitive" exchange rates for a $2 fee per check. Go to the office at 1350 I Street, N.W., 10th floor, Washington, DC 20005 (800-424-2923, 202-408-1200 in Washington).

Staying Healthy on a Trip Abroad

There's always a chance of getting sick when you travel abroad. Contaminated food and water or infected people may expose you to bacteria and viruses to which your body has no resistance. Your risk is particularly high in tropical latitudes, in developing countries, and in other areas with poor sanitation. Any sickness when traveling can mean not only doctor's bills but a concealed cost—every day lost to sickness costs you $100 or so, the price of merely *being* abroad.

If you're going to Europe, there's no special risk in urban centers. But health hazards increase in rural areas and as you head south. Whatever your destination, a few sensible precautions can help keep illness from blighting your trip.

Traveler's Medications

Start by getting any immunizations required or recommended for the country you'll visit; your local or state health department will tell you what those are. Then put together a personal kit of traveler's medications, including a stock of any long-term prescription medicines you may be taking. Then consider some nonprescription candidates. (Caution: If you're pregnant or have any medical condition, be sure to read the label of any nonprescription product for contraindications before buying.)

Take along **acetaminophen, aspirin,** or **ibuprofen.** All are equally effective for fever and most kinds of pain. Aspirin and ibuprofen also reduce inflammation and so are better for arthritis, muscle strains, and similar woes. Ibuprofen is best for menstrual cramps but must be avoided if you have even mild kidney disease. Acetaminophen is preferred for children.

You might also want to consider packing some of the following: **antacid** tablets for upset stomach, heartburn, indigestion; an **antihistamine** for stuffed or runny nose, irritated eyes, allergic skin reactions; a **cough suppressant** syrup for persistent, dry night coughs; a **decongestant** for stuffed or runny nose caused by colds or allergies and to prevent ear pain when flying; a **diarrhea remedy;** a **laxative** (milk of magnesia tablets may be most convenient); a **motion-sickness aid;** and a **fungicide** for athlete's foot, jock itch, and other common fungus infections as well as rashes and minor skin irritation.

Once abroad, your best defense against food-borne illness is to avoid possibly contaminated food and drink. The chief liquid hazards are untreated water and unpasteurized dairy products.

In larger European cities, drinking water is usually safe. In regions where tap water isn't chlorinated and local sanitation is poor, you have two options:

- *Drink something else*—carbonated drinks, beer, wine, or citrus juices (bottled or reconstituted with purified water). If possible, drink from disposable paper cups. Beware of ice cubes, unless you're sure they have been made with purified water.
- *Treat the water yourself.* A 10-minute boil does the trick; an immersion heater (with a plug compatible with foreign sockets) will do it handily. Or add a drop or 2 of 2 percent tincture of iodine, sold in pharmacies, to a glass of water, or 5 to 10 drops to a quart (depending on how cloudy the water is). Let the water stand for 30 minutes—or longer, for especially cold water.

In poor-sanitation areas, avoid uncooked food and unpeeled raw fruits and vegetables. Even cooked foods that have been improperly handled (unclean hands; inadequate cooking, storing, or serving) can do you in. Your best defense is to be selective about restaurants—and to be wary of street vendors.

EIGHT

Keeping Your Auto Expenses Down

Chances are, you wouldn't dream of taking the first house that came along at the seller's asking price. But many people buy a car just that impetuously. More to the point, they succumb to "new-car fever," allowing the dealer to *sell* them a car—a car the dealer wanted to sell them, at the dealer's price.

Here are some tips to help you avoid new-car fever and some money-saving strategies for operating and repairing your vehicle thriftily.

New Cars

How to Deal with a New-Car Dealer

Remember these rules. Here's the overriding rule of new-car buying: If a dealer won't talk price, don't talk purchase.

Three other rules can help:

1. Don't fall in love with any one car. You'll lose your negotiating edge.
2. Learn what the car cost the dealer. Negotiate up from that factory invoice price.

3. Keep the deal simple. Don't complicate negotiations with immediate discussion of a trade-in on your old car or of an auto loan.
Save that for later, when you've agreed on the purchase price.

Be a dispassionate buyer. Before you go near a new-car showroom,
select a few models that suit your needs and be willing to consider any of
them.

Even if you zero in on just one model, you may still have alternatives.
For years, American automakers have offered the same car under different nameplates: **Ford Thunderbird** and **Mercury Cougar,** for
instance. Some similar cars have an international heritage. The new
Ford Escort and **Mercury Tracer,** for example, are mechanically similar
to the **Mazda 323 (Mazda Protege).**

Next, decide on equipment. Most models come in two or more trim
lines (Standard, LX, GXE, and the like), each with a different base price.

Sometimes it's cheaper to buy a domestic car in a higher trim line with
a long list of standard equipment than it is to buy a base model and add
a lot of options. (Imported cars offer few options.)

With domestic cars, options may be priced individually or grouped in
packages. The packages are often cheaper than options purchased individually—but that's assuming you want all of those options. (See page
224.)

The automakers' brochures list the equipment in the various trim
lines. But you may have to visit dealers to get prices (from the window
stickers affixed to new cars).

The dealer's costs. Prices on window stickers are, of course, list
prices. Multiply those numbers by the cost factors included in the Summary Judgments in the most recent April issue of *Consumer Reports* for a
rough idea of what the dealer paid the factory for the car. But the more
accurate your figures are, the stronger your bargaining position. Precise
cost information is available from the Consumer Reports Auto Price
Service. It provides printouts for any make, model, and trim line you
specify. You can order printouts for each trim line so you can determine
the most cost-effective way to outfit the car. To order a printout, send
a check for $11 for one car, $20 for two cars, or $27 for three cars
(each additional car is $5) to *Consumer Reports,* Box 8005, Novi, MI
48376.

Prepare a worksheet before entering a showroom. It should include
the complete name of the car—make, model, and trim line—and, next
to it, the dealer cost and list price as shown on the printout. Under that,

in column form, list the invoice number and name of each option you want, its dealer cost, and its list price.

Finally, jot down the destination charge in each column. (The amount is constant; there's no dealer markup on destination charge.) Add up both columns. The difference between the two totals is the room for negotiation.

The totals, however, may not be the bottom line. Check the newspaper to see if manufacturers' sales incentives are being offered. The automaker may offer the dealer $1,000 cash back on certain models. The dealer may pass along all or part of that money—or none—to the buyer. But if one Chevrolet dealer advertises a rebate, you can be sure General Motors has some sort of incentive that enables all other Chevrolet dealers to offer a rebate, too.

When you get to the showroom, hand the worksheet to the salesperson and ask him or her to add the lowest markup the dealership is willing to accept at the bottom of the dealer-cost column. The worksheet should save time and haggling, if you are special-ordering a car. If you are willing to compromise, it's usually cheaper to buy a car from the dealer's stock.

What should you pay? How much over invoice should you expect to pay? Ideally, on a mid-priced domestic car in good supply—as most are these days—you may be able to pay as little as 2 to 4 percent over invoice. But markups vary greatly from model to model and dealer to dealer.

You're likely to get the best deal if you find a car on the dealer's lot that meets your specifications. Even if a car has more equipment than you want, it can be a good buy if the dealer is willing to absorb the cost of the extras. A dealer that doesn't have the car you want—or a model close to it—may trade a car on the lot for one on another dealer's lot.

Beware the add-ons. Even if the price you're quoted during the initial negotiations is acceptable, watch out for last-minute changes. A conveyance fee—a charge for processing the paperwork—is common. But paperwork is part of the cost of doing business and should be included in the dealer's markup.

Extended warranties are another ploy. They're probably not worth the money.

Salespeople still try to sell overpriced and essentially valueless protection packages that include rustproofing, paint treatment, fabric finish, undercoating, and the like. And they still try to sell overpriced "options" such as floor mats, pinstriping, and roof racks.

We've also come across antitheft packs that consist of etching the vehicle identification number on the car's windows. Many local police departments offer the same service for $10 or so.

Automobile Brokers: A Better Way to Buy a Car?

Fast talk and slippery sales tactics are among the most dreaded aspects of car shopping. One alternative to buying a car from a dealer is using an automobile broker. They contact dealers directly and come back to you with the best price. Often, their price beats what you could get yourself from a dealer.

How brokers work. Auto brokers are usually listed in the Yellow Pages, but your fingers may have to do a little walking. In the San Francisco Yellow Pages, for instance, they're under "Automobiles—Broker." In the New York City area, the Yellow Pages list brokers under "Automobile & Truck Brokers."

Brokers come in several varieties. They range from American Automobile Association (AAA) affiliates to used-car dealers who become brokers of new vehicles as a sideline.

Some brokers act solely as a referral service, putting you in touch with the dealer who offers the lowest price. In return, the broker receives either a commission from the dealer or a fee from the customer. (AAA Potomac, the association's affiliate in the Washington, D.C., area, offers its referral service to members without charge.)

Other brokers find the car you want at a franchised dealer, formally take title to the car, and then sell it to you. (Because these brokers are licensed as new-car dealers, the car is still a new car when you buy it.) A handful of brokers buy cars in advance and display them in warehouse-type showrooms.

What brokers charge. When a *Consumer Reports* editor spoke with brokers across the country, he found a wide variation in their commission. A large broker in suburban Detroit said he generally buys cars for $50 over invoice and marks them up as little as $50 more. One in Portland said he gets cars at invoice and adds an average of $250. A used-car dealer in Houston who operates a brokerage business as a sideline told us he tacks on $200. AAA Colorado, the auto club's Denver affiliate, runs a brokerage business that buys cars and resells them to members at a $500 to $700 markup.

To see how brokers operate in practice, a CU reporter in San Francisco called five brokers to inquire about buying a specific sedan, with certain optional equipment, which, according to the Consumer Reports Auto Price Service, would cost a dealer $12,700 and carry a manufacturer's retail sticker price of $15,234.

One of the purported advantages of using a car broker is that you get a firm price, with no haggling. Of the five brokers we telephoned, four quoted us exact prices, ranging from $12,635 to $13,798. (In our opinion, the car we were shopping for was a good deal at any price under $13,300.) The fifth broker wanted our reporter to come to his office; the fee, he said, would be $125 if our reporter priced the car but didn't buy it and $325 if our reporter did buy. This broker indicated that the final price, including the rebate and broker fee, would be slightly over $13,000.

True to the reputation of car brokers, none of the five that we called would bargain. Our staffer told a broker who quoted a price of $13,424 that he could get the same car from another broker for $12,635. "If that's the real price, buy it," he said.

There's no guarantee, of course, that the price quoted over the phone is the price you'll end up paying once you go in to complete the transaction. But brokers often do have the leverage to make a dealership keep its word.

What about warranties? Most dealerships must perform repairs covered by warranty for all cars carrying the nameplate of the makers it represents. Nevertheless you may find dealers reluctant to make repairs on a car bought elsewhere.

If your car turns out to be a lemon, lemon laws in some states will help you secure a refund after repeated attempts at repair have failed.

Financing and trade-ins. You can finance the car yourself through a bank or credit union. Some brokers will also arrange financing or send you to the originating dealer for it. If a manufacturer offers a choice between a rebate and low-interest financing, often the broker can structure the deal so you can take advantage of whichever you choose.

If you don't want to sell your old car yourself, some brokers will arrange to wholesale it for you.

Final safeguards. If an auto broker acts simply as a referral service, you'll write your check to the auto dealer and pick up your car there. If the broker has a dealership license, the broker may buy the car from the original dealer and then sell it to you. In the latter case, be careful. Some brokers don't bother to become licensed. They may take your deposit and then leave town.

So ask some questions and do some checking: Does the broker have a state license? Has he or she posted a performance bond? How many years has the broker been in business?

Check with your local Better Business Bureau for complaints. Ask the broker for the names of some recent customers, and call a couple of them to make sure the broker is legitimate.

Which Options Should You Choose?

Only a few years ago, many options on domestic models were available only in expensive packages. But sales have slowed. Carmakers are increasingly letting you choose your options either in a package, with a verifiable saving in cost, or individually.

But selecting the right options can be tricky. The table on pages 224 to 229 lists 30 popular options, along with our comments and the 1991 price range to the nearest $5.

We haven't tabulated certain "packs," options packages installed by the dealer or distributor rather than the factory. The price usually appears on a separate sticker next to the factory price sticker. Packs are generally high-profit items that provide little or no benefit to the buyer. Some packs, such as rustproofing and undercoating, may do more harm than good, trapping moisture and promoting rust.

We suggest you order price printouts from the Consumer Reports Auto Price Service for the cars you're considering (see details on page 219). Each printout lists all factory options available for a given model, with both the sticker (list) prices and the invoice prices (what the dealer pays the factory). If the options you want aren't sold separately or in a reasonably priced package that meets your needs, look for a comparable model of a different brand.

Automobile Service Contracts

Plain logic suggests that automobile service contracts are apt to be mediocre or poor buys. Contract sellers make money only if the buyers pay more for the warranty than the cost of the claims they make. Of course, that is true of almost any insurance arrangement; companies try to take in more in premiums than they expect to pay out in claims. But in the case of health insurance or homeowners insurance, you should accept the unfavorable odds because the consequences of a lengthy hospitaliza-

NEW-CAR OPTIONS

As published in the April 1991 issue of *Consumer Reports*

Option	Price	Advantages	Disadvantages	Comments
Larger engine	$0–$1,280	Quicker acceleration, more power for towing a trailer.	Fuel economy suffers.	Usually not needed, even with air-conditioning.
Turbocharged engine	$695–$34,300	A way to gain extra power without moving up to a larger engine. Turbo has negligible effect on fuel economy at light throttle.	Could be trouble-prone. Requires more frequent servicing. Throttle response usually delayed. May require premium fuel.	Usually sold as a unique model or in a package with other extras. Not recommended for towing a trailer.
Automatic transmission	$0–$4,000	Helps reduce driver fatigue in traffic; allows braking with left foot for faster reaction time. Overdrive gear reduces engine noise and highway fuel consumption.	Hurts fuel economy; automatic with overdrive and lock-up gearing harms fuel mileage least. Increases engine noise in some small cars.	Standard in large cars and many medium-sized models. Especially recommended in cars with foot-operated parking brake.
Four-wheel drive (all-wheel drive)	$800–$11,300	Markedly improves traction and directional stability in snow and mud.	Added weight and complexity. May add to maintenance costs. Lowers fuel mileage, even when not in use. May reduce cargo room.	Doesn't enhance traction and stability when braking. Limited-slip differential no substitute. Sometimes sold as unique model.
Traction control	$220–$2,475	Improves traction and directional stability from standstill and at low speeds on slippery roads.	Added complexity.	Recommended in rear-wheel-drive models, which tend to have poor traction on snow and ice.
Power steering	$235–$600	Quickens steering response in most cars. Eases parking.	Usually reduces feel of the road.	Standard in most cars. Often desirable even in small cars.

Feature	Price	Advantage	Recommendation
Antilock brakes	$680–$1,280	Markedly improves directional stability in braking, especially on slippery roads.	Brake pedal may pulsate slightly when the antilock feature functions.	Highly recommended; standard in some models. Limited but growing availability.
Air suspension	$650–$1,500	Smoother ride. Compensates for variations in load and terrain.	Added complexity.	Available in only a few luxury models.
Automatic level control	$170–$250	Adjusts height of rear suspension to keep car level, regardless of load. Improves road clearance, ride, and headlight aim when car is loaded or towing a trailer.	Adjustments may disconcert passengers. Added weight and complexity. Encourages overloading.	Standard in some luxury models. Optional in some large cars. Desirable if you frequently carry a full load or tow a trailer.
Outside mirrors	$20–$150	Electric remote-controlled mirrors are convenient to adjust. Heated mirrors, often sold with rear-window defroster, are a boon in winter.	Nonpower remote-controlled mirrors can be hard to adjust, and control for the passenger-side mirror is often out of the driver's reach.	Convex mirror on passenger's side needs no adjustment to suit different drivers, but objects appear farther away than they are.
Intermittent wipers	About $55	Clears light drizzle without needless wiper wear and driver annoyance.	None.	Standard in all but low-line domestic models. Recommended where optional.
Rear-window defroster	$35–$200	Essential for clearing fog and frost in moist and cold climates.	Defroster elements can be damaged if objects rub on inside of glass.	Strongly recommended in most climes. Some states require it.

(Continued)

NEW-CAR OPTIONS (Continued)

Option	Price	Advantages	Disadvantages	Comments
Rear-window wiper/washer	$85–$320	Improves rear visibility.	None.	Recommended for most hatchbacks and wagons. Better than an air deflector, which can increase fuel consumption.
Heated windshield	$250–$310	Clears windshield much faster than defroster; eliminates need for prolonged idling or scraping.	Impairs night vision; reduces range of devices such as garage-door openers.	Available only in a few Ford and General Motors models.
Optional seats	$0–$5,725	Multiple seat adjustments can tailor driving position to suit a variety of physiques. Heated seats are a blessing on cold mornings.	Power-operated seats add weight and mechanical complexity and can cut rear-seat foot room. Vinyl or leather not as comfortable as cloth.	The more adjustments the better. Divided front seats help comfort for two but reduce it for three.
Adjustable steering	$80–$335	Lets you position steering wheel comfortably. Eases access to driver's seat.	None.	Tilting column offers more adjustment than tilting steering wheel. Some columns tilt and telescope.
Air-conditioning	$670–$1,495	Increases comfort, reduces noise and fatigue, improves window defogging.	Reduces fuel economy. Increases service costs.	Desirable. Automatic temperature control ($65–$185 extra) gives added convenience.

Auto sound system	$30–$1,405	Can provide near-hi-fi sound. A tape player offers consistent sound quality; a radio may not.	Elaborate, costly sound systems are attractive to thieves; consider antitheft device or added insurance.	Factory- and dealer-installed systems aren't your only options.
Cruise control	$200–$235	Helps driver observe speed limits. Helps an erratic driver improve fuel economy. Reduces driver fatigue on long trips.	Can lull driver into inattention. Can be dangerous on slippery roads and in congested traffic. Best for long trips on lightly traveled roads.	Resume feature makes it easy to go back to preset speed, but some models lose their memory below 25 or 30 mph.
Theft-deterrent system	$150–$610	Burglar alarms, headlamps that flash, auto sound systems that self-destruct if yanked from dash, window glass coded with identifying marks—all help deter thefts.	Inadvertent alarms, whether from careless disarming or an electronic glitch, can disturb your neighbors.	Standard in some theft-prone models. Especially recommended in high-crime areas. Check your insurance company for theft history of model you plan to buy.
Electronic instrument- panel display	$90–$495	Large speedometer digits are easy to read.	Light-bar gauges and 1-mph increments of digital speedometer give less sense of changes in conditions than moving-needle dials. Displays may dazzle or confuse the driver.	Usually packaged with trip computer and vehicle monitor. Duplicate speedometer, projected on windshield of some models, is distracting. Choose only if you find standard displays hard to read.
Trip computer/ vehicle monitor	$90–$1,295	Computer can tell fuel consumption, miles to Empty, average speed, elapsed time and distance, etc. Monitor warns of door ajar, burned-out taillight, or engine malfunction.	Added complexity. Inaccurate data can cause needless apprehension. May distract the driver's attention from the road.	Often grouped with or linked to an electronic instrument panel display and cruise control. An expensive gimmick.

(*Continued*)

227

NEW-CAR OPTIONS (Continued)

Option	Price	Advantages	Disadvantages	Comments
Power windows	$245–$390	Convenient. Some models offer one-touch lowering of the driver's window, a nice feature.	Added weight and complexity. Switches can be confusing and hard to find at night. Power windows could injure small children.	An expensive nicety.
Central locking system	$125–$535	Increases safety and security. In some models, driver's control can lock all doors at once or just the left front door.	Added complexity.	Very desirable. Some models offer automatic locking, infrared remote locking, or keyless entry.
Courtesy lights	$25–$195	Lights conveniently stay on a few seconds after doors are closed.	Lights with a time-delay feature may take some getting used to.	Sometimes available only in an options package.
Sun roof	$0–$1,540	Can enhance ventilation. May add to resale value.	May cut head room critically. Open, it increases interior noise.	Test-drive car to be sure head room and noise are tolerable.

Item	Price	Benefit	Caution
Body trim, bumper protection	$0–$70	Vinyl body-side moldings protect a car from parking-lot nicks. Bumper guards help protect bumpers.	Metal moldings may offer more glitter than protection.	Sometimes available only in package or on higher-trim-line models with other decorative options.
Wheels and wheel covers	$0–$2,005	May make car easier to resell.	May attract thieves. Some covers hard to remove; others may fall off if car corners hard or brakes overheat. Alloy wheels easily damaged or defaced in tire-changing.	Strictly cosmetic. Functionally, wheel covers are no better than hub caps.
Aftermarket rustproofing; paint/ upholstery preservatives	Dealer-installed; price varies	Preservatives briefly improve luster of paint and stain-resistance of upholstery.	Rustproofing protection, if any, depends on installer's competence; can promote corrosion. Preservatives are grossly overpriced.	Dealer packs; not recommended. Added rustproofing won't help most cars. Preservatives are no better than treatments you apply yourself.
Service contract	Dealer-provided; price varies	Extends vehicle warranty.	Fine print may contain major exclusions and ambiguities.	Only for models with poor reliability *and* short factory warranty. Buy at end of warranty. Be sure contract can be canceled.

tion or a tornado can be financially devastating. That is not the case if your car's transmission breaks down.

You can avoid a great many repairs—and thus much of the need for a service contract—by buying a reliable car. But even if you do purchase a defect-free model with a good maintenance record, you may be worried about an unexpected major repair bill. An alternative to a service contract is to build a separate fund to pay for such major repairs—"self-insuring," as some people call it. That way you keep your money if nothing goes wrong.

If you do opt for a service contract, make sure that you can cancel it, just in case you have second thoughts. Most contracts allow you to cancel during the first 30, 60, or 90 days and get most of your money back. After that, you can still cancel, but you will be charged for the time the contract was in effect and for any claim already made. You may also be charged an administrative fee.

Other questions to ask if you decide to buy: Does the contract include labor? Where can the repairs be done? Is the contract transferable if the car is sold? Are towing and a rental car included? Is the repairer reimbursed, or do you have to wait for the check? If there's a disagreement, what is the arbitration process?

In any case, don't allow yourself to be pressured into buying a service contract, especially when you've purchased a brand-new car. During that first year you'll get very little for your money, considering most new-car warranty provisions.

Regardless of where you shop for a service contract, insist on getting the actual contract, not just a summary. Read it carefully before signing. Unfortunately, it may be difficult to know if your insurer is going to be around for the rest of the contract. Too many private insurers have taken the money and left the business. For that reason, a contract backed by the automaker may be more expensive, but it also may be a safer investment.

Automobile Warranties

It's easy to waste money on repairs you could get free—if you knew how. Some automakers provide "secret" warranties—informal extensions of the regular car warranty—usually to cover components that have proved particularly troublesome. It is often hard to discover whether those extensions apply to your car, since the automakers usually pass the word to their field representatives or dealers while leaving car owners in the dark.

If your car is suffering from a problem that might be covered by a secret warranty, send a self-addressed envelope with 52 cents postage to the Center for Auto Safety, 2001 S Street, N.W., Suite 410, Washington, DC 20009. The center compiles information about secret warranties by gathering automakers' dealer bulletins and by cataloging reports from car owners. Describe your car and the problem you are experiencing, and the center will send you specific information on any secret warranties that may apply.

If you can't resolve the problem with the dealer's service manager, contact the nearest factory regional office (listed in the car owner's manual) and ask a factory representative to help out. As a last resort, consider suing the dealer in small claims court.

New-Car Loans: How to Pay for Your Car Almost Forever

New-car loans are turning into long-term affairs. Seven-year loans, reportedly offered first in Florida, are spreading to other parts of the country.

The longer the loan term, the lower the monthly payments—but the more you pay in interest over the life of the loan, as the table below shows. Worse, you get no tax break for the loan: As of 1991, interest paid on auto loans is not deductible from your federal income taxes. Worse yet, a long-term loan may force you to keep the car for the long haul. If you own an average-priced car financed with a five-year loan, you'd have to make 51 payments to have equity in the car. If you trade in the car sooner, you may owe more than the car is worth.

THE COST OF A $14,000 AUTO LOAN AT 12% INTEREST (Rounded to nearest dollar)

Payments over	3 years	4 years	5 years
Your monthly payment is	$311	$274	$247
Total interest charges	$4,685	$5,707	$6,760
The total cost of loan	$18,685	$19,707	$20,760

Auto Insurance

In some cities, it's possible to pay more over time to insure a car than to buy one. For a couple with a 17-year-old son and two cars, premiums of as much as $4,000 a year are not at all unusual in urban centers such as

New York and San Francisco. Percentage increases in the cost of auto insurance have often outstripped the increases in the cost of living. Small wonder, then, that more and more motorists are driving "bare"—without insurance—even though that's illegal in most states.

Not only is the cost of insurance high, so too is the likelihood that you won't be completely satisfied with the way an insurance company handles your claim when you apply for the protection you thought your premiums were buying. In a 1987 survey of 62,000 *Consumer Reports* subscribers who reported on their most recent claim, some 40 percent reported that they were less than completely satisfied with the insurer's service. But with some companies, the likelihood of being less than completely satisfied was as high as 60 percent.

Given the potentially high cost and the levels of dissatisfaction shown, it makes sense to shop for auto insurance at least as carefully as you'd shop for an auto.

What Coverages Do You Need?

An auto-insurance policy is a package of seven types of coverage, each with its own premium. The sum of those premiums is the total you pay for your policy. You can raise or lower the price tag by taking higher or lower amounts of these coverages. Here are the details of the seven coverages:

1. Liability. In most states, the only type of coverage you must carry is liability coverage—insurance that protects others against damage you may cause by driving negligently. That is also the most expensive coverage and, unfortunately, the most necessary.

Despite years of effort to reform the insurance system, it's still more the rule than the exception that people seek legal redress, claiming the other driver was at fault and demanding thousands of dollars in compensation for personal injury. The "no-fault" movement, which swept through half the states nearly 20 years ago, was an attempt to hold down the cost of insurance and to speed financial compensation to those who suffered injury in accidents. In theory, no-fault insurance would pay the out-of-pocket medical costs and some additional benefits to an injured policyholder without regard to which party caused the accident. It would not pay for nonquantifiable costs such as the dollar value of "pain and suffering." Thus, no-fault insurance would reduce the size of claims and eliminate expensive and time-consuming lawsuits. The resulting savings would be passed through to policyholders as lower premiums.

In state after state, however, organized trial attorneys, who had the most to lose from this consumer-oriented initiative, succeeded in watering down most no-fault laws to the point where the tort system—the system of laws and legal remedies for alleged wrongs—remained intact. Under weakened no-fault laws many victims could continue to sue for compensation beyond that available from their own insurance companies, and no real savings resulted. Thus, liability coverage greater than that required in most states remains an auto-insurance essential.

There are two types of liability coverages—bodily injury coverage and property-damage coverage.

Bodily injury coverage pays for losses resulting from death or injury in an accident that's your fault. People you injure can collect against this coverage to pay their medical bills and lost wages and to cover pain and suffering. Awards for pain and suffering can be high enough to bankrupt you if you're underinsured.

Depending on the company providing the policy, you can buy liability coverage with a multiple, or "split," limit or with a single limit. Multiple-limit policies pay a certain amount to each person injured in an accident. The total amount paid out, however, is subject to a maximum for each accident.

If the policy pays a maximum of $100,000 per person and $300,000 per accident, and one person suffered damages of $200,000, the policy would pay only $100,000 to that person. If four people suffered injury in a single accident, the policy would pay up to $300,000 for damages.

A single-limit policy pays one amount per accident, regardless of how many individuals are involved. This form is slightly more expensive than the equivalent amount of multiple-limit coverage because it provides more benefits per person. If the driver carried $300,000 of single-limit coverage, one injured person could collect up to $300,000.

Most states prescribe the minimum liability coverage drivers must carry. (Drivers who don't carry insurance must post a bond if they're involved in an accident.) Judging by the size of some court settlements, however, those limits are very low. New York, for instance, requires minimum coverage that pays up to $10,000 to each injured person subject to a $20,000 maximum per accident.

In 1988 *Consumer Reports* subscribers appeared to carry far more coverage than most state minimums, and properly so. For a single-limit policy, the typical amount of coverage our readers carry is $100,000. For a multiple limit, the typical amount is $300,000 ($100,000 per person and $300,000 per accident). These amounts are in line with our own recommendations that you buy as much liability coverage as you can afford.

People who own a house or other assets generally should have minimums of at least $100,000 per person and $300,000 per accident.

In states with no-fault laws, injured parties first look to their own coverage to pay for their medical treatment, regardless of who was at fault. But an injured party still has the right to bring a suit, usually including claims for pain and suffering, if damages exceed some threshold established in the law. Because the potential for high awards still exists in no-fault states, most drivers carry bodily injury coverage in amounts comparable to those carried by drivers in states without such laws. The typical cost of $300,000 worth of bodily injury liability coverage for an adult driver with a good record, insuring one car in a suburban town, is about $200 per year from State Farm, a company with relatively low premiums.

Property-damage coverage pays if you damage someone else's property, usually another car. States require drivers to purchase minimal amounts of coverage, usually $5,000 or $10,000—not enough if an accident wrecks a new car beyond repair. Thus, $25,000 of property-damage coverage should be the minimum. An adult suburban driver would pay about $100 a year for $10,000 of property-damage coverage from State Farm. Increasing coverage from $10,000 to $25,000 adds less than $10 to the premium.

Together, the cost of bodily injury and property-damage makes up between 40 and 50 percent of the total insurance premium.

You can supplement the liability coverage with a so-called umbrella policy providing $1 million or more of coverage. Umbrella insurance "floats" above your other coverage—that is, you must carry the underlying liability coverage before you can buy an umbrella policy.

Umbrella policies are surprisingly inexpensive. For $1 million of coverage from State Farm, a person who is a good risk will pay about $100 (provided he or she has purchased the underlying policies from State Farm). Such policies are generally purchased by people whose assets far exceed the limits of, say, $300,000 liability coverage—those people need to protect their assets from big court awards.

2. Medical payments. Coverage that pays the medical bills for drivers and their passengers is not usually required in states without no-fault laws. Many people who already have medical and hospital insurance for themselves and their families forgo duplicate coverage in an automobile policy. Most people who buy medical-payments coverage do so in $1,000 or $2,000 amounts rather than the $50,000 or more of coverage possible. A small amount of additional coverage makes sense because the medical-payments coverage often includes a funeral benefit.

Even if you have a good health-insurance policy for yourself and your family, you might want to consider additional coverage through your auto insurance to cover nonfamily members who may be injured while riding in your car. Their medical bills will then be paid immediately by your carrier. Without that coverage, injured passengers would have to sue to collect against your liability coverage.

States with no-fault laws require you to buy personal-injury protection, or PIP, a more comprehensive form of medical-payments coverage. PIP covers not only medical bills but often lost wages while an injured person is unable to work, replacement services while a person is unable to perform routine tasks such as caring for young children, and some funeral expenses. Drivers in no-fault states generally can buy as much as $50,000 of PIP coverage, but most buy only $10,000. A few no-fault states require companies to provide for unlimited PIP benefits, which will cover all of a person's medical and rehabilitation expenses. A few states make drivers buy a minimum amount, such as $5,000.

You might save on PIP premiums if your state's no-fault rules allow policyholders to "coordinate benefits" with their health-insurance policy. By electing to make your health insurance "primary"—that is, to seek reimbursements for medical expenses from your health insurer before applying to your auto insurer—you could shave as much as 40 percent from the premium for personal-injury protection.

3. Collision. Collision coverage pays for physical damage to your car. It accounts for as much as 30 percent of the insurance premium on a new car or on an older model that has had a high frequency of claims.

Collision coverage is always limited by the deductible, which is the amount you pay before the coverage kicks in. Deductibles between $100 and $250 are the most common, but the deductible can be as high as $1,000.

One way to save on auto insurance is to take the highest deductible you can afford. The price of collision coverage with a $500 deductible is 15 to 25 percent less than the price for coverage with a $200 deductible.

The saving can be significant where insurance rates are high. In New York City, for example, State Farm would charge you $547 per year for collision coverage on a 1990 **Toyota Camry** if you took a $200 deductible. Take a $500 deductible and the premium drops to $410, a saving of $137.

It makes sense to drop collision coverage entirely on an older car with a low resale value, since the resale, or "book," value of a car also represents the maximum insurance settlement possible. It usually pays to carry collision for cars less than three years old; for those older than seven years, it usually doesn't. And if the car is between three and seven years old, the decision about whether or not to carry collision coverage at all depends in part on how much risk you're willing to assume and in part on how well your car has retained its resale value.

4. Comprehensive. As its name implies, this coverage is a catch-all that pays for damage resulting from such things as vandalism, hailstorms, floods, and theft. Comprehensive accounts for about 12 percent of the total premium, and 70 to 80 percent of all policyholders carry it. It is also usually subject to deductibles, which range from $50 to $500.

As with collision coverage, you can save some money by taking a higher deductible, and save more by dropping comprehensive when the book value of your car declines.

5. Uninsured motorists. This reimburses you for bodily injury (but not for property damage) in accidents caused by drivers who carry no insurance. Instead of looking to the motorist's policy for coverage, you look to your own. The minimum coverage companies offer usually matches the minimum required by state law. But many people carry coverage comparable to the amounts carried for bodily injury liability coverage.

In most states, uninsured-motorist coverage is part of every insurance policy, though you may elect in writing to reject the coverage. We advise you to keep it. However, this coverage may not be necessary in states with a good no-fault law. A vicious circle fuels rate increases for this coverage: As premiums rise, more drivers do without insurance (which is against the law in most states). That increases the number of claims against uninsured-motorist coverage, which in turn contributes to higher premiums and more drivers doing without insurance.

Similarly, the rise in rates has increased the need for a related coverage—*underinsured-motorist* coverage. Suppose you're injured by a person who carries the minimum liability coverage required by the state. Your damages exceed the limits of the driver's policy. If you have underinsured-motorist coverage, it will kick in where the other party's coverage leaves off. It pays only up to the limits of the coverage you buy, however. Usually you can buy coverage similar to that for liability.

Underinsured-motorist coverage may be offered as a separate coverage with a separate premium, but it's sometimes sold as part of the uninsured-motorist coverage. We think it's a good addition to your insurance package.

A typical premium for both uninsured- and underinsured-motorist coverage is about $40 to $45 a year.

6. Rental reimbursement. This coverage usually pays $15 to $20 a day, for a specified number of days, to rent a car while yours is being repaired. It costs around $12 a year.

7. Towing and labor. This coverage pays the costs of towing your car to a repair shop subject to the limits of your policy, usually $25 to $50. The premium runs, on average, $5 to $10 a year. If you're a member of an auto club, you probably already have this service and may not want to duplicate the coverage.

Watch Out for Packaged Policies

Insurance companies sometimes imply that policyholders should buy homeowners or tenant's policies from them before they will issue or even continue an auto policy. For the insurance company, homeowners and tenant's policies are generally profitable; auto insurance policies may not be. If a company can capture both policies, there's a good chance the entire account will be profitable and the policyholder will stick with the company longer.

In some states, these "tie-in" sales are illegal. In 1988, for instance, the Pennsylvania State Insurance Department accused a major broker, Alexander and Alexander, and two major companies, Harleysville Mutual and the Reliance Insurance Company, of illegally requiring customers to purchase homeowners insurance in order to obtain an auto policy. New York prohibits tie-in sales if such arrangements are not clearly spelled out in the policy forms approved and on file with the state insurance department.

Tie-ins should not be confused with "cross-sell" discounts, which companies must file with state departments. These discounts are legal, though they have the same effect as tie-in sales—they induce policyholders to put their eggs in one basket. Under cross-selling, a company encourages a policyholder to buy both policies by offering a discount on one or both of the coverages.

Both tie-ins and cross-selling discounts appear to save money, but you may save more and enjoy better service if you price-shop for insurance yourself.

Premiums—and How They're Set

You can save a lot of dollars by price shopping for insurance instead of automatically renewing with the company that insures you now. We rec-

ommend that you use the worksheet on page 240 to make a list of the
four or five highest-rated companies that sell auto insurance in your
state. Then ask for a premium quote from each of them. You may be
surprised to discover that the rates quoted differ by hundreds of dollars
a year in the annual premium for identical coverage.

How they rate you. To determine the premium you will pay, an insurance company sizes you up as a risk. The basic premium is determined
by your record of accidents and traffic violations and the make and
model of your car. Initially, someone in the company called an underwriter will place you in one of three risk tiers—preferred, standard, or
nonstandard. (Some companies have only two tiers while others have
four or five, the additional tiers being further refinements of the preferred tier.)

To figure the exact premium you will pay, the underwriter then delves
further into the risk you present, taking into consideration such factors
as your recent driving record. For example, drivers with one at-fault
accident, or perhaps two traffic violations, will usually qualify for the
standard tiers—and a premium some 20 percent higher than the preferred tier.

Underwriters also scrutinize the car that goes with the driver. Many
companies place drivers with high-performance cars in the highest-cost
tier. And drivers of some cars, such as the **Camaro IROC-Z,** will have
trouble buying insurance in any tier.

Most companies reject the worst drivers of all ages, such as those with
drunk-driving convictions. Such people must buy insurance from companies specializing in substandard drivers or from state-operated insurance pools or facilities.

Fine-tuning the rate. Once a company determines your rate tier, it further refines the basic premium by multiplying the rate for each type of
coverage in that tier by a numerical factor. That numerical factor is
based on such criteria as where the car is garaged; the age, sex, and marital status of the drivers; the age, make, and model of the car; use of the
car; how many cars are being insured; and the operators' driving records. In effect, the company uses the same criteria to refine your premium as its underwriters used to fit you into a basic risk tier. Discounts
for such items as good bumpers and antitheft devices are also figured
into these multipliers.

In sum, then, each company sets its own premiums by making certain
judgments about who drives, where the driver lives, what the driving rec-

ord is, and the make and model of car. Those judgments are based largely on generalizations about you drawn from the company's and the industry's experience with people the company thinks are like you.

Who's the driver?

Age: In 1987, drivers between the ages of 20 and 24 had the highest overall accident rate—37 accidents per 100 drivers—while those between the ages of 55 and 64 had the lowest—12 per 100 drivers. Young drivers therefore pay higher insurance rates than older drivers.

Gender: Young male drivers pay more than young females. Depending on the company, a single male will first qualify for the adult rate between the ages of 25 and 30.

Marital status: Single men under age 30 pay more than married men of the same age and generally a little more than single females of the same age. A few states require companies to offer unisex rates; that is, they prohibit the use of gender or marital status in rating drivers.

Smoking: Many underwriters believe smoking predicts driving behavior. "People who get the nonsmokers discount seem to have fewer accidents," says James Nikolai, a vice president at Farmers Insurance Exchange, one of the companies that uses smoking as a rating factor.

Business or pleasure use: Someone driving to work 40 miles a day on a crowded expressway obviously has a greater chance of having an accident than a retiree driving to the grocery store once a week. So companies consider how many miles the car is driven when they calculate premiums—the fewer the miles, the lower the premium. Someone using a car for business, such as an insurance adjuster, will pay about 25 percent more than a person driving a car for pleasure or to work fewer than 3 miles each way.

Breaks for students: Companies may allow families with young drivers to benefit from discounts for students with good report cards (B averages or better), students away at college without cars, and students who have taken driver-training courses. Depending on the sex of the students, such discounts can result in a saving of some 20 to 30 percent on the total premium the parents pay, so those discounts are worth asking about.

One car or two: If you insure more than one car, you might get a discount of 20 to 25 percent. Companies say that families with several cars generally exhibit more stability and responsibility, which means fewer accidents and traffic violations. Furthermore, each car may be driven less, reducing its chances of being involved in an accident.

Worksheet for Auto-Insurance Buyers

	Write amount of coverage here	Write premium quotes here	
COMPANY NAMES		1.	2.

Minimum coverage your state requires for

Bodily injury liability	_____	_____	_____
Property-damage liability	_____	_____	_____
Personal-injury protection (no-fault states)	_____	_____	_____
Uninsured motorist	_____	_____	_____

Subtotal A

COST OF MINIMUM COVERAGE

Level of coverage you desire for

Bodily injury liability	_____	_____	_____
Property-damage liability	_____	_____	_____
Medical payments	_____	_____	_____
Personal-injury protection (no-fault states)	_____	_____	_____
Collision			
1. $100 deductible	_____	_____	_____
2. $250 deductible	_____	_____	_____
3. $500 deductible	_____	_____	_____
Comprehensive with no deductible	_____	_____	_____
1. $50 deductible	_____	_____	_____
2. $100 deductible	_____	_____	_____
3. $250 deductible	_____	_____	_____
Uninsured motorist	_____	_____	_____
Underinsured motorist	_____	_____	_____

Cost of coverage you desire

Subtotal B* _____

Other coverages you might consider

Towing and labor _____

Rental-car reimbursement _____

Subtotal C _____

Do any other charges apply?

Membership fee _____

Surcharges _____

Subtotal D _____

How do the companies compare (Add subtotals B, C, and D)

Total premium _____

Does company have accident-forgiveness program?

Yes____ No____   Yes____ No____

After how many years does it apply? _____ _____

*Choose one Collision and one Comprehensive coverage when you add the premiums to reach Subtotal B.

Where do you live? Insurance companies have data on the number of claims for each of their territories, often by zip code location. That allows them to go beyond the simple fact that cars garaged in congested, urban areas get into accidents more often and are more likely to be stolen than cars garaged in rural areas. Insurers can single out one neighborhood, cite higher losses than in an adjoining neighborhood, and justify a higher premium. In New York City, for example, you'd pay a good bit more for certain coverages if you lived in the Williamsburg section of Brooklyn than if you lived across the river in Manhattan.

This kind of "territorial rating," however, is under attack by consumer groups. California's Proposition 103, an insurance-reform initiative, was the first effort to eliminate territorial ratings. The proposition was passed in November 1988. Its proponents are hopeful that it will achieve its aim and set an example for other states.

What's your record? At many companies, an accident that results in death, bodily injury, or property damage in excess of $400 or $500 triggers a surcharge on your premium. The charge, which lasts for three years, varies from company to company and ranges from mild to severe.

At State Farm, one at-fault accident results in a 10 percent surcharge in most states. Two such accidents add another 20 percent, and more than two tacks on 50 percent for each additional accident. At other companies, a single at-fault accident could bring a surcharge of 30 or 40 percent, and several accidents could add 150 to 200 percent.

Other companies don't levy a surcharge on policyholders who have been insured for a number of years. At Aetna, in most states, a policyholder who has had one at-fault accident will not receive a surcharge if he or she has been insured with Aetna for at least five years and has been accident-free up to that point. At State Farm, drivers insured for nine years without an accident will not find a surcharge tacked onto their premiums.

If surcharges are the sticks, these "accident-forgiveness" programs are the carrots to induce policyholders to stay. Companies know that long-time policyholders generate fewer losses than new ones. And once a policyholder has been around for a while, the company has recouped the costs involved in making that first sale. Forgiving an accident or two also deters policyholders from shopping for better rates.

What car do you drive? Most drivers would be surprised at the precision of the records maintained by insurers on almost every make and model of car driven. Data on the price of the car when new, how easily it's damaged, how easily it's repaired, how accident-prone, and how popular it is with thieves are folded into an elaborate numbering system.

As soon as a new model is introduced, companies assign it a number based on the car's price. More expensive cars have numbers that translate into higher premiums. Numbers change from year to year once a company begins to gather evidence of a model's damage, repair, and theft record. A poor record can translate into as much as a 15 percent price increase in collision and comprehensive coverages.

Small, two-door foreign cars, especially sports and high-performance models, have poor experience after they've been on the market for a year or two, reflecting their higher frequency and cost of repairs. Full-size four-door models and station wagons have good records, resulting in lower collision and comprehensive rates for their owners.

Before buying a car, you might want to check with your insurance agent to find out what the collision and comprehensive premiums would be for the car you're considering. You might avoid an unpleasant surprise on an already expensive purchase.

At State Farm, our Indianapolis driver could pay $255 for collision coverage with a $100 deductible on a 1990 four-door **Chevrolet Caprice** or $562 for the same coverage on a **Chevrolet Corvette.** For full comprehensive coverage, that driver could pay $125 on a 1990 **Toyota Camry SW** or $358 on a **Volkswagen Cabriolet.**

Are You a "High Risk"?

If you find yourself labeled a "high risk," possibly because you've had one too many at-fault accidents, your carrier might try to shunt you to a subsidiary rather than write you a policy itself. These subsidiaries often have names similar to the parent company's. You may think you're insured with State Farm Mutual Auto, Allstate, or the Erie Insurance Exchange, but if your policy is written by State Farm Fire and Casualty, Allstate Indemnity, or the Erie Insurance Company, you're with a subsidiary and you're probably paying higher rates than you would with the parent company.

You should shop around before accepting a company's offer to insure you through a subsidiary. Farmers Insurance Exchange, for example, places its high risks in a subsidiary called Mid-Century. High-risk drivers insuring through Mid-Century in the state of California would pay far more than if insuring through many other companies.

Used Cars

What to Buy, and Where to Buy It

Performance cars, luxury models, and convertibles are expensive even when secondhand, and many are packed with trouble-prone options. Your dollar will generally go further when you buy a small or medium-size sedan.

If you can, buy a used car with a known history—from a trusted relative, friend, or neighbor. Be more wary with other private sellers. Ask about the car's condition and mileage, and ask to look at repair bills. Ask whether the car has ever been in an accident. Ask why the car is being sold; the seller may divulge a problem you'd rather not cope with. If the seller is, in fact, a dealer, and the ad you're responding to hasn't clearly stated that fact, the dealer's ethics are questionable. Shop elsewhere.

You can't really recognize a bargain unless you know what the going prices are on specific models. A good source of such information is *Consumer Reports* Used Car Price Service, a call-in service. Whether you're buying, selling, or trading in, the price you'll hear is updated frequently for your region and takes into account mileage, major options, and general condition. When you call, have this information ready:

- your Zip Code
- mileage
- model name or number
- number of cylinders
- major options
- condition of vehicle

The service will cost you $1.50 per minute (expect five or more minutes for a typical call). Call 1-900-446-1120, seven days a week between 7:00 A.M. and 2:00 A.M. EST (no service available for Alaska and Hawaii).

Shop only for models with a proven record of reliability; avoid models likely to prove troublesome. See box on pages 245 to 249.

Look Them Over First

Never buy a used car without checking it out thoroughly on a sunny day. Bring along a helper (if possible, one with some car expertise), and check the following:

Fluids and leaks. While the car is parked, look for dark stains or puddles on the pavement underneath. They can mean leaks from the cooling

USED CARS: GOOD BETS, BAD BETS

The list of Reliable Used Cars includes 1985–1989 models whose overall repair record has been considerably better than average for a particular model year. Prices are averages in the Midwest for cars with average mileage, air-conditioning, AM/FM cassette stereo, and an automatic transmission (for cars) or a manual transmission (pickups and sport/utility vehicles). The list of Used Cars to Avoid, below, includes models whose overall repair record is considerably worse than average. Problems with the engine, transmission, clutch, and body rust have been weighted more heavily than others. RWD indicates rear-wheel drive; FWD, front-wheel drive; 4WD, four-wheel drive. (All judgments based on *Consumer Reports* reader experience with more than 806,000 cars, as reported in Consumer's Union's 1990 Annual Questionnaire and published in *Consumer Reports,* April 1991.)

RELIABLE USED CARS

$2500–3000

85 Chevrolet Nova
85 Honda Civic (2WD)
86 Isuzu pickup (2WD)
85 Mazda GLC
 (FWD) ☐
85 Mazda pickup
 (2WD) ☐
86 Mitsubishi pickup 4
 (2WD)
86 Subaru hatchback
 (2WD)
85, 86 Toyota Tercel
 (except wagon)
85 VW Golf Diesel

$3000–3500

87 Chevrolet Sprint
88 Dodge Colt (2WD)
88 Ford Festiva
85 Honda Civic CRX
86 Mazda pickup
 (2WD) ☐
86 Mercury Marquis
 V6
87 Mitsubishi pickup 4
 (2WD)
85 Nissan pickup 4
 (2WD)
86 Plymouth Colt
 (2WD)

85 Toyota pickup 4
 (2WD)
85 VW Jetta Diesel

$3500–4000

86 Chevrolet Nova
88 Chevrolet Sprint
87 Dodge Colt (2WD)
86 Honda Civic (2WD)
85 Honda Civic (4WD)
87 Isuzu pickup
 (2WD) ☐
86 Mazda 323
86 Nissan pickup 4
 (2WD)
87 ☑, 88 Plymouth
 Colt (2WD)
86 Toyota pickup 4
 (2WD)
87 Toyota Tercel
 (except wagon)
86 Toyota Tercel
 wagon (2WD)
86 VW Golf Diesel

$4000–4500

87 Chevrolet S10
 pickup V6 (2WD)
87 Dodge Ram 50
 pickup 4 (2WD)
89 Ford Festiva
86 Honda Civic CRX

88 Isuzu pickup (2WD)
87 Mazda pickup
 (2WD) ☐
87 Nissan pickup 4
 (2WD)
86 Nissan pickup V6
 (2WD)
87 Nissan Sentra
 (2WD)
86 Nissan Stanza ☑
86 Toyota Corolla
 (FWD)
87 Toyota Corolla FX
85 Toyota Corolla SR-
 5 (RWD)
86 VW Jetta Diesel

$4500–5000

87 Chevrolet Nova
89 Daihatsu Charade
89 Dodge Colt (2WD)
85 Honda Accord
86 Honda Civic (4WD)
87 Mazda 323
88 Mazda pickup
 (2WD)
88 Mitsubishi pickup 4
 (2WD)
88 Nissan Sentra
 (2WD)
89 Plymouth Colt
 (2WD)

86 Toyota Corolla SR-5 (RWD)
87 Toyota pickup 4 (2WD)
88 Toyota Tercel (except wagon)
87 Toyota Tercel wagon (2WD)
86 Toyota Tercel wagon (4WD)

$5000–6000

88 Chevrolet Nova
88 Dodge Ram pickup 4 (2WD)
88 Ford Ranger pickup V6 (2WD) ①
89 Geo Spectrum
86 Honda Accord
87 Honda Civic (2WD)
87 Honda Civic CRX
88 Mazda 323
87 Mazda 626 ①
89 Mitsubishi pickup 4 (2WD)
88 Nissan pickup 4 (2WD)
87 Nissan pickup V6 (2WD)
87 Nissan Stanza
88 Subaru sedan, wagon (2WD)
87 Toyota Corolla (FWD)
88 Toyota Corolla FX
87 Toyota Corolla SR-5 (RWD)
86 Toyota MR2
88 Toyota pickup 4 (2WD)
89 Toyota Tercel (except wagon)
87 Toyota Tercel wagon (4WD)

$6000–7000

86 Acura Integra
88 Chrysler Le Baron GTS

87 Dodge Raider
89 Dodge Ram 50 pickup 4 (2WD)
89 Eagle Summit
86 Ford LTD Crown Victoria
88 Honda Civic (2WD)
87 Honda Civic (4WD)
88 Honda Civic CRX
89 Mazda 323
87 Mazda 626 Turbo ①
89 Mazda pickup (2WD)
86 Mazda RX-7 ②
86 Mercury Grand Marquis
89 Mercury Tracer
89 Mitsubishi Mirage
87 Mitsubishi Montero 4
89 Nissan pickup 4 (2WD)
89 Nissan pickup V6 (2WD) ①
87 Nissan pickup V6 (4WD)
89 Nissan Sentra
87 Nissan Stanza wagon (2WD)
87 Olds Cutlass Supreme V6 (RWD)
89 Subaru sedan, wagon (2WD)
88 Subaru sedan, wagon (4WD)
88 Toyota Corolla (FWD)
89 Toyota pickup 4 (2WD)
87 Toyota pickup 4 (4WD)
85 Toyota Supra
87 Toyota Van (2WD)

$7000–8000

87 Acura Integra
87 Ford LTD Crown Victoria
87 Honda Accord

88 Honda Civic (4WD)
86 Honda Prelude
87 Jeep Cherokee, Wagoneer 6 (2WD)
88 Mazda 626 ①
88 Nissan 200SX 4
87 Nissan 200SX V6
88 Nissan Stanza
86 Toyota 4Runner 4 (4WD)
87 Toyota Camry 4 (2WD)
87 Toyota Celica (2WD)
87 Toyota MR2
88 Toyota pickup 4 (4WD)
89 Toyota pickup V6 (2WD)
88 Toyota pickup V6 (4WD)

$8000–10,000

88 Acura Integra
88 Buick Le Sabre V6
88 Chrysler New Yorker, E-class 4 (FWD)
88 Dodge 600 Turbo
89 Dodge Colt Vista (2WD)
88 Ford LTD Crown Victoria
89 Ford Probe 4
88 Honda Accord
89 Honda Civic (2WD)
89 Honda Civic CRX
87 Honda Prelude
88 Isuzu Trooper II 4 ①
89 Mazda 626
89 Mazda MPV 4
89 Mazda pickup (4WD)
87, 88 Mercury Grand Marquis
89 Mitsubishi Galant 4
87 Nissan Pathfinder (4WD)

89 Nissan pickup 4
(4WD) ☐
89 Nissan pickup V6
(4WD) ☐
89 Nissan Stanza
88 Nissan Stanza
wagon (2WD)
89 Subaru sedan,
wagon (4WD)
88, 89 Toyota Camry 4
(2WD)
88 Toyota Camry V6
88 Toyota Celica
(2WD)
89 Toyota Corolla
(FWD)
88, 89 Toyota Corolla
(4WD)
86, 87 Toyota Cressida
88 Toyota MR2
89 Toyota pickup 4
(4WD)
89 Toyota pickup V6
(4WD)
88 Toyota van (2WD)
87 Volvo 240

$10,000–12,000

89 Acura Integra
86 Acura Legend
88 Audi 80,90 4
85, 86 BMW 325
(2WD)
88 Buick Electra V6
89 Buick Le Sabre V6
87 Cadillac Eldorado
89 Ford Probe 4 Turbo
89 Honda Accord
89 Honda Civic (4WD)
88, 89 Honda Prelude
89 Isuzu Trooper II 4
87 Lincoln Continental
(RWD)
87 Lincoln Town Car
89 Nissan 240SX
87 Nissan 300ZX
88 Nissan Maxima
89 Nissan Pulsar NX

87, 88 Toyota 4Runner
4 (4WD)
88 Toyota Camry 4
(4WD) ☐
89 Toyota Camry V6
89 Toyota Celica (2WD)
89 Toyota MR2
87 Toyota Supra
89 Toyota van (2WD)
87 Volvo 740

$12,000–15,000

87, 88 Acura Legend
87 Audi 5000
87 Audi 5000 Quattro
Turbo
87 BMW 325 (2WD)
87 BMW 5 series ☐
89 Buick Riviera V6
88 Cadillac Brougham
88 Cadillac Deville,
Fleetwood
88 Lincoln Town Car
88 Mazda 929
89 Mazda MPV V6
(2WD)
88 Mazda RX-7
85 Mercedes-Benz 300
Turbodiesel
89 Mitsubishi Montero
V6
89 Nissan Maxima
88, 89 Nissan
Pathfinder (4WD)
89 Toyota 4Runner 4
(4WD)
88, 89 Toyota 4Runner
V6 (4WD)
89 Toyota Camry 4
(4WD)
88 Toyota Cressida
88, 89 Toyota Land
Cruiser
88 Toyota Supra
87, 88 Toyota Supra
Turbo
88 Volvo 240

$15,000–21,000

89 Acura Legend
88, 89 Audi 5000,
100,200
89 BMW 325 (2WD)
88 BMW 5 series ☐
88, 89 Cadillac
Eldorado
89 Cadillac Seville
89 Mazda 929
89 Mazda RX-7
89 Toyota Cressida
89 Toyota Supra
89 Toyota Supra
Turbo

Over $21,000

89 Mercedes-Benz
190E
87, 89 Mercedes-Benz
260
86–89 Mercedes-Benz
300
86, 87 Mercedes-Benz
420
86–89 Mercedes Benz
560

USED CARS TO AVOID

BMW

7 Series, 88, 89

Buick

Century 4, V6, 85, 86
Electra V6, 85, 86
Estate Wagon, 86, 89
Le Sabre V6, 86, 87
Regal V6, V6 Turbo (RWD), 87
Regal V6 (FWD), 89
Regal V8 (RWD), 86
Riviera V6, 86
Skyhawk, 85–89
Skylark 4, V6, 85
Somerset, Skylark 4, 86, 87; V6, 85, 86

Cadillac

Cimarron 4, 85; V6, 86, 87

Chevrolet

Astro van V6 (2WD), 86, 88, 89
Blazer, 85, 87–89
Camaro V6, 85–89; V8, 86–89
Cavalier 4, 85, 89; V6, 86–89
Celebrity 4, 85, 86; V6, 86
Chevette, 85, 87
Corsica, Beretta 4, V6, 88, 89
Corvette, 85–89
Monte Carlo V8, 86–88
10-20 pickup V6 (2WD), 88, 89; V6 (4WD), 89; V8 (2WD), 87–89; V8 (4WD), 85–89
S-10 Blazer 4 (4WD), 87; V6 (2WD), 89; V6 (4WD), 85, 88, 89

S-10 pickup 4 (2WD), 89; V6, 89 ①
Spectrum, 85
Sportvan V8, 86–89
Suburban, 85–89

Chrysler

Conquest, 87
Laser, 85, 86; Turbo, 85
Le Baron Coupe, 89; Turbo, 87, 89
Le Baron GTS Turbo, 85, 86

Dodge

Aries, 85, 89
B150-250 Wagon van V8, 85–89
Caravan, Grand Caravan, 89
Colt Vista (2WD), 85 ①; (4WD), 86 ①
D100-250 Ram pickup V8 (2WD, 4WD), 88, 89
Dakota pickup 4, 87–89 ①; V6 (2WD), 88; V6 (4WD), 88, 89
Daytona, 85 ①, 86, 87, 89; Turbo, 86–88
Dynasty 4, 89
Lancer, 85 ①
Omni America, Charger, 85, 86 ①, 87, 89
Shadow, 87, 89; Turbo, 87

Eagle

Medallion, 88
Premier, 88, 89

Ford

Aerostar van V6 (2WD), 86–88
Bronco V8, 85–88
Bronco II (2WD), 87, 88 ②; (4WD), 85, 86 ②, 87 ②

Club Wagon van 6, 85; V8, 85–89
Escort, 85–87
F150-250 pickup 6 (2WD), 87 ①; V8 (2WD), 88, 89
F150-250 pickup V8 (4WD), 87–89; V8 diesel (4WD), 85, 89
Mustang 4, 87, 88; V8, 89 ①
Ranger pickup V6 (4WD), 86 ②, 87
Taurus 4, 86–88; V6, 89 ①
Tempo (2WD), 85 ②, 87, 88; (4WD), 88, 89
Thunderbird 4 Turbo, 88 ②; V6, 89

Geo

Metro 89 ②

GMC

S15 Jimmy V6 (4WD), 85 ①, 88 ①, 89

Hyundai

Excel, 86–88
Sonata 4, 89

Isuzu

I-Mark, 85 ①

Jaguar

XJ6, 86–89

Jeep

Cherokee, Wagoneer 4 (4WD), 85, 86 ②, 89; 6 (2WD), 89; 6 (4WD), 85, 86 ②, 87 ①, 89 ②
Grand Wagoneer, 85–89
Wrangler 6, 87–89

Lincoln

Continental V6 (FWD), 88
Mark VII, 89

Mazda

626 Turbo, 88 ②
MX-6, MX-6 Turbo, 88 ②

Mercedes-Benz

190E, 86

Mercury

Cougar V6, 89
Lynx, 85, 86 ②
Topaz (2WD), 85 ②, 87, 88

Merkur

XR4Ti, 85, 86
Scorpio, 88

Mitsubishi

Galant 4, 87 ②
Precis, 87, 88
Starion, 87

Nissan

van, 87, 88

Oldsmobile

Eighty-Eight V6, 86, 87
Ninety-Eight V6 (FWD), 86
Custom Cruiser, 85, 86, 88
Cutlass Calais 4 (FWD), 86; V6 (FWD), 85–87
Cutlass Ciera 4, 86; V6, 85, 86
Cutlass Supreme V6 (FWD) 88, 89
Firenza 4, 85, 86
Toronado V6, 86, 87

Peugeot

505 4, 86

Plymouth

Horizon, Turismo, America, 85, 86 ①, 87, 89
Reliant, 89
Sundance, 87 ①, 89; Turbo, 87
Voyager, 89
Grand Voyager, 89

Pontiac

1000, 85 ①, 87 ①
6000 4, 86, 87
6000, 6000STE V6, 85, 88
Bonneville (FWD), 87
Fiero GT V6, 88
Firebird V6, 85 ①, 86–89; V8, 86–89
Grand Am 4, 86; V6, 85–87
Grand Prix V8 (RWD), 86
Grand Prix V6 (FWD), 88, 89
Le Mans, 88, 89
Sunbird, 2000, 85, 86, 87 ②, 88 ②

Renault (AMC)

Alliance, Encore, 85–87

Saab

900, 900S, 88, 89
9000, 9000S, 87, 89; Turbo, 87, 88 ②

Sterling

825 model, 87, 88

Subaru

Justy (2WD), 89 ②
sedan, wagon Turbo (4WD), 85–87
XT Coupe 4 (2WD), 86 ①

Volkswagen

Golf, 88 ①

① Manual transmission only.
② Automatic transmission only.

249

system, transmission, engine, or elsewhere. With the engine cold, remove the radiator cap and look inside the radiator; the fluid shouldn't be rusty. Greenish-white stains on the outside of the radiator indicate pinholes and the prospect of growing leakage.

Body. Blistered or peeling paint usually signals rust. If rust eats through the car or trunk floor, it can let deadly exhaust fumes inside. Left unchecked, it may affect not only the driver's health but the structural integrity and safety of the body and suspension of the car.

Place a small magnet against the wheel wells and the rocker panels under the doors—areas most likely to rust—and elsewhere on the car's body. If the magnet doesn't stick, it may indicate a "quick and dirty" patch-up job with plastic putty to cover rust or accident damage. Patchy or uneven color and poorly fitted doors, trunk lid, or hood may also be evidence of an accident.

Tires and suspension. A car with 25,000 miles or less on the odometer should still have its original tires. If the tires are bald (or brand-new, for that matter), someone may have rolled back or disconnected the odometer. Unevenly worn tires may signal accident damage or simply improper wheel alignment. Check the spare tire and make sure the jack and other tire-changing gear are present. A musty odor or water stains in the trunk may mean leakage.

Push and pull each front tire while holding it at the top. If you hear a clunk or feel play in the wheel, the wheel bearings or suspension joints may be worn.

Push down hard at each corner of the car a few times to bounce it up and down, and then let go. If the car needs more than one rebound to level off, the shock absorbers are suspect.

Stand about 10 feet behind the car to see whether one side is lower than the other. Then do the same from the other side to see whether the front or rear sags. A lopsided car may need new springs.

Interior. The seats should be free from broken springs and rips in the upholstery, and they should not sag. A musty odor may signal water seepage, which is hard to find and even harder to plug. Examine the pedals; rubber pedal pads that are badly worn (or brand-new) belie a low odometer reading.

Check out all controls and accessories: safety belts, heater and air conditioner, radio/cassette player, horn, wipers and washers, seat adjusters, power windows and door locks, remote-controlled mirrors, dashboard indicator lights and gauges, and alarm system, if any. Have your helper stand outside to verify that the headlight high and low beams, parking lights, turn signals, backup lights, and license-plate lights are working.

The Road Test

If everything checks out so far, spend at least half an hour test-driving the car along various roads and at various speeds. Note the following:

Engine. The car should start quickly and easily, even when the engine is cold. Drive-away should be smooth, with no lurching, coughing, or odd noises. The car should accelerate smoothly and maintain power when climbing hills. Pings or knocks may mean the engine needs higher-octane fuel or a tune-up; leave the diagnosis to a mechanic.

With the engine warm, accelerate to about 45 mph, take your foot off the accelerator for a few seconds, and then tramp down hard on the accelerator. Your helper should watch through the rear window. Black smoke from the tailpipe may mean only that the fuel system needs adjusting. But blue smoke means that the car is an oil burner and that an expensive engine rebuild or replacement lies ahead.

Persistent billowy white smoke is another bad omen. It tells you that coolant may be getting into the engine's combustion chambers, probably through a blown head gasket or a crack in the cylinder head or engine block. (But white vapor exiting the tailpipe briefly when you first start up on a damp, frosty morning is nothing to worry about.)

Transmission. Smooth shifting is the key here. A manual clutch should engage smoothly, without bucking or juddering. If the clutch doesn't engage until the pedal is nearly all the way up, or if the pedal doesn't have an inch or so of free play at the top, you could face an expensive clutch job.

If the car has an automatic transmission, inspect it with the transmission dipstick. The fluid should be reddish, with a faint odor of chestnuts. A dark-brown color, a rancid smell, or metal particles on the dipstick bode ill.

Steering. The car should hold the road nicely. Steering should be smooth and precise, without much free play or vibration.

Have your helper kneel in the road in a safe area and watch from behind as you drive straight ahead. The front and rear wheels should travel precisely in line. If the car sidles along like a crab, an accident has probably bent the body or frame. Give up on that car. If the car's steering simply pulls to one side, though, a wheel alignment may save the day.

Brakes. Accelerate to 45 mph on a flat stretch of empty road and brake fairly hard, without locking the wheels. In each of three consecutive tries, the car should stop quickly, with no swerving, grabbing, or vibration. With the engine idling, press firmly on the brake pedal for about 30 seconds. It should feel solid and rock steady. If it feels spongy or keeps sinking, the hydraulic system may be leaking.

Comfort and noise. Cruise down a bumpy road at 30 or 40 mph. Does the car bound, bottom out, or hop sideways? The suspension could be faulty. Do you hear squeaks and rattles? They can be hard to trace and eliminate.

With the engine running, listen from outside the car for sputtering or rumbling from the exhaust pipe, manifold, muffler, or catalytic converter. Replacing those parts, especially the catalytic converter, can be pricey.

Excise Taxes Hit Gas-Guzzlers Harder

Changes in the tax code have made running an inefficient car even more financially punishing. Over the five years starting in 1991, Americans will pay an extra $66 billion in higher excise, or usage, taxes. For the average household, that means about $100 more in 1991 for taxes affecting:

- *Gasoline.* As of December 1990, drivers are paying 5 cents more per gallon in federal gasoline taxes. For an average car using 500 gallons of gasoline per year, that translates to $25.
- *Gas-guzzlers.* You'll now pay an excise tax of between $1,000 and $7,700 if you buy an inefficient car, double the earlier penalty. The rule targets new vehicles weighing under 6,000 pounds that get fewer than 22.5 miles per gallon, such as a **Cadillac Brougham** with a 5.7-liter V8 engine. Limousines are also subject to the tax, regardless of their weight.

Automobile Leasing

Not Such a Bargain After All

Will you save money, as some ads contend, by leasing a car rather than buying it? Probably not. Leasing a car usually isn't as good a deal as owning one. True, monthly lease payments may be lower than installment-buying payments. But if you buy, you own a car worth a considerable amount of money when it's paid up. If you lease, you may own nothing after the same period. People who lease a car usually don't avoid the normal responsibilities of ownership, either—insurance, maintenance, and sometimes repairs of any unusual damage.

Leasing does buy convenience for people who trade in cars often or who dislike borrowing money. A lease is also the only way to drive a new car when you can afford the monthly payments but not the down payment.

Your Lease Responsibilities

If you sign a lease, you will be responsible for the following expenses:

Security deposit. Usually equal to one or two months' payments but refundable (usually without interest) at the end of the lease, if the car is in good shape.

Advance payment. You'll probably have to pay for the first month or two in advance.

Title and registration. Usually about $100. Try to negotiate to have the company pay those fees.

Monthly payments. Most leases run for 36 to 48 months. Monthly payments on a four-year lease are usually 10 to 15 percent lower than on a three-year lease.

Insurance. Most leasing companies set minimum limits that are higher than those required in most states. A few leasing companies offer insurance to their customers. But we recommend you shop around for prices from at least three insurance companies.

Maintenance and repairs. Try to negotiate to have the leasing company share the burden of the car's upkeep and repair. For an additional monthly fee, some leasing companies will cover all or part of the maintenance.

The Consumer Leasing Act requires companies to disclose any warranties provided by car manufacturers and to tell you if any additional warranties are available.

In some states, you also have protection under state "lemon laws," which cover new cars that turn out to be duds. According to most state laws, a car is a lemon if it has been taken in for repair of the same problem four times without success during the first 12,000 miles or one year, whichever comes first, or if the car has been out of service at least 30 days. If you have a lemon, the prescribed remedy is a new car or your money back.

Lemon laws don't apply to leased cars in every state. To find out the law in your state, contact the department of motor vehicles or the state attorney general.

Mileage charges. Leases also include a limitation on mileage—with an added cost for each mile over the limit. For example, if a lease allows 18,000 miles a year but you log 20,000, you may have to pay 12 or 15 cents or more per mile for the excess. That's an additional $240 to $300 a year.

Wear and tear. When you return the car, you will have to pay for any unrepaired damage, missing equipment, or excessive wear and tear. The Consumer Leasing Act requires the company to define unreasonable damage, but the language is often vague. If the lease is unclear, ask for a detailed description of the damage you're responsible for.

Disposition charge. Some leases make you responsible for a "disposition charge" of $150 to $250 or so—the cost of the cleaning and repair needed to prepare the car for resale. Try to negotiate the disposition charge out of the lease.

Early termination. The Consumer Leasing Act requires the company to tell you under what conditions you can get out of the lease early and what the penalties will be, but it does not limit the penalty.

The sooner you break a lease, the stiffer the penalties. In the early part of a lease, the car depreciates more than the amount covered by your monthly payments. So the leasing company levies an early termination fee to make up for the shortfall.

Charges if the car is lost or stolen. Many leasing companies consider a stolen or totaled car an early termination. They then slap you with fees for expenses in excess of the amount paid by your insurance coverage. Never sign a lease that will penalize you if your car is lost or stolen.

Shop Carefully for a Lease

You can lease from a new-car dealer who sells the make you want, or you can choose from almost any make and model by shopping at an independent leasing company. It's best to collect estimates from at least three companies, carefully comparing the total price and terms of each lease.

Don't hesitate to challenge the first monthly price quoted by a leasing company. You shouldn't expect to pay the first price quoted for most car leases.

Haggling pays; a small reduction in the monthly payment can make a big difference over the life of a lease. Consider paying a small, fixed, up-front charge in exchange for a reduction in the monthly payment. For example, a $25-per-month reduction would save you $1,200 over the life of a four-year lease.

Maintenance and Repair

Which Gasoline for Your Car?

Premium-grade gasoline is not "more powerful" than regular. Nor does it burn more easily. Nor does it generally improve fuel mileage. Buying gasoline with a higher octane number than your car needs is a waste of money.

Most cars run happily on unleaded regular (87 octane) gasoline. Only about 10 percent of today's cars need a mid-grade (89 octane) or premium (91 octane or higher) gasoline. To find out which grade of gasoline your car was designed to use, check the octane recommendation in your car owner's manual.

If your car knocks on the recommended gasoline, a tune-up may be more in order than a higher grade of gasoline—at least in older cars, where ignition timing and fuel mixture can be adjusted. Most cars built in the last few years, however, don't permit such adjustments; all of their engine functions are electronically controlled. In those models, a mid-grade or premium fuel may be the only answer.

If your car has a carburetor, you needn't be concerned about a gasoline's detergents. Just about all gasoline sold today has a detergent package effective enough to keep carburetors clean. Buy the cheapest gasoline that has sufficient octane.

If your car is a recent model with a fuel-injected engine, you need a gasoline with a detergent package that keeps the fuel injectors and intake valves relatively free of fuel deposits.

The closest thing to a standard test for a gasoline's ability to keep valves clean is one developed by the German automaker BMW. A gasoline can pass at either of two levels: "unlimited mileage," in which the deposits average less than 100 milligrams per valve, or "50,000 miles," in which the average weight gain is more than 100 milligrams but fewer than 250. Many national and regional brands are said by their refiners to meet BMW's unlimited-mileage standards, though not all grades of a particular brand may pass.

Fill-up hints. When you fill up, stop after the first or second click of the nozzle's automatic shutoff. Letting the gasoline overflow the filler not only wastes money, it's a fire hazard. It can also damage the car's paint unless you promptly rinse with water. And as the gasoline evaporates, it pollutes the air.

Always unscrew the fuel-filler cap slowly, letting the pressure in the fuel tank vent gradually. In some cars, rapid removal of the cap can let gasoline spurt out of the tank. Such spurting has caused fires in automobiles and at service stations.

Don't let your car's fuel tank get below half-full in cold weather. The more air in the tank, the more chance of condensation. Water in the fuel can freeze in the fuel line and prevent the engine from starting.

Motor Oils

Attention to minor maintenance and use of the proper fluids can extend a car's life markedly. Oil, for instance, is an engine's lifeblood—it seals, cools, cleanses, lubricates, and helps fight corrosion. But you must use the proper product for your car and climate. The label on the container tells what you need to know.

The Society of Automotive Engineers (SAE) sets many motor-oil standards. The letters and numbers following the letters SAE on an oil container define the oil's viscosity grade. For example, oil labeled SAE 10W-30 is a multigrade oil. The first number, 10, refers to flow properties at low temperatures (the lower the number, the thinner the oil). The second number, 30, tells the high-temperature flow properties. The W denotes an oil recommended for winter use.

Oil thins out, sometimes excessively, as it heats up, so multigrade oils contain additives called viscosity-index improvers. These additives make a multigrade oil behave, when warm, like a relatively thick SAE 30 oil.

However, some viscosity additives can cause damaging deposits. A 10W-40 oil contains more viscosity additives than a 10W-30 oil. It's best to stay away from multigrade oils with a wide spread in numbers, such as 10W-50. Use the narrowest spread that's suitable for the climate in your area.

If the container reads "Energy Conserving," the oil probably has friction-modifier additives that can help improve fuel economy by a fraction of a mile per gallon.

Most oil containers also carry an API (American Petroleum Institute) symbol that refers to performance or service level. Take API Service SF/CC, for example. The S means the oil is suitable for gasoline engines. The next letter, on a scale from A to G, indicates the oil's performance level. Some oils carry a designation such as API Service CC or DD. The C means the oil is suitable for diesel engines; the performance scale (the next letter) runs from A to D. (CD is designed for more severe service than CC.)

For gasoline engines, the SG performance level is the newest type of oil on the market. It promises the best protection against wear, oxidation, and sludge buildup. In cars made before the SG level was introduced, the owner's manual may recommend an earlier level, such as SE or SD. SG oils may be used—and, in fact, are preferable—in such cars.

To increase an engine's life expectancy, change its oil more frequently than the interval recommended by the automaker—every three months or 3,000 miles is a good rule of thumb. If the recommendations in your owner's manual allow, use a 10W-30 oil. It can give slightly better fuel economy than 10W-40 oil and produces fewer engine deposits. And, while under stress, it can provide a thicker film between moving parts than most 5W-30 oils. Also, the thicker film provided by a 10W-30 oil will benefit an older engine.

A brand name of oil sold at a discount store is no different from the same brand name sold at a service station. So, buy motor oil at the lowest price available.

Batteries

An auto battery should present no mysteries to the consumer. Ideally, you need know only the size your car requires. Then you can shop by comparing the manufacturer's specifications and prices for batteries of the same size.

In the real world, however, mysteries abound. It's a mystery to us, for example, why six dozen of the batteries CU tested for a 1991 report delivered less current than the manufacturers claimed they would. Batteries can lose some power with age. But we tested relatively fresh batteries, fewer than six months old.

Mysterious, too, for the typical consumer, is the age of the battery at the point of sale. Although our shoppers asked for fresh batteries, more than 15 percent of the ones originally sold to us were more than six months old. We scrapped that batch and sent the shoppers out to do more buying, this time armed with manufacturers' information that allowed them to crack the date codes on the batteries. Only with that extra sleuthing could we avoid testing old batteries.

If you have to replace a battery, you'll have to confront the same kinds of mysteries we did.

The principal types of battery on the market today are the following:

Low-maintenance. This type, sometimes termed a "dual alloy" or "hybrid" battery, has caps or covers over each cell to permit periodic refilling. Some low-maintenance batteries have a translucent case, through which you can check the electrolyte level. Most of the batteries we tested are low-maintenance.

Maintenance-free. The name implies that this type never needs water; indeed, some maintenance-free batteries have no caps. Maintenance-free batteries, sometimes termed "calcium/calcium," may not fare as well as low-maintenance batteries after deep discharges.

Dual. Of the three we tested, two combine a standard low-maintenance battery with separate backup cells for emergencies or for when you need extra power. A switch on the battery case activates the backup. The third, the **Champion Switch,** is a unique two-in-one design.

Manufacturers further categorize batteries by group number, which denotes the size of the case. Within a group size, power output varies from brand to brand and even among models of the same brand.

You probably won't find the group-size number in your car's owner's manual, so you'll have to check the label on the old battery or refer to the battery dealer's handbook for the group size appropriate for your car.

Finally, manufacturers use two specifications to characterize a battery's power output:

Cold-cranking amps (CCA). This describes how much current the battery can deliver to the starter motor for a specified time. Manufacturers offer several CCA levels for the batteries in their line, to accommodate the differing demands of automobile electrical systems. The batteries we tested—one group with 455 to 550 claimed CCA, another with 600 to 650 claimed CCA—cover popular power ranges.

Reserve capacity. Listed in minutes, this describes a battery's ability to continue supplying power to the engine and the headlights if the charging system fails. A battery's reserve normally helps supply power to accessories when the engine is close to idle speed—in stop-and-go driving, for example, with the lights, wipers, and other accessories running.

Power loss. Unless a retailer periodically charges the batteries in stock, they will gradually lose their charge as the days pass. They can lose much of the original charge in something like six months and can then begin to age permanently because of internal chemical changes. Obviously, you don't want to pay a new-battery price for one that's prematurely middle-aged.

The industry's own test procedures call for batteries no more than 60 days old to serve as test samples. We had set a more realistic cutoff age of six months for our samples. As we noted, we couldn't find a sufficient number of batteries even that fresh in our first round of buying, when we took the retailers at their word that they were selling us fresh batteries. We discarded the first 84 batteries purchased. And even when we sent the shoppers out armed with the shipping-date codes to judge age, we ran into problems. In the end, we had to buy what was on hand for the **Sears DieHard DualStart** and the **Interstate X2 Booster** dual batteries; we had difficulty dating samples we saw and couldn't always find fresh samples. All the other batteries we tested were fewer than six months old when we bought them.

We made sure each battery was fully charged before we began testing. Then, using standard industry tests, we checked each brand's actual cold-cranking amperage and reserve capacity. We tested eight samples of each battery. Half failed to match their claimed cold-cranking ability. Only the **Delco Freedom 24-60,** the **Interstate 24-42,** and the **Energizer** consistently delivered the power they claimed. The others fell short—some far short. The dual batteries were among the worst.

Our tests for reserve capacity produced more encouraging results. Nearly every model met or exceeded the capacity claimed, though results for some brands varied considerably.

Refunds, full and partial. Every auto battery comes with a complicated warranty. In most cases, it provides for a free replacement if the battery fails within the first 3 to 12 months. If the battery fails further down the road, manufacturers offer a prorated warranty, in effect a partial credit toward a new battery based on the number of months the failed one was in service.

The prorating isn't always straightforward. Suppose, for example, that you paid $60 for a battery with a $100 list price. If the battery failed halfway through its warranty period and if the prorating were based on that $100 list price, you would have to pay $50 for a replacement— almost as much as you paid for the original.

Recommendations. If your old battery has served you well, you should replace it with one that's comparable—not necessarily the same brand, but one that has a comparable cold-cranking amperage. There's usually no reason to pay for a more powerful battery; you'll pay for power your car may never need.

The models to consider first are the **Delco Freedom 24-60,** the **Interstate 24-42,** and the **Energizer.** Those three, with a cold-cranking capacity ranging from 455 to 525 amps, were the only ones to deliver consistently the power they claimed to have. The **Delco** also surpassed comparable models in its reserve capacity. The higher-amperage batteries to consider first are the **Deka 624MF** and the **Sears DieHard 43224,** rated at 650 and 600 cold-cranking amps, respectively. Most of the samples delivered the power claimed. The **Deka** did better than the **Sears** in our reserve-capacity test.

Batteries that failed our cold-cranking test may perform reliably in your car. (In particular, the backup feature on the dual batteries may bail you out if you sap the main battery by leaving the lights on overnight.) With those batteries, though, you won't get all the power you've paid for.

List prices in our 1991 test ranged from $40 to $132, but discounts are common.

Check the new battery periodically, just as you would the engine oil or coolant levels:

- Check the electrolyte level in a low-maintenance battery every month or so at first. Do the same for a maintenance-free battery with caps over the cells. You can check it less often as you become familiar with its rate of water loss. Top off the cells with distilled water as needed and replace the vent caps securely.

- Inspect the battery terminals periodically. Corrosion buildup degrades the electrical contact, which can reduce the current flow to the starter motor. Use a wire brush to keep the terminals and posts clean.

- Check the hold-down hardware that keeps a battery from vibrating. Vibration can shorten a battery's life.

- Neutralize sulfuric acid on the battery case by washing it with a baking-soda solution. Always use eye protection when working around batteries and be aware that the acid can burn your skin. Don't smoke or use an open flame near an auto battery; it could explode.

Sometimes, automotive electrical problems aren't the battery's fault. If the battery is properly maintained but too weak to crank over the engine, suspect the alternator and voltage regulator. Check the charging system and the drive belt, along with the starter solenoid, the ignition switch, and the wiring.

If the battery does need to be replaced, be sure to return it to the dealer for recycling. Don't throw away an auto battery with other household trash.

CRACKING THE CODE
FRESHNESS DATES

In 1991, a CU staff member who has a five-year-old car with its original battery decided to start shopping for a replacement. The first store he visited had a sale on batteries in progress. He spotted a promising model on the shelf—the right size, the right amount of power, an attractive price. Stamped on top of the case was the date code "6JN."

Our battery testers cracked that code for him. Turns out the battery had been gathering dust for as long as he had been driving his car. It was shipped to the dealer in October 1986.

Granted, most stores don't sell five-year-old batteries. But they do sell batteries that have been sitting on the shelf for six months to a year.

It is possible to buy a fresh battery, if you know how to decipher the shipping code. (A battery is generally shipped within three months of manufacture.) The code can appear on a sticker affixed to the battery or stamped on the case. It may be a string of letters and numbers, but all the information you need is in the first two characters.

All the batteries we tested, with the exception of **Delco** and **Douglas,** start the code with a letter that represents the month: A for January, B for February, and so on. Next comes a digit for the year—1 for 1991. So A1 or A1X stands for January 1991; B1 would represent February 1991. Some codes skip the letter I, so M would represent the month of December.

Delco batteries use the first character to represent the year and the second the month. So, 1CN1 would be 1991, March. **Douglas** uses the letters in its name to encode the year: U equals 1989, G equals 1990, and L equals 1991. The second character represents the month. Thus, the code L-9 stands for September 1991.

Clearly these codes are not intended to help you buy fresh batteries.

Ratings of Auto Batteries

As published in the October 1991 issue of *Consumer Reports*. Listed by types. Standard batteries are listed in groups by manufacturers' cold-cranking amperage range; within groups, listed in order of performance in CU's test of cold-cranking amperage.

❶ Brand and model. We chose batteries from most major brands, in popular sizes for replacement batteries.

❷ Price. The manufacturer's suggested retail price. Discounts may be available.

❸ Group size. Batteries are classified into group sizes based on physical dimensions. Group size 24, the one we tried to find for each brand, is the most popular size. Group size 26 is a common alternative. Two of the dual batteries come only in group size 34.

❹ Cold-cranking amps. This factor reflects a battery's ability to start an engine in the dead of winter. These columns give both the manufacturers' *rated* cold-cranking amps and a judgment that reflects *performance* in our test. The higher the score, the more samples had the rated amperage. Numbers in parentheses for the dual batteries are the rated cold-cranking amps for both portions of the battery. Our judgments are for the main battery only.

❺ Reserve capacity. Indicates how many minutes a fully charged battery could keep the engine and electrical accessories running in the event the charging system fails. These columns give the manufacturers' *rated* reserve capacity and the median value we *measured*. Numbers in parentheses for the duals are the reserve capacities for the main battery plus the backup.

❻ Warranty. The number of months each marketer offers a *full* warranty and a *prorated* (partial refund) warranty.

❶ Brand and model	❷ Price	❸ Group size	❹ Cold-cranking amps Mfr. rated	Performance	❺ Reserve capacity Mfr. rated	Measured	❻ Warranty period Full	Prorated	Comments
Standard batteries									
Delco Freedom 24-60	$68	24	525 amp	●	95 min.	114 min.	3 mo.	60 mo.	A,B
Interstate 24-42	56	24	455	●	90	91	6	42	—
Energizer	40	26	525	●	80	85	—	60	—
Douglas 24-6000	56	24	535	◒	100	106	12 ☐1	60	E
Motorcraft Tested Tough BX-24	62	24	550	◒	105	108	3	60	F
Deka 524MF	75	24	525	◒	80	93	3	60	A,E
GNB High Energy 26HE60	50	26	530	◒	85	92	—	60	A
Exide Motorvator	40	26	530	◒	—	79	3	65	G

| | | | ④ Cold-cranking amps | | ⑤ Reserve capacity | | ⑥ Warranty period | | |
① Brand and model	② Price	③ Group size	Mfr. rated	Performance	Mfr. rated	Measured	Full	Prorated	Comments
Napa Power 9460	$ 73	24	515 ②	◐	80	85	3	60	—
Exide The Driver's Edge 24-60	62	24	515 ②	●	80	81	3	60	—
Deka 624MF	85	24	650	◐	110	115	3	65	A,E
Sears DieHard 43224	60	24	600	◐	115	118	12	60	—
Exide The Driver's Edge 24-72	72	24	600 ②	○	85	100	3	72	—
Napa The Legend 7524	83	24	600 ②	○	115	112	3	75	—
Douglas 24-7000	67	24	650	○	115	124	12 ①	70	E
Dual batteries									
DieHard DualStart 43501	120	34	525(800)	◐	70(105)	77(128)	12	60	D,H,I
Interstate X2 Booster	132	34	525(800)	◐	70(105)	81(132)	6	60	D,I
GNB Champion Switch	70	24	③(640)	◐	③(108)	70(107)	12	12 ④	C

① Without warranty card and proof of purchase, 90 days.
② Ratings taken from code on battery case.
③ No CCA or reserve-capacity claim for main battery; tested at 480 CCA.
④ Dealer may add 60 mo. prorated warranty period.

Features in Common
Except as noted, all are "low-maintenance" batteries, with removable covers for access to cells.

Key to Comments
A—"Maintenance-free" battery. The **Delco Freedom 24-60** is fully sealed.
B—Has built-in hydrometer that gives approximate charge status of 1 cell only.
C—Sealed "Pulsar" technology battery.
D—Vent caps awkward to remove for servicing.
E—**Deka** available east of the Mississippi; **Douglas** available east of the Rockies.
F—Distributed by Ford Motor Co.
G—Available at K Mart.
H—Available only at Sears.
I—Comes with side-terminal adapters for group size 78 use.

Automobile Polishes

Some people feel the need to replace a car when it starts to look dowdy. Ironically, they may have contributed to the car's tired look by overpolishing it.

Paint, not polish, is what protects a car's finish. So be careful not to polish away the car's paint when restoring a smooth finish. If your buffing cloth is picking up much color, the polish you're using contains an abrasive that's grinding away the paint. Here are some other tips on maintaining a car's finish:

- Wash the car thoroughly before polishing it, since most road dirt is a good deal harder than a car's finish. If you don't, you'll only grind dirt into the paint, causing small but unsightly scratches.

- Polish that has dried too long on the surface can be difficult to buff. Polish dries very quickly on a hot, dry day, so you should tackle only small sections at a time.

- To see whether a polish is holding up, observe what happens to water on the car's surface. Beads of water that form on a well-sealed surface are rounded and have a small contact area. As the polish wears away, the beads spread and flatten. When the polish is completely gone, water doesn't bead at all but merely lies in a sheet on the surface of the car.

- Although you may not need to polish a new car, you should wash it often. Bird and tree droppings, salt, tar, and even plain dirt can eventually mar the finish. Frequent washing is especially important in the summer, when high temperatures increase the damaging effects of contaminants.

Safety Belts

If you keep a car for more than a few years, the safety belts can become worn and need replacement. The major automakers make replacement belts for any car that originally had them. The new belts may not match the car's upholstery, but they will help protect the car's occupants in the event of a crash.

Tire Care: Buy a Good Tire-Pressure Gauge

Improperly inflated tires can cause poor handling and even blowouts. They may also wear out prematurely.

Significantly underinflated tires can suffer from uneven, accelerated tread wear, as well as from excessive flexing, which causes overheating and may lead to early tire failure. Overinflated tires also wear unevenly, give a harsher ride, and can cause blowouts.

To maintain your tires properly, buy a good gauge. Get one for each car you own, keep it in the glove compartment, and use it once a month or so. It will safeguard the life of your tires and help ensure safe driving.

You can't rely on a gas station's air hose. The station's air dispenser may not be accurate. What's more, if you've driven any distance to the station, your tires will have warmed and therefore increased their pressure by as much as 4 to 6 pounds per square inch (psi).

The recommended pressure for your car's tires (the *maximum* pressure is embossed directly on the tire sidewall) is usually for cold readings. A tire gauge lets you read the pressure right in your own driveway. If tires are underinflated, you can then drive to the gas station and inflate each tire by the requisite number of pounds, using the tire gauge as the measuring instrument.

While you are checking, don't neglect the spare. Air slowly seeps through the pores of any tire. A spare sitting in the trunk can become so underinflated as to be useless.

The War over Bent Fenders

These days, even a little fender bender can cost you hundreds of dollars to repair. Manufacturers warn you against using parts that weren't made by the automakers. But your insurance company insists that you use cheaper parts or pay the difference. What do you do?

Over the past eight or so years, cheap replacement parts—fenders, hoods, and other sheet-metal parts costing 25 to 40 percent less than parts manufactured by the automakers—have begun to show up. Insurers have welcomed the cheaper parts. But automakers are conjuring up the specter of poorly fitting parts that corrode easily and are possibly unsafe.

The Motor Vehicle Manufacturers Association has even urged state legislatures to require insurance companies to notify policyholders who file claims that parts not supplied by original-equipment manufacturers are "inferior." So far, 14 states require car owners to receive some sort of notification when parts not supplied by the original manufacturer are used.

Insurers have countered with a certification program to test parts for strength, corrosion, and fit and to certify them for quality. Most insurance companies give policyholders a choice of auto parts. But some insurers make it hard to turn down a cheaper replacement part if it's the same kind and quality as the original and comes with a guarantee from the part's distributor (as most do). Policyholders who insist on original equipment must pay the difference.

Car owners who want to save money by using cheap replacement parts should make sure they are stamped with a yellow oval sticker bearing the word CAPA (Certified Automotive Parts Association). The sticker indicates that a particular part has passed the auto insurer's certification tests.

How to Keep Your Car Happy and Healthy

How do people keep a car running smoothly for 100,000 miles or more, over years of driving? Experiences vary, but we can offer some commonsense tips that may give you a shot at cracking the 100,000 barrier with your car:

- *Change the oil frequently.* While some new-car manufacturers recommend changes only every 7,500 miles, changing your oil every 3,000 to 3,500 miles, particularly with city driving or smaller, higher-revving engines, is a wise policy. You might also consider replacing the oil filter each time you change the oil.
- *Don't wait for trouble.* Take care of routine maintenance—checking fluid levels, inspecting belts and hoses, and so on—at least as often as the car owner's manual recommends.
- *Keep the car garaged.* Parking the car indoors, particularly in the winter, makes work easier for just about every mechanical component, especially the battery, the starter motor, the oil, and the transmission fluid. Garaging the car also helps protect the body from the damaging effects of sunlight, road salt, air pollution, and the like.

Drive Right and Save Money

You can save fuel—and money—by driving wisely.

- Instead of driving short distances, walk or ride a bicycle. A car burns more than twice as much gasoline during the first few minutes of operation as it does at other times.
- Combine several short trips into one long one, to drive as little as possible with a cold engine.
- Drive off at a moderate speed as soon as the engine runs smoothly. You don't need to let the engine warm up for several minutes.
- Inflate the tires properly. Underinflated tires cause drag, which can raise fuel consumption by as much as 6 percent.
- Keep your car tuned properly, and have its emissions system inspected regularly.
- Replace the air filter at least every 15,000 miles.
- When traffic permits, limit your speed to 55 mph on highways; the car will burn at least 15 percent less gasoline than at 65.

- Limit use of your car's air conditioner.
- If you expect your car will be idling for more than 30 seconds, turn off the ignition.
- Try to anticipate traffic conditions and drive at a constant speed; braking and accelerating waste fuel.
- In a car with manual transmission, downshift only when needed to make the car accelerate adequately. When you want to slow the car, use the brakes instead of downshifting; using the engine to decelerate the car wastes fuel. And if the car has an overdrive top gear, use it whenever it will pull the car smoothly. Overdrive can save you fuel around town, not just on the expressway.
- Traffic conditions permitting, accelerate briskly until the car is in top gear, then drive with a delicate touch.

Should You Join an Auto Club?

Does it pay to join an auto club? That's apt to depend on where you live and your life-style. You probably don't really need an auto club if you live outside the freeze-and-snow belt and don't do much traveling.

In any case, many auto-insurance companies offer inexpensive optional coverage of emergency road-service costs. An individual membership in an auto club will probably cost considerably more.

Membership in an auto club, however, may be worth it to you because of the reassurance it provides—along with some services that may not be readily available otherwise. In addition to road maps and advice about routes, some clubs offer members a range of travel-planning services.

If you decide to join, you'll have a choice between a full-service club and a limited-service club.

- The advantage of a full-service club is that it usually provides no-cost road service—you don't have to pay for service and then apply for reimbursement. An affiliated garage or service station will try to get your car back into operation on the spot or will tow it to the garage if necessary. The club picks up the bill for that basic service, though you'd have to pay for parts and any extensive repairs.
- The advantage of a limited-service club is that you're free to

choose any garage you want. If your car won't start when you want to leave home, for example, you can call your local service station for help even if the station isn't affiliated with your club. The limited-service club will reimburse you, up to a preset limit, after you've made your own arrangements for service.

NINE

Enjoying Leisure for Less: Electronics and More

The retailing motto "Only suckers pay list" applies with particular force in the electronics and camera markets: Substantial discounts are almost always available, if you know where to look. This chapter points you toward the best buys in those products—and in some others that can brighten your leisure time as well.

Home Electronics

Setting Up a Home Theater

Choose a center for your system. First, decide whether the TV set or the receiver will be the center of the system. Until recently, there was really no choice: It had to be the receiver. But sophisticated TV sets, costing $700 to $1,000 for the 27-inch size ($1,500 to $2,000 for 31- and 32-inch sets, $3,000 or more for 35-inch sets), can deliver amplified sound to four or five external speakers. Such sets may be worth considering if you don't have a convenient stereo system in the same room as the TV, especially if you're in the market for a new TV. The drawback of a TV-based system: It ignores the entertainment possibilities of CDs, radio, and tapes.

A receiver-based system can cost much less, especially if you already have a TV with an audio output. If your stereo and TV occupy the same room, you may just need to connect the two systems with a cable (cost: about $5). You can beef up TV sound with a pair of self-amplified speakers for as little as $150. For a separate receiver, expect to pay at least $200. For an A/V (audio/video) receiver that decodes Dolby Surround sound, figure $300 or more.

Speakers. Expect to pay $350 to $400 (after a discount of about 20 percent off list price) for a pair of good speakers. The second set (the "rear" ambience speakers) for a Dolby setup can be cheaper speakers, since the rear channels carry only untaxing midrange frequencies. Increasingly, manufacturers are selling small speakers specifically for use as rear speakers. We've seen some, from Yamaha and Radio Shack, that sell for less than $100 a pair. They'd do fine. For the fifth speaker in a Dolby Pro-logic setup, you'd want something in between, in the $200-to-$250-a-pair range—$100 to $125 for one. To accommodate the market for home theater, many companies now sell their speakers individually as well as by the pair.

In a surround-sound setup, placement of the rear speakers is less critical than that of the front speakers. Rear speakers can be on the floor and pointed at the ceiling or side walls, or they can be mounted high on the wall.

Playback devices. At a minimum, you'll need a hi-fi VCR. They're now fairly inexpensive, available at discount for less than $400. Models with high-quality sound can double as audio tape recorders. Their ability to record for up to six hours at EP speed gives them an advantage over audio cassette decks. If you have this sort of use in mind, buy a VCR with record-level controls. If you want to edit your own tapes, look for a machine with assemble-editing capability (it lets you put glitch-free video segments end to end), front-panel jacks, and perhaps a remote capable of controlling two VCRs.

The price of laser-disc players and the discs themselves has also dropped significantly. The best bet for most people is a "combi" player, which is a carousel-style CD changer that plays both CDs and video laser discs. **Sony, Philips, Magnavox, Panasonic,** and **Pioneer** are the most popular brands. Players start at $500, discs at about $20.

Remote control. If all the components in a home-theater setup are of the same brand, there should be little problem in running at least its basic functions with just one remote—probably the TV's or the VCR's, since those remotes are typically the most advanced.

In a setup of mixed brands, you may want a programmable, or "learning," remote to run the system. The "universal" remotes now come with high-end TVs and VCRs, and they can be bought separately for $70 to $150. But don't plan on throwing away all the dedicated remotes. There will undoubtedly still be a few esoteric functions only they can control.

Videotapes: Little Difference Among Major Brands

Standard-grade tape is well made, but not very profitable. So the push is on to sell more "premium" tapes. But if you buy standard-grade videotapes, you're doing the right thing.

Manufacturers' grade designations don't help much in identifying the best tape. One company's "super-high" grade is often no better than another company's—or even its own—"high" grade. The performance of each brand's various grades is often indistinguishable. The overall quality of brand-name videotape is quite high, regardless of grade.

Gaps, scratches, or a poorly applied magnetic coating cause the intermittent flecks and streaks called dropouts. All videocassette recorders have circuitry that replaces missing bits of picture lines with corresponding bits from the line above, a trick that ordinarily goes undetected by the viewer.

Sound. Until recently, all VCRs used the "linear-track" method to record sound; in this process, a narrow strip was reserved along the tape's edge for the sound track. However, the tape's low speed made good audio quality difficult to achieve.

A few years ago, high-fidelity sound was introduced in VCRs, using the tape's full width. In response, tape manufacturers introduced new tape grades with names that sound as though the tapes have been engineered especially for hi-fi VCRs. In fact, almost any brand-name tape should give excellent audio results with any hi-fi VCR.

Licensed tapes. The JVC and Sony companies, originators of the VHS and Beta tape formats, respectively, license other manufacturers to produce videotape. These tapes carry an official VHS or Beta logo. Before buying an unfamiliar tape brand, check the packaging to see if the tape is licensed. Unlicensed tape may tend to have defects—excessive dropouts, considerable noise, and the like.

Some unlicensed tapes avoid using an official logo. Others skirt the legal edge by using the logo in a sentence rather than having it stand alone. Another tip-off is the absence of an address for the manufacturer or distributor.

Buying wisely. Since there is very little difference among major brands of VHS tape, it pays to shop by price and stock up when tapes are on sale. You can often find tape at 40 to 50 percent off list.

CD Changers: No Costlier than Single-Play Models

If you want to add a compact-disk player to your hi-fi system, a changer makes more sense than a single-play model. Changers often cost about the same as single-play models and have been just as reliable; they come with ample features, and they can provide hours of music without interruption.

Magazine changers typically accommodate 6 to 10 discs in a special holder that pops into the front of the machine. Most magazines are compatible with autosound CD changers, so you can move discs from home to car. And because you can store CDs in the magazine, you don't have to handle them as often. A magazine-type changer also makes sense for those who want their CDs grouped—piano concertos in one magazine, symphonies in another, and so on.

If all you want is a player that's simple to use and relatively inexpensive, consider a carousel changer. Such changers hold five CDs arrayed on a revolving platter. Some carousels put the platter on top of the console, under a dust cover. These top-loaders have to be on top in a stack of components. Other carousels—front-loaders—have a wide slide-out drawer to hold the discs and can fit anywhere. Some carousel changers let you change the other discs on the platter even while one disc is playing.

You can spend anywhere from $200 to $800 for a CD changer. Spending a lot will get you gear with names like **Luxman, Carver, Nakamichi,** and other brands best known to audiophiles. But those units aren't necessarily better than cheaper ones with more familiar names—**Sony, Pioneer, Technics,** and so on. Even if you spend only $200, you will get hardware that delivers superb sound. You will also get a player that lets you repeat, delete, or rearrange the selections on any or all of the discs you've loaded.

Tape Decks: Analog or Digital?

In 1990, digital audio tape (DAT) decks made their debut in the American market. DAT delivers sound similar to that on compact discs, and it leaves music free of disturbances such as hisses and pops, which can crop up in analog recording. Nevertheless, conventional analog tape decks remain popular:

- Good analog decks cost about half as much as DAT models, which list for $800 to $1,200.
- Analog decks can play any of thousands of inexpensive prerecorded tapes. DAT-deck owners must choose from fewer than 200 prerecorded classical and jazz tapes selling for about $25. (That is, if they can find such tapes. Two major New York City stores we called didn't have any in stock.)
- Because analog decks frequently boast some form of noise reduction, many people find that analog sound is good enough for most purposes.

In our view, the best analog decks for the money list for between $350 and $750. Cheaper models don't perform as well; more expensive ones have frills most people don't need.

There are two types of midpriced analog decks: single and dual. In past tests, we've found that single-deck models deliver better sound quality. Dual-deck machines can copy prerecorded tapes or play two without interruption. But when we last tested them, in March 1989, quite a few suffered from flutter, a defect that makes music sound wavery or fuzzy.

What features to look for. Here are some especially useful features:

Autoreverse. This feature reverses the tape automatically when it reaches the end, so you can play or record both sides. Some dual-deck models play both sides of two tapes with only the slightest break. As a result, you can listen or record for up to three continuous hours with C-90 tapes.

Music search. This feature can search for the gap between selections, allowing you to tell the deck to skip songs you don't care for.

Tape scan. This allows you to browse through a tape by listening to the first 10 or 15 seconds of every selection.

Recording meter. If you do a lot of recording, look for a deck with a bar-graph recording-level meter that has 12 or so segments. The more segments, the easier it is to monitor loudness.

Automatic bias adjustment. This assures recording accuracy on all types of tape.

Noise reduction. Tape-it-yourselfers should also consider a deck's noise-reduction and sound-improvement circuitry. On the models we've tested, Dolby C has proved effective, but it will be eclipsed any day now by Dolby S, which promises to be even better.

HX Pro, circuitry that expands a tape's dynamic range in the treble, provides still another way to improve recordings. Then there's DBX, a noise-reduction system that lets you make excellent live recordings or copies of CDs. Nowadays, though, it's not found very often in the kind of tape decks consumers usually buy.

One limitation to tapes made with Dolby C and DBX (but not with Dolby S) is that they must be played on a deck with the same type of noise-reduction circuitry. On most car decks and portable tape players—equipped, at best, with Dolby B noise reduction—Dolby C recording would sound slightly unbalanced in tone. A DBX recording would sound even worse. If most of your recording will involve copying compact discs, consider buying the same brand of deck and CD player. You may be able to direct both units with a single remote control, and they may be able to interact, which simplifies the process of making tapes from CDs.

If you need to copy tapes quickly, there are decks with high-speed tape-to-tape copying. But the sound quality on tapes made that way is apt to be worse than it is on those recorded at normal speed.

Tape Decks: DAT or DCC?

A clear-cut choice between the relatively low price of analog tape decks and the superior performance of digital audio tape decks may well be blurred by a third option.

In fall 1990, Philips N.V., the electronics giant that helped develop compact discs, announced that it was working with the Tandy Corporation to develop a new tape technology, digital compact cassette, or DCC. It would do what digital audio tape cannot: let the same deck play both digital and analog cassettes. The owner of a DCC deck could continue using an existing analog tape collection while starting a new one in the digital format.

But DCC tapes are incompatible with DAT. Fear of betting the wrong way might lead consumers to stay away from digital altogether.

DCC is not yet in the marketplace, so for now, DAT is the only digital game in town. And it's apt to prove a formidable opponent in a faceoff between acronyms. When we tested two of Sony's new DAT models in 1990, they were everything digital tape decks are cracked up to be. They copied compact discs perfectly and exhibited features not found on most analog decks—for example, the ability to program selections to play in any order and to go quickly to a particular track.

When we made recordings from LPs and radio, DAT decks recorded far better than any conventional deck we had seen. Nevertheless, the price of DAT decks and tapes is steep and is likely to remain so.

Price is one area in which DCC could well gain an advantage over DAT. Philips has said its machines will list for $500 to $600 when introduced. Eventually, the price for bare-bones DCC models is expected to drop to about $200.

DCC has other factors in its favor. Five record companies have already agreed to issue pop titles in DCC. (Philips claims that the system's design allows for inexpensive mass production of digital tapes, not possible with DAT.) And the fact that Tandy, through its **Radio Shack** and **Memorex** brands, will manufacture DCC decks and tapes should ease the new technology's entry into the marketplace.

For a well-heeled audiophile who wants digital equipment now, there seems little reason to refrain from buying a DAT deck. DAT technology is sound, and there are certainly plenty of compact discs from which to record. For people with greater patience, DCC may prove worth waiting for.

Blank Audio Cassettes: Which Tapes to Buy?

You can save money by buying according to use.

- Use a low-priced Type I tape for basic recording—copying an LP, recording speech, or making a tape to play in the car.
- Use a Type I or a Type II tape for copying LPs or cassettes when sound quality matters, for copying compact discs to play in the car, or for making tapes to use in a walkabout tape player.
- Use a high-rated Type II or a Type IV "metal" tape for the most demanding tasks.

We tested C-90 tapes, which give you up to 90 minutes of recording or playing time. Other things being equal, the shorter C-40 and C-60 tapes should be comparable. So should the new C-76 and C-100 tapes, made to match the maximum playing time of a CD.

Electronic Piano: Inexpensive Practice Instrument

If you can't afford a piano or can't fit one into a cramped apartment, consider an electronic piano. Superficially, such instruments resemble the electronic keyboards so popular these days, but there are important differences.

The pianos lack the accompaniment and rhythm sections of electronic keyboards. But their salient feature is touch sensitivity. Their keyboards

respond to the force with which a player strikes the keys, yielding a sub-
tlety of touch similar to that of an acoustic piano. That, and their relatively realistic piano sound, makes them near-replacements for a
traditional piano. (Some electronic keyboards also offer touch sensitivity, but those are more expensive than the ones we tested.)

A number of the pianos have 61 full-sized keys, adequate for a learner
or as a practice instrument. Though the abbreviated keyboard is certainly a restriction (a piano has 88 keys), electronic pianos offer certain
advantages. These instruments are portable and compact. (Optional
stands are available to raise them to playing height.) They're much less
expensive than an acoustic piano, even a good used one. And what
acoustic piano can be stored in a closet?

€lectronic €quipment: Where the Buys Are

If you buy electronic gear in an audio salon with listening rooms and
attentive salespeople, you're apt to pay list price or close to it. You can
pay less, though the shopping conditions may not be as pleasant:

- Try a discount house. But try not to buy at the tagged price, which
  may be no bargain. Check newspaper ads to see if you can find the
  hardware you want advertised at an attractive price. Then ask the
  discounter to beat that price. You may be surprised at how fast the
  discounter's price tumbles.

- Check the audio magazines. There, you'll often find mail-order
  ads for components at attractive prices.

Don't Overspend for a Camera

It's a cinch to pay too much when you shop for a camera. You may buy
fancier equipment than you need. Or you may make the mistake of paying list price. Here's how to buy wisely.

Ask yourself this question: Do I need advanced equipment or just
something for snapshots? A 35-millimeter single-lens reflex (SLR) camera lets the photographer see what the camera "sees" (through whichever lens is being used) and thus compose a shot precisely. With most
SLRs, you can choose from an assortment of lenses and other accessories to "build" a camera customized to your precise needs. However, an
SLR may be more camera than you really need or want. If you take pic-

tures only on vacations and special occasions, you'll probably be happier with a simpler and less costly camera. Along the same lines, if you don't necessarily want to explore the variety of interchangeable lenses available for SLRs, there's less of a reason to own one.

Nevertheless, lots of people still want to have the latest and the best. If you fit that category, you will certainly want to consider an *autofocus* model. The automatic SLRs not only focus themselves with remarkable speed and precision, they also help with loading and winding film and with setting the shutter speed and aperture. These features enable beginners to get excellent results in most situations. Most of the automated cameras can still be used manually, so that advanced photographers can retain creative control.

As for creativity in general, if you already know how to use an SLR or are willing to spare some time to learn, you can find good value in a manual-focus SLR.

For Beginners

Until fairly recently, if you wanted a simple point-and-shoot camera, you had to buy a disc or 110 model. These cameras tend to have small negatives that don't enlarge well beyond snapshot size. The newer, automated, compact 35-millimeter camera is just about as small and as easy to use as any disc or 110 camera, and with it you can get the quality inherent in the larger frame of 35-millimeter film.

A compact camera makes picture-taking easy:

- *Automatic load.* You drop in the film cartridge, pull some film out, and a motor threads and winds the film through. The same motor winds film after each shot and rewinds when the roll is finished.

- *Automatic exposure control.* This helps prevent pictures from coming out too light or too dark. A compact usually "reads" the film's sensitivity from the metallic coding on the film cartridge and adjusts the camera accordingly.

- *Built-in flash.* This fires when it is needed.

The limitations of these cameras concern the advanced photographer more than the snapshooter. The exposure settings, for instance, are decided by the camera, not by you—a trade of control for convenience. On the other hand, a compact 35-millimeter camera is smaller and lighter than an SLR. That counts for a lot when traveling.

Buying Wisely

Forget about list price in photo equipment. It's pure fiction.

In major metropolitan areas, intense competition generates the lowest prices on cameras and photo supplies. But even if you live in a rural or suburban area, you needn't pay top dollar. You can order from a big-city mail-order house, often for as little as half of list price. Check the mail-order ads in the photography magazines.

But be wary, whether you buy in person or by mail. Don't assume that the lenses and other equipment in a "kit" are of the same brand as the camera. An exceptionally low price on a brand-name camera may mean the lens is a cheap off-brand. It may even mean a manual-focus lens on an autofocus camera. So ask for details.

Find out also whether any lenses you'll want to buy later actually exist. Some lenses that are originally announced with a given camera model are never marketed or become available much later.

Watch out for the classic bait-and-switch tactics practiced by a few shady dealers: The ad may feature a low price to catch your eye, but by the time you get to the store, the item is "all sold out." Or the low price may be valid only if you buy other equipment—a camera case or an electronic flash. Sometimes, such equipment actually comes with the camera, but the store tries to charge extra.

Ask about the warranty. If the equipment has been imported through authorized factory channels, the ad generally says "U.S. warranty." But much of the Japanese-made photo equipment sold in the United States is "gray market" merchandise, imported by someone other than an authorized distributor. That doesn't mean there's anything wrong with such goods, which tend to be less expensive than the factory imports. But they may come with an "international" warranty that requires you to send them overseas for warranty service or to deal with the retailer who sold you the camera.

A store may tell you that the sales slip is your warranty. That means the store, not the manufacturer, assumes responsibility for any problems during the warranty period. Some stores will sell you the same goods with or without a U.S. warranty. As you might expect, a U.S. warranty costs extra.

Cordless Phones Have Come a Long Way

Cordless phones used to promise more than they could deliver. Sure, they gave you freedom from the cord and freed you from phone wiring, making for easy-to-install "extensions" in rooms not wired for a phone. And cordless phones were a boon to people who have trouble walking. But past models often suffered in both performance and reliability.

Our tests on the latest models show that the best ones are practically a match for regular phones if the handset is close to the base. In general, the phones' reliability and performance have improved markedly in the past few years, and many models offer a wider array of useful features.

Cost is not necessarily a factor in performance. If you can do without the bells and whistles, you can find a dependable, less expensive model with good performance.

Before you spend $60 to $200 for a cordless phone, you might consider using a longer cord on your regular phone or its handset. Price: less than $10. And be aware that most cordless phones won't operate at all during a power outage (they must be plugged into a wall outlet), so we don't recommend a cordless model be used as your home's only telephone. Still, a cordless phone can make a nice addition to your phone system.

Some features have almost become standard on cordless phones, just as on regular phones: switchable pulse or tone dialing, last-number redial, and mute or hold buttons. Here's a rundown of the features that count most:

Ten-channel operation minimizes the risk of interference from nearby cordless phones and increases the chance of finding a clear channel. Most 10-channel cordless phones let you change channels "on the fly"— while talking. However, if you live where cordless phones are few and far between, choosing a model with fewer channels shouldn't hurt performance and will cost less.

A *speakerphone* gives you a separate microphone and speaker in the phone's base, letting you talk at both base and handset. You can make hand-free calls and use the base and handset as two ends of an intercom. (Some cordless phones have a speaker that is intended only for intercom use, not for calls.) Models that also have a dialing keyboard on the base are, in effect, two phones in one.

Two-way paging is found in many speakerphone models. Push a button on the base and the handset sounds a page signal; push a button on the handset and the base does the same. People sometimes use paging to find a missing handset or to signal the person at the other end.

A *ringer in the base* lets you know the phone is ringing even if the handset is away from the base. That way, you're less likely to miss incoming calls. Some models let you turn off the base ringer or change its volume.

An *out-of-range tone* warns you that the phone's functions won't work properly unless the handset is closer to the base.

A small, flexible antenna is less likely to break than a telescopic metal antenna. More and more models come with (or accept) the flexible type. In **Cobra Intenna** phones, the user's hand and arm function as the antenna, which works fine unless you cradle the handset on your shoulder.

Speed-call memory lets you store frequently called numbers so you can dial them using one or two buttons. Many phones can store more than 10 numbers. Usually, each number can contain up to 16 digits.

A mute or hold button lets you talk to someone nearby without letting the person on the other end hear what is said. On some phones, you must hold the button down; on others, you press it once to activate and again to deactivate. If you have call-waiting service, you can put a caller on hold with any of the phones by tapping the hook switch.

An extra battery in the base can keep charging even if the handset is elsewhere. When the battery in the handset runs down, you switch to the charged one. As of our November 1991 report on cordless phones, only the **Sony SPP-115** had this feature of the phones we tested. The extra battery allows this model to operate briefly during a power failure.

Dry-Cell Batteries: Which Type Is the Bargain?

If you buy only alkaline batteries, you'll be sure of getting your money's worth. All the alkalines we tested most recently were good, and all out-lasted the other types. Shop around—prices can vary widely from store to store.

If you're looking for ways to save on out-of-pocket expenses, you might consider a heavy-duty, nonalkaline model. They work fine in devices that don't draw a lot of power if you let them rest between uses. The only catch is you'll have to replace them more often than alkalines.

Rechargeable batteries can pay for themselves in a few months in devices you use frequently. AA-sized rechargeables are particularly practical because they last as long as or longer between charges than a heavy-duty battery.

Batteries aren't like bananas; you can't just look at them and tell whether they're about to go bad. To get the freshest stock, shop in stores that do a brisk business in batteries. If you ask, many electronics and dis-count stores will check the voltage in the batteries you're buying with a battery tester.

How to Buy a Computer

You'll have to determine the importance of price for yourself. Computer magazines are stuffed with mail-order ads for computers, printers, accessories, and software at discounts of up to 50 percent. A retail merchant probably won't offer more than 10 percent to 15 percent off (though sales on specific items are common), and some stubbornly stick to full list price.

The price advantage of ordering hardware by mail is undercut by several disadvantages.

First, the relationship between buyer and seller is reduced essentially to a telephone call or an order form. While some mail-order companies will discuss your purchase by phone with you at great length, it's not the same as having a salesperson at your elbow to point out a mistake or a feature.

Second, ordering by mail runs the risk of damage to the hardware in transit.

Third, problems are harder to iron out. If you buy a printer locally and it doesn't seem to work with your computer, you can cart the whole system back to the store for help. Repair help doesn't come by mail.

Still, we can suggest a money-saving strategy: You might buy the heart of a computer system—the computer, a monitor, and vital accessory hardware—at a computer store, but use mail-order for items unlikely to present repair problems, such as expensive software packages.

Once you've bought your computer, don't buy applications programs right away. Take the computer home first, work with the manual and the systems software until you are comfortable with them. Meanwhile, read computer magazines—especially publications devoted to your own make of computer—keeping an eye out for reviews of programs that seem worthwhile. Get a feel for advertised mail-order discounts on most software packages.

At the store, however, do check the range of software the store carries. Are several vendors represented for diversity? For serious applications such as word-processing, you will want to try more than one software package.

Check the store's service facilities. Ideally, the store should have its own service department. Service shouldn't take more than a few days.

If you live in or near a metropolitan area, attend a meeting or two of the many users' groups organized around most of the popular computers. Users' groups are mother lodes of straight talk. You can learn about the quirks of a particular computer, the best places to get discounted software, and merchants with reputations for helpfulness and reliability. After the purchase, a users' group can help you debug a troublesome program, provide free or cheap software through an exchange library, and offer a way to buy or sell used equipment. Most computer stores can give you information about users' groups in your area.

Mail Order: Handle with Care

Mail-Order Scams: Shearing the Suckers

From sex pills to $4 emeralds, mail-order scams still thrive; some basic mail frauds never seem to go out of fashion. You wouldn't fall for such schemes, you say? Millions do.

Sweepstakes swindles. You receive a solicitation letter that says you've won some sort of contest or sweepstakes. But to claim your prize you must pay a "redemption fee," ostensibly to cover the cost of insurance, shipping, and handling. The fee may be more than the prize is worth. In other cases, the prize serves as a come-on to get you to buy something else. You win a diamond, say, and the company wants you to pay to have it mounted.

Chain letters. You receive a letter asking you to send $50 (or some other amount) to the person at the top of a list of names. Then you're supposed to send a certain number of copies of the letter to other people, removing the name at the top of the list and adding your own to the bottom. If six names were on the list and the "chain" was unbroken, when your name reached the top of the list, 4,096 people would send you $50 each. You'd find $204,800 in your mailbox.

Nice theory, but it never works that way. The profits often begin and end with the first person on the list. It's mathematically impossible for everyone to benefit: Latecomers always lose. And (oh, yes) any chain that involves mailing money is an illegal lottery, even if the letter states, "This is not a chain letter."

Work-at-home schemes. Shut-ins, children, the elderly, and the handicapped are often lured by ads for "profitable work that can be done at home." Many offers refer to stuffing envelopes, although sophisticated mailing equipment has virtually eliminated the need for human envelope stuffers. The ads typically ask respondents to pay $2 to $10 for information. Instead of receiving information on envelope stuffing, respondents are often told to place a similar ad to attract other victims.

Work-at-home handicraft scams are often intended to sell sewing machines or crafts supplies. People must usually sign a contract requiring them to buy supplies from the company—but the company is not obliged to pay for work done at home.

A variation on this scheme is the "assembly work" scam. The advertisers sell materials to make aprons, ties, baby shoes, or other items, and say they will buy back the finished products. But the company then rejects the submitted work, saying it's of inferior quality.

Medical quackery. Swindlers peddle panaceas to cure just about any health problem. Thousands of people still waste their money on antiaging formulas, sex nutrients, cancer cures, and bust developers. None works. Some are dangerous.

C.O.D. scams. When you answer the phone, the salesperson says you're a winner. All you need to do is order a year's supply of vitamins (or ballpoint pens or whatever) and you'll win a gift—maybe a personal computer, a grandfather clock, or a motorboat with an inboard motor.

Lured by the prospect, you place an order. But you end up paying $15 to $100, sometimes much more, for the merchandise, insurance, shipping, and handling.

Your package arrives. When you open it, the prize isn't what you thought it would be. The "personal computer" has become a hand-held calculator. The motorboat has become an inflatable raft with a plastic motor. Whatever you've received, it isn't worth what you've just paid for it.

It used to be that you were stuck. When your package arrived, you had to pay for it C.O.D.—cash on delivery. The Postal Service then gave the shipper its money and couldn't refund it to you. But now, people who order C.O.D. can pay for the purchase directly, by writing a check payable to the sender. Therefore, if you've been taken, you'll only be out the fee for stopping payment on a check.

While C.O.D. rules still allow you to pay for packages with cash, certified check, or money order, those forms of payment for items bought sight unseen are inherently risky. Our advice is to steer clear of C.O.D. in the first place.

Smart, Thrifty Mail-Order Shopping

When you order merchandise by mail, you can save money and avoid headaches by following some commonsense rules:

- Before placing an order with an unfamiliar company, check with the Better Business Bureau, the postal inspector, or the state and local consumer-protection agencies nearest the company's headquarters.

- Fill out the order forms neatly and completely. Keep careful records of your orders, including the company's name, address, and phone number; a list of the items purchased, the costs, and the catalog numbers; and the order date and expected delivery date. Also keep a copy of the advertisement or catalog you ordered from. If you're placing an order by phone, record the name or station number of the operator.

- Check the company's return policy before ordering. Some companies have a no-questions-asked, satisfaction-guaranteed policy and accept returns even years after a purchase. Most companies limit their return period, usually to between 10 and 30 days after you receive the merchandise. Some companies exclude personalized items from full-return policies.

- Follow the company's instructions for returning merchandise. Some companies will pay return postage if they have sent the wrong merchandise or if the goods arrive damaged. But if you've ordered the wrong size or color, you'll probably have to pay the return postage. Insure items you're returning.

- When comparing costs, don't forget to consider shipping expenses. A few companies include the cost of shipping in the price of what they sell, but most charge separately—with a flat fee, a charge for each item, or a fee based on cost or weight.

- Most companies insure orders as a matter of course, but some companies try to pass the cost on to you directly by including a line on their order forms for an optional insurance fee. Save the money—it's the shipper's responsibility to make sure your merchandise arrives safely and on time.

- Include sales tax when you're comparing costs. In most cases, you're exempt from paying state sales tax on mail-order purchases if the company doesn't have a retail outlet or other facility in the state where you're ordering. If it does, the company must collect your local sales tax. (You'll also be taxed if your home state has a law requiring taxation.)

Companies that charge sales tax on handling, packing, and shipping charges aren't cheating. Most states tax those services as well as the actual cost of the merchandise.

Rules of the game. The Federal Trade Commission's Mail Order Rule protects you against the problems of late delivery and nondelivery of merchandise. The rule requires companies to send ordered goods within the time period stated in their advertisements or within 30 days if no shipping date is given. The clock starts ticking as soon as the company receives a properly completed order form, including payment.

If the company can't ship on time, it must notify you and provide a postage-paid reply card giving you the option of canceling the order and receiving a refund or accepting a new shipping date.

If you agree to a new shipping date and the company still can't meet it, the company must send a second postage-paid notice. Unless you sign and return this second notice, the company must automatically cancel the order and refund your money.

The 30-day rule does not apply to photofinishing services, magazine subscriptions (after the first issue), cash-on-delivery orders, seeds, plants, or book and record clubs and other serial deliveries. And it doesn't cover telephone orders when you pay by credit card. (But it does apply if you order by phone, then mail in the payment.)

If you pay by credit card, you're covered by the FTC's Fair Credit Billing Act, which allows you to withhold payment of disputed charges. To do that, you must write the credit-card company at the "billing error" address given on your bill within 60 days of the time you receive the bill. The letter must include your name, account number, the dollar amount of the error, and an explanation of the problem.

If you win the dispute, you don't have to pay the amount in question or any finance charges. If the company wins, you have to pay the bill in full, plus any additional finance charges.

How to complain. Most mail-order houses act quickly to settle a problem. But if you have a problem with an order, first write a letter to the company explaining what went wrong. Many companies provide toll-free customer-service numbers—but if you call to complain, be sure to write a follow-up letter so you have a written record of the action for your files. If you don't receive a satisfactory response in 30 days, start writing letters of complaint to other agencies, including these:

Direct Marketing Association (11 West 42 Street, New York, NY 10036). The DMA sponsors a "Mail Order Action Line" that will intervene with companies on your behalf and refer you to other agencies.

Better Business Bureau (Council of Better Business Bureaus, Inc., 4200 Wilson Boulevard, Suite 800, Arlington, VA 22203, 703-276-0100). The BBB can help you check a company's record and reputation before you place an order, and it accepts complaints if you've already ordered and have a problem. You must contact the BBB office nearest the company's headquarters, not the office in your area. To get a directory of BBB offices, contact the Council at the address above.

Federal Trade Commission (Pennsylvania Ave. and Sixth Street N.W., Washington, DC, 20585, 202-326-2180). The FTC does not act on individual complaints, but it does use them to build cases against companies.

U.S. Postal Service (475 L'Enfant Plaza, Washington, DC 20260, 202-268-2000). Send a copy of your complaint letter and all necessary documentation to the Chief Postal Inspector.

State and local consumer-protection agencies in your area should also be able to help.

Panty Hose: Bargains by Mail Order

You can generally get the best prices on panty hose by buying through the mail. The real bargains are the imperfects, also sold only through the mail. Companies say the flaws in these hose are cosmetic—a few strands less per square inch, a panty that's not quite the right hue, and so on. That is likely to be true. In most cases, you won't be able to find the imperfection. The companies also claim that the flaws won't affect wear. That is also likely to be true.

Nylon is just about the perfect material for hose. It's strong, resilient, resistant to abrasion, and capable of being spun very fine and smooth, and it's unaffected by perspiration. But manufacturing methods that emphasize one of those qualities often do so at the expense of others. So, until fairly recently, you couldn't find stockings that were simultaneously sheer, silky, stretchy, and strong.

Sheerness, support, and *control* don't have any standardized definitions, so those words on a hosiery package are often more advertisement than description. *Sheer,* for example, may mean the hose are sheerer than some other hose sold by the same company. Or it may mean the hose are sheerer than, say, a pair of cotton socks. Or *sheer* might carry the same meaning as it does in *sheer pleasure.* The word is often a part of the brand name.

Sheerness is often at odds with stretch as well as with strength. Both the elasticity and strength of nylon can be increased by adding even a small amount of a synthetic fiber called spandex. Stockings with spandex hold the leg in, supporting it and helping to keep ankles and feet from swelling. But until recent years, spandex made *support hose* bulky and thick—the hose of choice mainly for women who must be on their feet for long periods.

More than 10 years ago, manufacturers discovered how to spin spandex into finer strands and how to wrap the strands with nylon, a technique that makes the fiber silkier yet tougher than plain spandex. The result is the so-called *light-support hose,* which are popular as much for their comfort as for the support they provide. Encouraged, manufacturers knit even finer spandex threads into very sheer hose. Hose that really offer support usually say so somewhere on the label.

Adding spandex to the panty part of panty hose has produced yet another category of hose—*control-top hose.* This variety isn't girdlelike, however—the spandex serves more to smooth things over than hold it all in.

Features. There are several things to look for in panty hose:

- The color of the panty is the only difference you're likely to find between regular hose and products that advertise themselves as combination underpants–panty hose.

- A wide, reinforced waistband helps hold up sheer-to-the-waist hose and doesn't bind the way a narrow band does.

- A crotch panel usually makes hose fit more comfortably, especially in queen size. A panel made of cotton breathes better than one made of nylon—which is important whether or not you wear underpants.

- A hole in the toe can be a big nuisance. Buy hose with reinforced toes.

- Very sheer hose can be durable if they contain a bit of spandex.

- Washing panty hose loose in the washing machine shortens their life. Panty hose last longer if you wash them by hand or use a net bag in the washer.

Save on Makeup, Facial Products, and Skin Care

Good Mascara Needn't Cost a Lot

Women who use makeup have strong ideas about mascara. They like basic black, whether fashion calls for sixties-style sooty eyes or the eighties' clear-eyed look. And they want their eyelashes to look natural. They generally own just one mascara—and it's an inexpensive one. Drugstore variety brands such as **Maybelline** and **Cover Girl** outsell the pricier department-store brands—**Elizabeth Arden, Estée Lauder,** and **Lancôme**—by more than three to one.

Just as women approach mascara in a practical way, so did *Consumer Reports.* We convened a panel of 22 women—all volunteers who regularly use mascara—to evaluate more than 30 products. The women considered the appearance, durability, ease of application, and ease of removal of black mascara (the results may not apply to other colors). In the laboratory, we evaluated water resistance and resistance to flaking.

The five highest-rated products—**Max Factor 2000 Calorie, Chanel Cils Lumière, Almay One Coat, Christian Dior Diormatic,** and **Ultima II Extra Full**—ranged in price from $3.95 to $17.50, on average. It makes sense to try the cheaper ones first. The panelists particularly liked the applicator of the top-rated **Max Factor** ($4.67). The **Almay** ($3.95), they said, thickened lashes more than most. Both were low in water resistance, but that shouldn't be a problem for women who don't wear contact lenses or have sensitive eyes. Removal was a bit harder with the **Almay.**

Women with sensitive eyes or those who wear contacts may want better water resistance and resistance to flaking. **Avon Wash-Off Waterproof** was high in water resistance and moderate in resistance to flaking. At $4.50, it's certainly worth a try.

The panelists' judgments made it clear that they did not like products containing petroleum-based solvents rather than water. If you agree with their views, read the ingredients labeling. Water should be one of the first items listed.

Finding Happiness with Inexpensive Eye Shadow

Most eye shadows are powders that come in little compacts. (The style of the compact bears a direct relationship to price.) Powders are easy to apply and blend, but they tend to wear off quickly.

The typical applicator for a powdered shadow looks like a cotton swab but with sponges on the ends instead of cotton. Some applicators have a rounded sponge at one end, a tapered sponge at the other. You use the rounded end to apply shadow to the lid, the tapered end to outline the eye and shade the crease in the lid to create contour.

Makeup experts say a brush does a better job of applying and blending eye shadow, but hardly any cosmetics manufacturers include brushes with the powder. (And those that do tend to use low-quality brushes.)

There are cream eye shadows, too. They take the form of pencils, crayons, wands (like mascaras), and compacts. With the pencils, crayons, and wands, you draw or paint the color on your eyelid and blend it with your fingertip. With the compact variety, you simply dip your fingertip into the cream and smear it on your lids. Creams glide on easily and resist flaking, a bonus for contact-lens wearers. But because they're oil-based, creams smudge and crease easily, particularly in hot, humid weather.

For the most part, there's very little difference between one powdered eye shadow and another, between one cream and another. The ingredients are essentially the same, whether the shadow costs $2 or $15.

We retained the services of a professional makeup artist to evaluate 31 brands of eye shadow purchased in three colors per brand. He evaluated the intensity of the color, the ease of application, and the degree of shine. A number of colors weren't true to the color that appears in the case. And some were much less intense than others. Otherwise, differences were slight.

Expensive eye shadow in fancy packaging can be nice to use, but inexpensive eye shadows will do just as well. Simply choose a color you like and apply it with care. The most important part of achieving a good look is to prepare the eyelid properly. Cover the eyelid, from lash to brow, with a very thin layer of foundation followed by a generous dusting of face powder. The eye shadow will then go on more easily, blend better, and last longer without creasing. Women with oily skin would do well to apply a second dusting of face powder over the eye shadow.

Sponge-tipped applicators are good for covering broad areas, such as the eyelid or the brow bone. A makeup brush is best for fine work— outlining the eye and contouring the crease in the eyelid. Our consultant recommends buying good brushes with tapered, natural bristles.

When buying eye shadow, beware of the fluorescent lighting often found at cosmetics counters. Try to apply a small amount of shadow to your skin and go out into daylight to evaluate it. Since there are rarely "testers" in drugstores or mass-merchandise department stores, your best bet is to take the shadow in its bubble pack to a window so at least you'll get a true view of the color in the package.

Skin Moisturizers: Cheaper Is Better

Women use far more moisturizers than men do. (Most men have thicker, oilier skin than women do, and they don't need moisturizers as much.) Accordingly, women are the prime target of moisturizer advertising.

Most women don't expect a moisturizing lotion to cure dry skin, just to soothe it and make it feel softer. In choosing an all-purpose moisturizer, ignore the ads for expensive products. A cheap, plain lotion is likely to do the best job.

The only way to soothe and soften dry skin is to restore the proper balance of moisture to the *stratum corneum,* the very top skin layer. A moisturizer helps do that in two ways:

1. Most moisturizers contain oil, which helps retard the evaporation of water. Normally your skin produces enough oil on its own to form an adequate barrier. But various factors such as a harsh environment and soaps and detergents can strip the skin of its natural oils. Some people don't have much oil to begin with, having inherited a tendency toward dry skin. And oil production tends to slow down with age.

2. Moisturizers also work with the help of humectants—ingredients that attract and hold water as it passes through the *stratum corneum.* Humectants (glycerin is one) can also attract water from the air, but this works best in a humid environment, when you need a moisturizer least. The main objective of moisturizing is to get and keep water in contact with the skin, so the best time to apply a moisturizer is immediately after a shower or bath, while your skin is still damp.

Any effect a moisturizer has is only temporary, since it works only on the surface of the skin, smoothing, softening, and plumping up the dead cells. No matter how expensive a moisturizer is and what special ingredients it contains, it won't "penetrate deeply" into skin layers, "nourish" the skin, or "cure" dry skin.

Facial Cleansers: The Economic Performers

The main purpose of a facial cleanser is to remove makeup and grime. Soap and water do that, of course. But too much soap can remove a skin's natural oils, leaving it rough, chapped, and tender. Soap makes dry skin drier still. And soap and water have less clout than cleanser at removing heavy makeup.

A typical cleanser, whether cream or lotion, contains water; glycerin or other moisturizers; oils, fats, or greases (to give the product the right consistency and to dissolve grime); detergents (to wash away grime); preservatives (to forestall spoilage); and dyes and scent (to make it look and smell good).

The archetype of the breed is the traditional "cold cream"—thick, greasy stuff you massage into your skin, then wipe off. **Pond's Cold Cream** and its descendants—including wipe-off lotions—are still very popular. But years ago, **Noxzema** cream in the blue jar pointed the way toward a revolutionary alternative: a less greasy goop you can wash off with water. Today there are as many wash-off creams and lotions as there are varieties that you wipe off. And there are creams and lotions that can be removed either way. We bought all types.

We recruited a panel of 90 women who wear makeup. The women described their skin to us as normal, dry, oily, or "combination" (oily in one area and dry in another).

We put samples of each product into unlabeled jars to ensure objectivity. Any label instructions were typed on plain labels and affixed to the jars. The panelists tried two products a week for 10 weeks, judging each product for a variety of attributes and for overall quality.

The winners. If soap and water doesn't do the trick for you, try **Olay Beauty Cleanser.** Our large panel of women thought it was the best. And it costs much less than most other products the panelists favored. Like the other favorites, it can be washed off. (Our panel seemed to feel that cold cream has had its day.) **Olay** is conveniently packaged in a pump-top bottle.

Other products worth trying include **Elizabeth Arden Moisture-Rich Skin Wash** cream ($2.13 an ounce) and **Revlon European Collagen Complex** lotion ($1.19). The latter comes in a pump bottle and can be either washed or wiped off.

According to the panelists, the three products were easy to apply and remove, took off makeup efficiently, smelled pleasant, felt good on the skin during use, and left the skin feeling nice after use.

Expensive Balm for Chapped Lips

Skiers know that life on the chair lift leads to chapped lips. A tube of petroleum-jelly ointment, such as **Vaseline Lip Therapy,** solves the problem—but it turns out to be a surprisingly expensive solution. **Lip Therapy,** all 0.35 ounces of it, sells for about $1.30 a tube in our area, or a little more than $59 a pound. A one-ounce tube of plain **Vaseline,** priced at $1.50, runs about $24 a pound. Cheaper still, though not as convenient to apply: A pocket-sized jar of **Vaseline** petroleum jelly. It weighs 1¾ ounces and sells for about $1.40, or a mere $12 a pound.

How to Buy a Sunscreen

No sunscreen can prevent the sun from taking its toll on your skin or let you tan darker than your skin will allow. But any product with an SPF (sun-protection factor) of 15 or more can help prevent a painful sunburn. Any of them may also help protect your skin from excessive aging and reduce your chances of developing skin cancer.

Strictly speaking, SPFs higher than 15 are overkill for most situations in the continental United States. You probably wouldn't need an SPF of more than 26 even if you were, say, to lie motionless on top of Mauna Kea in Hawaii for a full day in midsummer.

Our tests have shown that label claims of SPF level and waterproofness or water-resistance are justified. Since one SPF-15 product ought to protect as well as another SPF-15 product, it makes sense to buy a sunscreen by price. Waterproof or water-resistant sunscreens don't cost anything extra, and they can provide some added protection on a hot day. So we'd choose the cheapest waterproof product we could find.

Among the sunscreens we've tested, the least expensive were store brands—K mart's **Sun Block, Eckerd,** and **Rite Aid.** Such store brands should provide good protection.

Products from the sun-care brands—**Coppertone, Hawaiian Tropic, Sea & Ski, Alo Sun Fashion Tan, PreSun,** and so forth—cost considerably more. The most expensive products tend to be the chic (**Bain de Soleil, Lancôme, Clarins),** the specialized (**Cancer Garde, Doctors' Choice for Babies & Toddlers),** or the small-packaged (**Bullfrog).**

It's important to protect children from overexposure, since they spend about three times as much time in the sun as adults. But you don't need to buy a special sunscreen. The main difference between "baby" products and adult ones is that most baby products don't contain PABA, a potential irritant. But a number of nonbaby sunscreens are also formulated with chemicals other than PABA.

INDEX